FROM THE EYE OF THE STORM

Higher Education's Changing Institution

From the Eye of the Storm

Higher Education's Changing Institution

Edited by

Ben Jongbloed

Center for Higher Education Policy Studies (CHEPS),
University of Twente, The Netherlands

Peter Maassen

Center for Higher Education Policy Studies (CHEPS),
University of Twente, The Netherlands

and

Guy Neave

International Association of Universities (IAU),
Paris, France

KLUWER ACADEMIC PUBLISHERS
DORDRECHT / BOSTON / LONDON

A C.I.P. Catalogue record for this book is available from the Library of Congress.

ISBN 0-7923-6065-6

Published by Kluwer Academic Publishers,
P.O. Box 17, 3300 AA Dordrecht, The Netherlands.

Sold and distributed in North, Central and South America
by Kluwer Academic Publishers,
101 Philip Drive, Norwell, MA 02061, U.S.A.

In all other countries, sold and distributed
by Kluwer Academic Publishers,
P.O. Box 322, 3300 AH Dordrecht, The Netherlands.

Printed on acid-free paper

Printed in the Netherlands.

Contents

Contributors

Jeroen Bartelse is Research Associate at the Center for Higher Education Policy Studies (CHEPS) at the University of Twente, The Netherlands.

Eric Beerkens is Research Associate at the Center for Higher Education Policy Studies (CHEPS) at the University of Twente, The Netherlands.

Harry de Boer is Research Associate at the Center for Higher Education Policy Studies (CHEPS) at the University of Twente, The Netherlands.

Bas Denters is Associate Professor in Political Science at the Faculty of Public Administration and Public Policy at the University of Twente, The Netherlands.

Ian R. Dobson is Associate to the Deputy Vice-Chancellor at Monash University, Australia.

Leo Goedegebuure is Associate Director at the Center for Higher Education Policy Studies (CHEPS) at the University of Twente, The Netherlands.

Åse Gornitzka is Research Associate at the Norwegian Institute for Studies in Research and Higher Education (NIFU), Oslo, Norway. She was seconded to CHEPS from October 1997 to November 1999.

Oscar van Heffen is Research Associate at the Center for Higher Education Policy Studies (CHEPS) at the University of Twente, The Netherlands.

Jeroen Huisman is Research Coordinator at the Center for Higher Education Policy Studies (CHEPS) at the University of Twente, The Netherlands.

Ineke Jenniskens is Research Associate at the Center for Higher Education Policy Studies (CHEPS) at the University of Twente, The Netherlands.

Ben Jongbloed is Research Associate at the Center for Higher Education Policy Studies (CHEPS) at the University of Twente, The Netherlands.

Han van der Knoop is Head of the General Resources Division at the University of Amsterdam, The Netherlands.

Jos Koelman is Research Associate at the Center for Higher Education Policy Studies (CHEPS) at the University of Twente, The Netherlands.

Peter Maassen is Acting Director of the Center for Higher Education Policy Studies at the University of Twente, The Netherlands.

Lynn Meek is Professor at the School of Administration and Training at the University of New England, Armidale, Australia.

Christopher Morphew is Assistant Professor of Higher Education Administration at the School of Education, University of Kansas, United States of America.

Guy Neave is Director of Research at the International Association of Universities (IAU) in Paris and Visiting Professor at the Center for Higher Education Policy Studies at the University of Twente, The Netherlands.

Karen Sorensen holds a Doctorate in International and Comparative Education from the University of Stockholm and has studied education in Poland since 1981.

Ulrich Teichler is Director of the Centre for Research on Higher Education and Work at the University of Kassel, Germany.

Jef Verhoeven is Professor of Sociology and Director of the Centre for Sociology of Education at the Catholic University of Leuven, Belgium.

Hans J.J. Vossensteyn is Research Associate at the Center for Higher Education Policy Studies (CHEPS) at the University of Twente, The Netherlands.

Piet de Vries is Assistant Professor of Economics at the Faculty of Public Administration and Public Policy at the University of Twente, The Netherlands.

Lieteke van Vucht Tijssen is Member of the Governing Board at Utrecht University, The Netherlands.

Egbert de Weert is Research Associate at the Center for Higher Education Policy Studies (CHEPS) at the University of Twente, The Netherlands.

Marijk van der Wende is Research Associate at the Center for Higher Education Policy Studies (CHEPS) at the University of Twente, The Netherlands.

Don F. Westerheijden is Research Associate at the Center for Higher Education Policy Studies of the University of Twente, The Netherlands.

Kurt de Wit is Researcher at the Centre for Sociology of Education at the Catholic University of Leuven, Belgium.

Preface

In order to celebrate the fifteenth anniversary – the third lustrum – of our Center, we at CHEPS decided to collectively write a book on the issue of how higher education institutions deal with the demand for change. Institutional change is without any doubt one of the burning issues for researchers in higher education and policy studies in general, but even more so for administrators at the institutional level (institutional leadership, deans) and planners of higher education in public life (government agencies, intermediary organisations, international organisations).

Whereas the *lustrumbook* we wrote for our second lustrum concentrated on comparative policy studies, many of them focusing on comparisons between different national higher education systems, this time the object of our analyses is the institution itself. Today's higher education institutions are faced by demands from a multitude of actors – from inside the institution (students, staff) as well as from the institution's environment (governments, employers, research councils, sponsors). These demands require changes in policy, practice, systems, and culture. The ways in which institutions respond to these demands and how their behaviour may be understood and predicted is the challenge tackled by the authors of this volume, each from their own perspective and each looking at different aspects of the educational organisation.

The chapters contained in this book have been written by teams of authors, generally consisting of a staff member from CHEPS and an author from outside CHEPS. This has allowed us to combine different theoretical and practical perspectives and to rethink previous CHEPS approaches. It also shows that we at CHEPS are open to new ideas and challenges ourselves. Writing the book has reminded us of how little we know of the 'inner life' of the higher education institution and has suggested areas we should target in our future research efforts.

We would like to express our gratitude to all of those who have been involved in the production of this book. Our list runs from the staff of our institute, going on to our close colleagues at the University of Twente, our collaborators in the various research projects that underlie some of these chapters, the Board of the University of Twente (for their financial support), to Kluwer Academic Publishers (represented by Joy Carp), who agreed to publish all of this. We would especially like to thank Di Davies who – although being as far away from us as Australia – did a wonderful job in proof-reading the chapters and improving our English. A final mention goes to Astrid Zuurman who transformed the different bits and pieces very professionally into a camera-ready manuscript. Now, forward to our next lustrum!

The editors

Chapter 1

Introduction
Organisational adaptation in higher education

PETER MAASSEN, GUY NEAVE AND BEN JONGBLOED

Key words: cultural dimension; institutional adaptation; organisational theory

1.   INTRODUCTION

How do universities and colleges adapt to changing circumstances, expectations, demands, and pressures, both from within and from outside? In this book we will discuss the topic of organisational adaptation in higher education. Before giving a brief overview of the various chapters contained in this volume, we will address the concept of organisational change, and the theories that may be used for studying this subject.

Universities have existed since the early Middle Ages. It can be argued that they are extremely successful organisations, given that they have been able to survive since their origin in more or less the same organisational form, despite the tremendous changes taking place in their external environments. Today, as in their early days, the universities' main organisational building blocks are the knowledge areas around which chairs, departments, schools, and faculties are created. Today, as at its beginning, the university is populated by administrators, academics, and students, whose interactions determine the university's day-to-day internal life. The relatively stable organisational structure, consisting of units that operate more or less independently of each other, and the dynamic internal interaction between the three main groups populating the university, are features that can still be found in any university around the world. All universities have faculties, departments or comparable organisational units, while they also have

1

students, administrators, and academic staff whose main ranks are (the equivalents of) full professor, associate professor, and assistant professor. In addition, whether he or she is called rector, president, or vice-chancellor, all universities have a prominent academic at a core place in their leadership structure, either as the individual institutional leader, or in the case of the Netherlands, as a member of the central institutional governing board.

Other types of higher education institutions, e.g. the German and Austrian *Fachhochschulen*, the Dutch and Flemish *hogescholen*, the South African *technikons*, the *colleges* and *polytechnics* to be found in many countries in the world,[1] also show a remarkable similarity when it comes to their organisational structure and their internal interpersonal dynamics. The terms used for their organisational units and for the members of their academic staff may not always be the same as those used in universities, but colleges have also created organisational units around knowledge areas and are also populated by academic staff, administrators and students. The mission of a college may differ from that of a university, but the similarities as regards organisational structure and internal dynamics are such that it was, for example, relatively easy from an intra-organisational perspective for specific Norwegian colleges to develop and introduce traditional university functions, such as PhD programmes, or for the former British polytechnics to transform into universities.

Next to an *internal* life, universities and colleges have an *external* life. Martin Trow introduced the terms *public* (external) and *private* (internal) lives for the two sides of a higher education institution's existence. The characteristics of their internal life and the nature of the relationship between their internal and external lives make these organisations unique and significant objects of study. Therefore, it is almost obvious that many important concepts and theories in the field of organisation theory have been developed in studies of higher education institutions. Examples are 'loose coupling' (Weick 1976), 'organisational saga' (Clark 1970), and 'garbage can decision making' (March and Olsen 1976). But the relationship, of course, works in two directions, as is underlined in the following quote from the chapter on *Organisation Theory* in the *Encyclopaedia on Education:* "[M]ost of the significant scholarship on higher education draws on organisation theory, sometimes explicitly, in reference to particular conceptual frameworks, and sometimes implicitly, in analysing organisations or organisation contexts" (Rhoades 1998). Why this emphasis on organisation theory, and why the growing interest in organisational adaptation?

---

[1]   In the remainder of this chapter these organisations will be referred to as *colleges*.

One of the possible explanations might be found in a generally acknowledged global trend implying that our societies are moving from being manufacturing based to being information and knowledge based. It is believed that we are witnessing not merely a temporal fluctuation, but a fundamental structural shift in our society. Even though the nature and impact of the information and knowledge revolution are far from clear,[2] and even though we are still only at the beginning of understanding the possible effects of the underlying technological developments on our daily life, we cannot but accept that a country's productivity and competitive position in the global marketplace are more and more linked to the capacity of that country to produce, handle and transfer knowledge and information. Given its traditional role in the handling, transfer and production of knowledge, it is obvious that higher education is (or at least should be) a core social institution in our expanding knowledge and information society. If they fully want to live up to their role, higher education institutions will have to adapt to the needs of the knowledge and information society – without these needs being perfectly clear. The question is, whether the traditional strong adaptive power of higher education institutions is capable of this. As a consequence, examining and understanding the way higher education institutions adapt to changing circumstances has become an important part of the field of higher education research. In order to understand the way higher education institutions adapt, we (i.e. CHEPS) are moving gradually from an emphasis on system level issues, such as governmental policies and steering models as well as quality assessment mechanisms, towards a focus on institutional level issues, with governmental policies representing one of the external variables to take into account.

Many observers argue that the adaptive power of higher education institutions is not strong enough. They suggest that the current economic, political, and technological developments that underlie the move towards the knowledge and information society form an unprecedented threat to universities and colleges. These developments are expected to radically alter the shape and function of these organisations, or even make them obsolete. Casper (1997: 1), for example, discusses the question whether in the future we will have "a world without universities", while Drucker and Holden (1997: 1745) even go one step further, suggesting that in the light of technological developments, "thirty years from now big university campuses will be relics".

---

[2] Even though many manifestations of today's information society had their origin in the laboratories and libraries of the higher education institution itself.

However, despite these and other claims that the university is an endangered species and might disappear, especially as a consequence of technological developments, the counter arguments are equally convincing. Throughout the centuries, it was suggested on many an occasion that the then threats to higher education were unprecedented and would lead to the end of the university. Time and again, however, the university has overcome the crises it faced, and also today the current crises and threats don't seem to reach the core functions of the university. Castells (1996: 397), for example, suggests that

> *[S]chools and universities are paradoxically the institutions least affected by the virtual logic embedded in information technology. (...) In the case of universities, this is because the quality of education is still and will be for a long time, associated with the intensity of face-to-face interaction. Thus the large-scale experiences of "distant universities", ..., seem to show that they are second-option forms of education which could play a significant role in the future, enhanced system of adult education, but which could hardly replace current higher education institutions.*

In this book we will not adhere to the "doom-scenario" of a world without universities and colleges. We are not going to discuss the question whether the threats to which higher education institutions have recently been exposed are indeed unprecedented, or whether the adaptive capacity of higher education institutions is strong enough to deal with them. Instead, we will discuss the notion of organisational adaptation in higher education as such, assuming that it is of interest to examine this notion both from a scholarly and a practical perspective. From a scholarly perspective it is of interest because of the unique organisational characteristics of universities and colleges. Examining these organisations will add to our knowledge of organisational change in general. As far as the practical perspective is concerned, studying organisational adaptation is of interest because of the suggested key function of higher education as a social institution in today's knowledge and information society. Increasing our understanding of how these organisations adapt may lead to more realistic efforts to steer or control these institutions – efforts undertaken by external stakeholders, such as governmental agencies, and internal managers alike.

2. UNDERSTANDING ORGANISATIONAL ADAPTATION

Academic and administrative institutional leaders have to assess regularly how and when to deliberately adapt (part of) their university or college to its changing environment, that is, whether to reshape the external life of their institution. In addition, the dynamics of the internal life of higher education institutions are such that they also lead to adaptation processes. These, however, are in general emerging processes instead of deliberately designed ones. In order to analyse the nature and effects of both types of adaptation processes, it is important that these processes are monitored by individual universities and colleges themselves, as well as examined by academic researchers from various disciplines. To this end, many universities and colleges have installed special units, such as offices for institutional research, through which their own internal aspects and the external trends relevant to the organisation can be monitored and analysed. Also in social science research in general and in the field of higher education research in particular, over the last years the interest in organisational adaptation has grown.

In addition to the structural organisational aspects and the composition of the institution's population, we would like to point to a third element that is relevant for understanding organisational adaptation in higher education, namely the concept of *culture*. This element can be attached to different organisational aspects, i.e. the culture of the institution as a whole, or of parts of the institution (e.g. departmental or faculty cultures), or to the human dimension – be it of individual academics or of the collective of the academic staff (the academic culture).

What do we mean by organisational adaptation? In the context of this book it refers in the first place to deliberate attempts of a university or college to change any aspect of its organisational structure as a reaction to or in anticipation of external developments. Structure is interpreted broadly in this respect, including, amongst other things, the institution's teaching programmes. In the second place it refers to any major deliberate change taking place in the composition of the population of the university, i.e. in the group of administrators, academics, or students. This type of change may originate from internal reasons and sources, for example as a consequence of the introduction of new teaching programmes or the start of a new faculty, as well as from external ones, for example, as the result of the introduction of a new law on governance structures for all universities. Third, it refers to institutional efforts to adapt the culture of (part of) the institution, or to change the (collective or individual) academic culture of the institutional academic staff. Fourth, it refers to gradual, non-planned (in other words, emergent) changes that take place either in the organisational structure or the cultural dimension of an institution, or in the composition of its staff. These kinds of changes are in general bottom-up and often are the result of disciplinary developments.

In table 1, the main sources and objects of change are presented.

Table 1: Sources and objects of change

Sources of change	Objects of change
Belief systems (Clark 1983)	Organisational structure
• Discipline (incl. knowledge production)	• Teaching structure (incl. curricula)
• National/supranational system (e.g. governmental policies; national laws)	• Research structure
	• Management structure (incl. budgetary framework, quality management, human resources management)
• Academic profession-at-large	
• Institution itself (e.g. scale, age, complexity, etc.)	• Governance or decision making structure
	• Organisational matrix
Additional sources	Composition of population
• Student organisations	• Administrators
• Market partners	• Students
• Alumni	• Academic staff
• Employers of graduates	
• Media	Cultural dimension
	• Institutional culture
	• Faculty/department culture
	• Collective academic culture
	• Individual academic culture

Deliberate adaptation or change processes consist of three successive stages. First, somewhere in the organisation there has to be the realisation that there is a need for change. Second, there has to be the willingness to change. The person or group realising that there is a need to change has to be able to get this need on the institutional agenda, to operationalise this need in a recognisable and realistic way, and to mobilise interest groups in order to get sufficient internal support for the change process. Third, the institution has to be able to implement the intended change. It needs to have the resources, the skills and the capacity to carry out an effective change operation.

3.   ORGANISATION THEORY

In the field of organisation studies, various theories have been developed and applied over the years. These theories enable us to examine and understand different aspects of organisations. A number of the theories have also been used in research projects undertaken by the authors of this book. It has to be stressed that in the CHEPS research programme and its research activities we do not limit ourselves to using one theory. We feel that our aim to understand organisational phenomena is served better by applying competing theories than by assuming that one specific theory is superior. In the chapters included in this book various theories have been used. Given the excellent overviews on organisation theory that are available[3] we will not discuss these theories (or: models, perspectives, approaches) in this chapter. It suffices to briefly characterise them and refer to some of the existing overviews.

The first of the theories applied by CHEPS researchers over the years is the population-ecology, or natural selection, approach (see, for example: Hannan and Freeman 1977; Aldrich 1979; Carroll and Hannan 1989). This approach "posits that environmental factors select those organizational characteristics that best fit the environment" (Aldrich and Pfeffer 1976: 79). This approach does not deal with individual organisations, but focuses on forms or populations of organisations. Organisational forms that have the appropriate fit with the environment are favoured over those that do not fit or fit less appropriately (Hall 1994).

The second theory we want to mention is the resource-dependence model (Pfeffer and Salancik 1978). The basic starting-point of the resource dependence theory is that decisions are made within the internal political organisational context of the organisation as part of the attempts of the organisation to manipulate the environment to its own advantage. Rather than being passive recipients of environmental forces, as the population-ecology approach suggests, resource dependency theory implies that organisations will make strategic decisions about adapting to the environment.

The contingency model is the third theory to be mentioned here (Lawrence and Lorsch 1967). Scott (1981: 114) has characterised this theory as follows: "The best way to organise depends on the nature of the environment to which the organisation must relate." This implies, for example, that the more

---

[3]   See, for example, Pfeffer (1982), Astley and Van de Ven (1983), Morgan (1986), Hall (1994).

uncertain and complex its environment, the more differentiated an organisation has to be in order to be successful.

Finally, we want to mention the neo-institutional theory. Scott (1995: 33) defines an institution as consisting of "cognitive, normative, and regulative structures and activities that provide stability and meaning to social behaviour. Institutions are transported by various carriers – cultures, structures, and routines – and they operate at multiple levels of jurisdiction." It is suggested by DiMaggio and Powell (1991) that the focus on the cognitive dimension of institutions is the major feature of the new institutionalism in sociology (incl. organisation studies).

Next to these four main theories, also a number of approaches or theories from other fields have been applied in the chapters in this book. We mention, for example, cultural theory (Thompson, Ellis and Wildavsky 1990) and theories originating from economic science (neo institutional economics, management control).

4.   STRUCTURE OF THE BOOK

The perspectives used in this book for discussing organisational adaptation relate to the sources and objects of change presented in table 1. It will be obvious that we do not cover every possible relationship between any of the sources and objects included. We have limited ourselves to those relationships that have been the subject of CHEPS research. These can be summarised under the following main headings.

Relationship between national/supranational policy aspects and institutional management structure.
       This relationship forms the starting-point for chapters 2, 3, 4, and 12. In chapter 2, Westerheijden and Sorensen discuss the way Central European higher education institutions have adapted themselves to radically changing environments. Higher education institutions, it appears, indeed have different ways of reacting to the opportunities opened after 1989, depending on market needs and on the idiosyncratic constellation of its belief system (Clark 1983). De Weert and Van Vucht Tijssen (Chapter 3) focus on the consequences of the growing autonomy of higher education institutions for the working conditions of their academic staff. The authors argue how these and other external effects challenge higher education institutions to reconsider traditional practices and to develop new policies in the area of

human resource management. In chapter 4, by Van der Wende, Beerkens and Teichler, an analysis is presented of the way in which internationalisation is likely to cause organisational changes within institutions of higher education. Finally, in chapter 12 by Van Heffen, Verhoeven and De Wit, changes in steering strategies, policies and university policy plans in Flemish higher education are examined from two theoretical perspectives: instrumental theory and cultural theory.

Relationship between national policy aspects and institutional governance structure.
An example of trying to understand the attempts of universities to change their organisational structure – one of the objects of organisational change mentioned in section 2 of this chapter – is Chapter 10 by De Boer and Denters. The authors employ a set of dimensions to classify the main characteristics of university governance systems. Their classification scheme, based on notions of democracy, guardianship, and the concentration and separation of powers, provides a basis for a systematic description of university governance systems. They use their classification scheme to analyse post-war changes in the Dutch system of higher education governance.

Relationship between national policy aspects and institutional organisational matrix.
This relationship is at the core of chapter 11, in which the authors, Bartelse and Goedegebuure, discuss the institutionalisation of the graduate school in a number of European countries. The approach they take to understand the change processes is derived from innovation theory and centres around the concepts of compatibility and profitability.

Relationship between national policy aspects, national funding mechanisms and market partners, and institutional management structures.
This relationship is discussed in chapters 7, 8 and 9. Chapter 7, by Jongbloed and Van der Knoop, focuses on budgeting processes at the institutional level. The purpose of the chapter is to examine the principles of resource allocation at the institutional level and to look directions into which budget systems are changing. Koelman and De Vries in their chapter (Chapter 8) discuss changes in universities and colleges that have resulted from the fact that these institutions are increasingly orienting themselves on the market. Consequently, the character of these organisations is becoming *hybrid* (part non-profit, part for-profit). This will have implications for accountability and, therefore, the principles of academic accounting. Chapter 9, by Vossensteyn and Dobson, focuses on the student and looks at ways in which

higher education institutions have sought to respond to student needs. Institutional responsiveness to student demands is a phenomenon that is expected to manifest itself even stronger in the coming decades, in which students are expected to contribute even more to the costs of their training. Again, this is an effect of changes in relationships between government and higher education. Many of the policy changes can be characterised as leading to market-type mechanisms that determine the course of the higher education sector.

Chapters 5 (Jenniskens and Morphew) and 6 (Huisman and Meek) examine, on the basis of various theories, the factors that are argued to affect academic programme development in universities and colleges. In chapter 5, the concept of academic drift is discussed. The authors are especially interested in analysing the factors faculty members cite as leading to the introduction of new degree programmes. They examine how these factors relate to arguments derived from the literature on academic drift and propositions offered by neo-institutional theory. In chapter 6, the authors apply both the resource dependency model and neo-institutional theory to understand the emergence of new study programmes in Dutch universities.

Finally, in Chapter 13 by Gornitzka and Maassen, a number of theoretical notions underlying an international comparative research project on the relationship between governmental policies and organisational change in higher education will be presented.[4] The authors of chapters 6 and 12 have used empirical material gathered in the framework of this European Commission-sponsored research project.

References

Aldrich, H.E. (1979) *Organizations and Environments*. Englewood Cliffs, NJ: Prentice Hall.
Aldrich, H.E. and J. Pfeffer (1976) Environments of Organizations. *Annual Review of Sociology* Vol. 2, Palo Alto, CA: Annual Review.
Astley, W.G. and A.H. Van de Ven (1983) Central Perspectives and Debates in Organization Theory. *Administrative Science Quarterly* 33: 245-273.
Carroll, G.R. and M.T. Hannan (1989) Density Dependence in the Evolution of Populations of Newspaper Organizations. *American Sociological Review* 54: 524-541.
Casper, G. (1997) *Eine Welt ohne Universitäten?* Werner Heisenberg Vorlesung, Bayerische Akademie der Wissenschaften und Carl Friedrich von Siemens Stiftung, Munich (Quoted from a broadcast script of the Tele-Akademie of the Südwestfunk, issued on January 26).
Castells, M. (1996) *The rise of the network society*. Oxford: Blackwell Publishers.
Clark, B.R. (1970) *The Distinctive College: Antioch, Reed and Swarthmore*. Chicago: Aldine.

---

[4] An extended version of this chapter was published in the journal *Higher Education*.

Clark, B.R. (1983) *The Higher Education System. Academic Organization in Cross-National Perspective*. Berkeley: University of California Press.

DiMaggio, P.J. and W.W. Powell (1991) Introduction. In: W.W. Powell and P.J. DiMaggio (eds.) *The New Institutionalism in Organizational Analysis*. Chicago: University of Chicago Press.

Drucker, P.A. and C. Holden (1997) Untitled. *Science* 275 (5307), 1745.

Hall, R.H. (1994) *Organizations. Structures, Processes, and Outcomes*. Seventh Edition. Englewood Cliffs, NJ: Prentice Hall.

Hannan, M.T. and J.H. Freeman (1977) The Population Ecology of Organizations. *American Journal of Sociology* 82 (March): 929-964.

Lawrence, P.R. and J.W. Lorsch (1967), *Organization and Environment*. Cambridge, MA: Harvard University Press.

March, J. and J. Olsen (1976) *Ambiguity and Choice in Organizations*. Bergen: Universitetsforlaget.

Morgan, G. (1986) *Images of Organizations*. Beverly Hills, CA: SAGE Publications.

Pfeffer, J. (1982) *Organizations and Organization* Theory. Boston: Pitman.

Pfeffer, J. and G.R. Salancik (1978) *The External Control of Organizations: A Resource Dependence Perspective*. New York: Harper & Row.

Rhoades, G. Organization Theory. *In: Education: The Complete Encyclopedia*. Amsterdam: Elsevier Science.

Scott, W.R (1981) *Organizations: Rational, Natural, and Open Systems*. Englewood Cliffs, NJ: Prentice Hall.

Scott, W.R. (1995*) Institutions and Organizations*. Thousand Oaks, CA: SAGE Publications.

Thompson, M., R. Ellis and A. Wildavsky (1990) *Cultural Theory*. Boulder, CO: Westview Press.

Weick, K. (1976) Educational Organizations as Loosely Coupled Systems. *Administrative Science Quarterly* 21: 1-19.

Chapter 2

People on a bridge
Central European higher education institutions in a storm of reform

DON F. WESTERHEIJDEN AND KAREN SORENSEN

Key words: autonomy; institutional culture; transformation

> *Dziwna planeta i dziwna na niej ci ludzie.*
> *Ulęgają czasowi, ale nie chcą go uznać.*
> A strange planet with its strange people.
> They yield to time but they don't recognise it [1].

1.   THEY YIELD TO TIME: INTRODUCTION

Arguably, the demise of communism in Central and Eastern Europe was the largest environmental change for higher education institutions in the last half-century. Hundreds of higher education institutions in tens of countries were challenged, *inter alia,* to:

- change their governance and management structures to more democratic ones that would allow more autonomous behaviour;
- change their curricula to match the transformation from socialist economies to market economies;

---

[1] This quotation as well as part of the title of this chapter are taken from Wisława Szymborska's poem *People on a Bridge*.

13

- change their mission from mainly teaching-oriented to incorporate research; and
- compete with a new sector of private higher education institutions of varying kinds.

Not all of these changes were present in all Central and Eastern European countries; in the Czech and Slovak Republics, for example, private higher education was not allowed. And in some countries (e.g. those that became independent after the demise of the USSR), there were even more challenges involving adjustment to a new political state of affairs. Regaining autonomy would seem to be the simplest way to characterise the changes in the higher education systems under study (see Amsterdamski & Rhodes 1993: 397). Indeed, even at first glance the leap from strict central control under communist rule to extreme autonomy and fragmentation — tendencies ever present in higher education (cf. Clark 1983) — is striking.

How do higher education institutions react to these changes in their environment, and how can differences in reactions among various higher education institutions be explained?

We attack this question by first examining two contrasting case studies of how higher education institutions give shape to their new autonomy. We then consider some theoretical approaches which help to explain the differences. Some environmental factors are kept constant in the two case studies, that is, they are placed in a single country (Poland), are mono-disciplinary institutions and are in the same discipline (economics). At this juncture, we seek to broaden the discussion by asking: what would happen if these constants became variables? This question is explored through empirical illustrations of how four other higher education institutions in Central Europe responded to the environmental challenges posed by the developments of 1989.

The best name for the period, the *Velvet Revolution*, was coined in Czechoslovakia, but '1989' clearly began in Poland. It was there, with the government's initiation of 'roundtable discussions' with the Solidarity trade union, that the first cracks in the communist system appeared. As Garton-Ash (1999) explains: 'When Gorbachev gave an inch, the Poles took a mile'. In this chapter, therefore, institutions in Poland will be the starting point of our discussion, against which we shall try to compare and contrast some developments in institutions in the Czech and Slovak Republics and Hungary.

2. PEOPLE ON A BRIDGE IN THE STORM: TWO POLISH ECONOMICS ACADEMIES EN ROUTE TO THE MARKET[2]

Changes in the higher education system in Poland came almost as quickly as the political change ushered in by the defeat of communist candidates in the June 1989 elections. By the autumn of 1989, a new law was already being drafted in Poland which would allow marked changes in the relationship between the state and higher education institutions. This relationship under communist rule had been characterised by strong state control of a highly centralised system, where major organisational and curricular decisions were taken at the ministerial level to support the centrally planned economy.

With the passage of the Act on Higher Education in September 1990, institutions of higher education were granted 'full' or 'partial' autonomy in their internal affairs, according to a formula based on academic staff qualifications. Institutions with full autonomy were free to write and enact their own statutes; those with partial autonomy were to have their statutes approved by the Ministry of Education. Irrespective of the relative degree of autonomy granted, the election of all internal authorities, the determination to offer certain study programmes, the design of syllabi, the assessment of tuition fees for non-regular classes, and the standards for accepting new students were all matters to be relegated to the institutional level. In addition, the Act restored the right of institutions to elect their own rectors and, notably, provided the basis for the establishment of private higher education institutions.

Two subsequent pieces of legislation — the Act on Academic Titles and Academic Degrees (also passed in September 1990) and the Act on the State Committee for Scientific Research (passed in January 1991) — completed the legal boundaries under which changes in the system might be made. The latter law changed the basis of research funding from a wholly statutory grant system to one in which a portion of the state budget would be awarded on a tender basis, with institutions or units competing for the funding of projects.

Thus, from a very early stage in the societal transformation begun in 1989, higher education institutions in Poland were free to chart their own paths to change. In the absence of a centrally designed plan for reform, they were

---

[2] This section is based on Sorensen (1997).

challenged to adapt to a new environment characterised by flux and uncertainty.

While all institutions would react in some way to the freedom won under the new legislation, it was the economics academies which were particularly pushed to change. The restructuring of the nation's banking system, the creation of a capital (stock) market and the formulation of a new monetary policy, as well as insurance and social security reforms, required the input of specialists which a curriculum linked to a centrally planned economy could not provide. In May 1990 Leszek Balcerowicz, Minister of Finance under the Mazowiecki government, foreseeing the long-range need for professionals in the new economy, called for proposals for the reform of higher economic education (Beksiak *et al.* 1991: 4).

2.1   The Warsaw School of Economics

Known during the period of communist rule as the Central School of Planning and Statistics (*Szkoła Główna Planowania i Statystyki,* SGPiS), the Warsaw School of Economics (WSE) can trace its origins to 1906, when it was founded as a school of Private Commercial Courses for Men. Prior to its nationalisation and transformation in 1949 into a state economics university which would prepare students for work in the new centrally planned command economy, the school functioned as a private university, funded by foundations and private sources, but with the same legal status as the Polish state universities.

When the school was nationalised, the old curriculum was eliminated and one based on the Soviet Union's model of economic studies was implemented. Many of the school's junior faculty members were replaced by stalwart Communist Party members. Four faculties (planning of trade, planning of industry, planning of finance, and statistics) were created, offering courses heavily indoctrinated with Marxist-Leninist theory. Over the years, the school earned the epithet 'The Red Fortress'. However, intermittently, in periods when Soviet influence waned, some of the senior faculty who had distinguished themselves in the field were able to use their prestige to organise visits from Western economists. In this way, the school also gained a reputation as the 'Polish Cambridge'.

In 1980, a chapter of the Solidarity trade union was organised at SGPiS but, contrary to what happened in some other Polish higher education institutions, few academics joined the union. Nonetheless, in September

1981, Solidarity members held two of the five deanships. When martial law was imposed in December 1981, Solidarity activity continued underground at SGPiS. Courses in the latest economic theories were offered and discussions were held on how the school could be reformed if a more benevolent political atmosphere prevailed. By the late 1980s, travel restrictions were again eased and many faculty members travelled abroad. When the Solidarity union became legal again in April 1989, however, only one dean was not a member of the Communist Party.

In this period, the administration of SGPiS consisted of a rector (nominated from among the ranks of the full professors and appointed by the Ministry) and the academic senate. The senate consisted of the rector, two pro-rectors, the deans of the faculties, the administrative director, the bursar and representatives of the junior faculty and the student government.

The internal structure of faculties at SGPiS was in accordance with branches of the public economy. The five faculties — foreign trade, internal trade, economics of production, finance and statistics, and social economics — offered one or more of the lines of study which were approved by the Ministry.

The faculties were headed by deans who also headed their respective faculty councils, composed of senior academic staff in the faculty and representatives of the junior staff. The councils supervised the thesis work of candidates for doctor and *habilitacja* (post-doctorate) degrees, while the deans were responsible for the students' progress through the official study lines. Faculty members generally taught courses only in the faculty to which they were admitted.

Students were accepted into a particular faculty and, with rare exception, finished their line of study completely within that faculty. Entrance exams, set by the Ministry, consisted of a written test and an oral interview. Students following a given study line all took the same courses, up to the level where they began their masters thesis work. From the first day of classes, students would enter into a certain group and remain with that group until graduation, except for special thesis seminars in their final year. Students who maintained above average exam results were allowed to vary their programmes in their final years and these variations might include courses in a second faculty.

In December 1989, in anticipation of the autonomy proposed under the draft legislation, a small group of reform-oriented faculty members and students began to plan structural changes at SGPiS. As members, for the most part, of the academic section of the Solidarity union, this group was well-informed of the planned legislation, since a draft of the law on higher education was sent to all trade unions. Meeting to discuss the draft of the law, they established that the new provisions for the free election of rectors opened the possibility for fundamental reforms. They decided to mount an election campaign based on the idea of building a new school, and chose one of the members of their group to be their candidate.

The programme of change which was decided upon took into account the fact that supporters of reform were nearly a majority in the academic senate, but a clear minority in the faculty councils. Since faculty councils could block changes, the power of the councils would have to be broken. Moreover, the fact that faculties could have great influence over students' programmes meant that the reform should include a way to take the students out of the grasp of the conservative councils.

The idea of admitting students to a *studium* of basic studies then evolved, and was refined to include the concept of a *studium* of graduate, or specialised, studies, so that students would continue outside the rule of faculties. New units, *kolegia*, were conceived to take the place of faculties, linking academic staff with similar specialities and common research interests, as the old faculties had done. This programme of restructuring, then, formed the basis of the campaign to elect the new rector. The incumbent rector of seven years, who had been active in the Communist Party, stood for election as well.

When the November 1990 election of the rector was not decided in the first round, the candidates opened special dialogues with the student groups to enlist their support. The candidate supported by the Solidarity faction won with a 54 per cent majority. If the students were eliminated from the ballot, the vote would have gone against him.

At the first meeting of the academic senate, the new rector proposed the establishment of a reform committee to organise the process of restructuring. He appointed those who had conceived the original plan for changing the school to the committee, as well as others supporting the reform.

The reform committee presented its plans for restructuring, both formally at senate meetings and through 'information bulletins' (published periodically and made available in the staff and student lounges). Early in 1991 the senate (now augmented by the reform-minded rector), the pro-rectors and student government representatives passed a declaration outlining some of the basic features of the reforms. The school would be restructured: the basic units would be departments and institutes, and faculties would be abolished. At the middle-level, *kolegia* would be the units responsible for staff development and research undertakings. The academic staff of the school were invited to declare their membership in a particular *kolegium*.

In April 1992, on the basis of the declarations received, the senate passed a resolution, establishing five *kolegia*: economic analysis, world economy, social science, enterprise science, and management.

In subsequent meetings of the reform committee, the proposed restructuring was further refined. The *Studium* of Basic Studies would encompass three semesters of 'core' courses which were intended to provide the basis for future specialised studies. Students would enter into the *Studium* of Diploma Studies in their fourth semester, and begin to take courses in the specialisation (study line) of their choice. The students would have progressively more choice in constructing their programmes as their level of study advanced and they could enrol in courses offered in a variety of departments according to the requirements in their chosen line of study.

Lines of study would not be offered by any faculty, or department or institute within it. Students in the *Studium* of Diploma Studies would follow a line of study by completing the courses (credits) required in the line. The courses would be drawn from various departments, and students would be guided through their chosen line by individual tutors (advisors).

The senate established a programme committee to coordinate matters relating to the new curricula. It had the responsibility of proposing the requirements for the different study lines and determining the balance of free vs. elective courses within them. Also, since the abolition of the faculties meant that certain basic courses (such as micro and macroeconomics, finance and statistics) would be offered by different departments, the programme committee had the task of supervising the standardisation of these courses.

In November 1991, the senate recognised the creation of seven new study lines, viz. economics, finance and banking, management and marketing, quantitative methods and information systems, public economy, international relations, and business administration. These were submitted to the Central Council on Higher Education (a representative academic national body which approves new study lines).

The staff were invited to propose courses which they felt qualified to teach, and these would be approved by the programme committee. When this committee perceived a gap in the offerings in a particular area, it suggested courses and solicited candidates to teach them. In this way, a host of new courses which would reflect the conditions in a market economy could be offered.

In the autumn of 1992, a catalogue explaining the new programme of studies was published. The courses were listed according to the level at which students were eligible to register for them and, within these levels, alphabetically. This type of listing was devised as a strategy to sever the connection between courses and *kolegia* or their units — while the course instructor was listed, his or her affiliation was not. It was expected that students would 'vote with their feet' to eliminate courses which were not applicable to their needs in the new economy.

By February 1993, then, the basic structural reforms at WSE had been accomplished. During 1992, agreements were made with a consortium of Canadian universities as well as the University of Minnesota in the US to enter into faculty exchanges. The latter eventually resulted in the joint offering of an MBA. Tempus[3] projects were initiated as early as 1991. In May 1991, the senate approved the setting of fees for evening classes commencing in the new academic year. Enrolments in these courses exceeded expectations, and over the next few years continued to rise steadily, even as fees increased. In both day and evening classes, students could complete three-year *licencjat* degrees as well as *magister* degrees.

As the value of fixed academic salaries decreased with inflation, the majority of staff supplemented their income with lucrative work in private enterprise or consulting. This was seen to bring a much-needed practical input to courses, but also raised concerns that outside work was jeopardising the staff's commitment to the school and that it would be increasingly difficult to recruit new staff.

---

[3]   Tempus stands for *Trans-European Mobility Scheme for University Studies*. This is the European Union programme for cooperation with higher education in Central European countries.

2.2　The Oskar Lange Academy of Economics in Wrocław

Founded in 1947, in the period between the end of World War II and the communists coming to power, the Oskar Lange Academy of Economics (*Akademia Ekonomiczna im. Oskara Langego we Wrocławiu,* AEW) began as a private professional school, The Higher School of Commerce, with one faculty, that of national economy. In 1950 it was nationalised as the Higher School of Economics, and was renamed in honour of Oskar Lange, 'the Father of Socialist Economics', in 1974.

The influence of Stalinism permeated the institution in the early 1950s, much the same as at other higher education institutions across Poland. By the end of the 1950s, however, senior professors who were invited to conferences in the West (often by virtue of pre-war contacts) were granted permission to attend. Connections with academics in East and West Germany predominated, due to Wrocław's identity as the German city of Breslau before the realignment of Polish borders in 1945.

After 1968, AEW had more contact with the West and Western publications. British and American nationals were allowed to teach English at the institution and Western economics books were made available to students as a vehicle for English language study. In the 1970s, staff began translating American economics textbooks.

The majority of faculty members belonged to the Communist Party. During the Solidarity period, many of the younger staff declared their support for the union. However, the general consensus today is that the influence of Solidarity at AEW was not strong. Dissatisfaction with the system, however, led an estimated ten per cent of the teaching staff to emigrate in the 1980s.

At the close of the 1980s, there were four faculties at AEW offering eight different lines of study. The faculty of industrial economics and engineering, introduced in 1950, was the only one of its kind in the country. Three lines (social economics, the economics and organisation of production, and the economics of trade turnover and services) were duplicated in two faculties, but some specialities within these lines differed and one of the two faculties was located in an external branch of the academy located in Jelenia Góra.

Under the 1990 law on higher education, AEW was granted partial autonomy since it did not employ the 60 full professors necessary to be accorded full autonomy. This meant that the institutional statute, after being passed by a two-thirds majority of the senate, had to be confirmed by the Ministry of Education before coming into effect. The AEW statute was passed by the senate in April 1991, and confirmed by the Ministry in August 1991.

The aspects of autonomy which were readily acted upon included the democratic election of a rector and pro-rectors in November 1990, and the assumption by the individual faculties of responsibility for entrance exams. At AEW the incumbent rector (a member of the Communist Party) was re-elected, defying a national trend. No major structural changes were undertaken, and institutional leadership remained close to its pre-1990 configuration.

Changes to align courses to the emerging market economy were at first largely confined to amendments to the study lines offered. In July 1990, it was decided that altogether four study lines would be eliminated by 1994. Four new lines were proposed: finance and banking, regional economy, economics, and management in enterprises and marketing. New courses, such as computer programming and the psychology of management, forecasting in the management of enterprises, and business ethics were approved by separate senate votes. Changes in the number of hours allotted to certain courses were also made. The extent to which students could compose individual study plans, and the possibility of interfaculty cooperation in the teaching of basic courses were debated in the senate. There were two basic subjects (mathematics and macroeconomics) being taught over three faculties and students could choose among lecturers in these subjects.

In this period, a motion was put before the senate by the student and staff chapter of Solidarity to drop 'Oskar Lange' from the name of the institution. This motion received only one positive vote, and was thus defeated.

In September 1991, a two-year fee-paying professional programme for secondary school graduates, The Lower Silesian School of Business, was created. It was intended to provide training for managers and specialists in economics and administration.

With the development of new courses and programmes being proposed by individual faculties, some overlap of courses was evident. The same specialities or lines were to be offered by three faculties. A committee to study the organisational structure of the faculties was formed in response. Its report pointed out that the structure of the academy was not uniform: while the basic unit of the academy was the department, in the Institute of National Economy some departments belonged to institutes, and some were independent. In the other faculties, all departments had independent status.

In subsequent sessions, the senate acted decisively to abolish two departments which were understaffed, and to create a department of business law, headed by a professor (instead of a habilitated doctor, as had been the case until then). There was much debate and less resolution about the matter of dividing and amalgamating departments. Temporary closure on the matter was achieved with the senate exhorting the deans of faculties to consider the structure of the faculty before creating new departments.

Debate about the assessment of tuition fees for weekend classes set the rector against many members of the senate who noted that the other economics academies had already set tuition fees for these courses. This issue loomed large in the rectorial election of autumn 1993, with the incumbent losing to a reform-oriented candidate supporting tuition fees for weekend classes. The intake of weekend students continued to rise substantially.

Short-cycle courses were introduced, including a day programme in economics at the *licencjat* level, offered externally in the town of Świdnica, and an executive MBA programme open to graduates of tertiary institutions (in any discipline) and to prospective graduates of (the new) professional institutions offering *licencjat* degrees. This latter programme was offered in coordination with McGill University in Montreal and the Université du Québec.

In 1994, twenty-five students who had completed three semesters of study were accepted into an innovative two-year programme termed the School of Small Business, offered in conjunction with the Catholic University of Breda, the Netherlands, and the University of Bristol. After four semesters in the programme, the students would have the option of concluding their studies with a *licencjat* degree or returning to their studies at the sixth semester level and continuing for a *magister* degree.

By 1994, then, the changes at the academy included the addition of two *licencjat* programmes, offering professional courses, and an executive MBA programme. The four faculties offered a total of six different study lines (with two lines duplicated in two faculties), and were composed of departments which, depending on the faculty, were independent or functioned under an institute.

3.   VISIBLY QUICKENING THEIR STEP:
EXPLANATIONS FOR DIFFERENT REACTIONS

The two institutions considered here responded notably to the challenge
presented in the early 1990s to change their curricula, governance, mission
and behaviour. From the larger perspective, the changes they undertook were
similar: their curricula are now geared to prepare students to enter a market
economy, their management structures are independent of state authority,
and their degree offerings as well as general teaching and research activities
indicate a heightened responsiveness to their environment. A closer
perspective however reveals significant differences between the institutions
particularly in the pace and process of change.

Sorensen (1997) set the data from the two cases first against Clark's (1983)
categories of work, belief, authority and integration in order to elicit the
particulars of change in each institution, and then against Clark's
propositions concerning change in higher education institutions. As well,
concepts from the field of institutional and organisational theory were used
to interpret the differences in the pace and process of change.

The differences between the Warsaw School of Economics (WSE) and the
Oskar Lange Academy (AEW) which are most relevant to the research
questions here are, in particular, the adoption of major structural change, the
early introduction of fee-paying courses, and the introduction of new
programmes of studies which allocated a good deal of choice to students at
WSE *versus* the maintenance of old structures (faculties), the delayed
introduction of fee-paying courses and the espousal of regional initiatives at
AEW. In terms of pace and process, AEW, in its evolutionary and adaptive
approach to change, differs sharply from WSE where rapid, radical change
was intentionally initiated.

The change, or lack of change, in structures at the institutions — in Clark's
terms the way the *work* of higher education institutions is organised (e.g.
from a faculty to a *kolegia* sectional structure at WSE) — is best
characterised with reference to March and Olsen's (1989) categorisation of
intentional change in institutions. At WSE the change appears to be a
textbook example of what they describe as the process of *radical shock*,
wherein 'major structural changes in institutions are made in the hope that
such changes will destabilize political arrangements and force a permanent
realignment of the existing system' (1989: 64). Although the circumstances
that aided the process of change at WSE — the general societal
transformation of 1989 — were themselves the result of a complex

combination of intentional and unintentional change, the concept of engineering fundamental structural change in order to disrupt the balance of power (held by the faculties) and initiate a comprehensive programme of reform was an intentional strategy of the reform group at the institution.

Other processes were at work as well: *bargaining and negotiation*, as coalitions of groups or individuals standing to gain or lose power readily formed; and *contagion*, as reformers called upon their experience in Western universities for ideas of different structures. And, in terms of what March and Olsen (1989) term the 'exploitation of the incompleteness of stable processes', there could be observed certain *anomalies* wherein changes were 'transformed by the process of change' and unanticipated consequences resulted from the intentional changes introduced. For example, when exchanges with Western universities were initiated, it was expected that the contact would accelerate the process of curricular reform and bring new instructional materials to the school. It was not expected, however, that the contact would result in new teaching methods being adopted as well. When students were given more choice in their programmes and the opportunity to choose among instructors offering the same course, it was expected that the most popular instructors' courses would be filled first. It was not expected that students would propose class registration on a meritocratic basis, asking that they be ranked so the better students would have first preference for courses (and instructors). Students are thus seen to have become more competitive in the new system.

At AEW, *bargaining and negotiation* and *contagion* were found to be the main processes by which change occurred. With most, if not all, of the initial moves towards curricular reform originating at the faculty level, but requiring approval by the academic senate, it may be said that many of the moves were negotiated in that arena. New courses which would have wide 'market appeal' were sought by each faculty, with some duplication and conflict arising. The decision to allow duplicate lines of study was an outcome of negotiation, with the eventual result that some basic courses would be offered on an interfaculty basis.

Programmes which were totally outside the traditional course structure, such as the MBA programme and the School of Small Business, had a later start at AEW than at other academies and are an example of change by *contagion*. The participation of representatives from AEW in the Coordinating Unit for the Reform of Economic Schools (at the national level), and the CHER Higher Education Advanced Training Course also facilitated the spread of innovative ideas by *contagion*.

At both institutions, there was evidence of what March and Olsen (1989: 80) term the 'garbage can' aspect of reorganisation, where 'highly contextual combinations of people, choice, opportunities, problems and solutions stimulate change'. The general transformation of the political and economic system brought a whole new range of actors to the fore, as well as a new range of problems and solutions. While some of the problems identified by reformers were approached with strategies which reflected rational planning, some solutions were rather the result of fortuitous circumstance. At WSE, the development of the MBA programme in cooperation with the University of Minnesota, for example, was largely the result of one professor's involvement with the Institute of Public Affairs there during the initial transition period. At AEW, as well, it was the serendipitous contact of individuals with Western institutions and other academies in Poland which sparked the creation of the MBA programme and several new courses.

4.   OTHERS ON THE BRIDGE: CASES FROM OTHER CENTRAL EUROPEAN COUNTRIES

What are the main themes for change that came out of the two Polish cases, and how do other higher education institutions in Central Europe take up these or other themes, seen from the point of view of regained autonomy? Broadly considered, the changes may be divided into those made in response to the removal of central steering, for example, change in internal structures and decision-making, and those which demonstrate a response to the new market environment, for example, changes in curricula, degree structures and personnel.

From CRE institutional reviews,[4] reports are available on four universities in the three countries that we selected. We will provide brief vignettes of each, based on these reports.

---

[4]   The CRE, the Association of European Universities, performs voluntary reviews of the quality management and strategic management capacities of universities which are used by universities as a tool for institutional leadership to prepare for change. Following a pilot in 1994–95, about 12–15 universities throughout Europe have been reviewed every year. Each review results in a 15–20 page report by the external review team, consisting of three former university rectors and another higher education expert as secretary. The review reports used in this section were CRE 1996a (CTU), CRE 1996b (JATE), CRE 1997 (KLTE) and CRE 1998 (STU).

4.1   Czech Technical University in Prague

The Czech Technical University in Prague (CTU), the largest of the Czech technical universities, traces its history back to the XVIIIth century, and portrays itself as the most research-oriented technical university of the Czech Republic. Its context was influenced heavily by the law on higher education, which dates back to the Czechoslovak times of the first months after the *Velvet Revolution*. It had passed through the parliament even faster than the Polish law had, in March 1990. Mistakenly applying academic freedom to collectives instead of to individuals, this law granted all faculties legal autonomy equal to universities, clearly in strong reaction to communist-time central control. The 1990 law on higher education furthermore, *inter alia*:

- changed the degree structure, opening up the possibility for technical universities to offer three-year *bakalař* degrees next to the traditional five-year *inženyr* degrees;
- required all study programmes to be accredited by a new accreditation committee; and
- stimulated reintegration of research into universities.

Leadership at CTU saw the low level of governmental funding, which made up 90% of CTU's total budget, as the main problem, because it was too little for normal operation. The national funding formula was mostly driven by student numbers, faculties being rewarded for accepting ever more students. Note that the autonomy of faculties included setting enrolment numbers and the concomitant entrance examinations.

CTU's internal funding allocation model mirrored the national one, with the exception that it doubled from 10% to 20% the part of the state budget reserved for research. Despite the financial constraints, until 1996 it had not proved possible to rationalise, for example, mathematics provision at CTU: each faculty clung to its own unit. Also, the faculties left only a very small portion of the state funding for the rectorate for strategic use (also extra-budgetary allocations such as research grants all went directly to faculties or departments, and university overheads were, it seems, regularly evaded).

Academic salaries were not competitive with the private sector, which at that time was taking a positive turn. The low salary level meant that academics had to engage in moonlighting, or they gave up their university job altogether in favour of more lucrative jobs in private companies (leading to brain drain). This led to an imbalanced personnel structure at CTU, with a large proportion of older full professors, some young assistants, but very few middle-aged associate professor-level personnel.

This situation also meant that reform policies could not be furthered by negative sanctions: leadership had to be glad that anyone was willing to remain working in a university at all. Encouragement of international contacts (e.g. through university grants for travel to conferences) was one of the few rewards that they could think of as a viable option.

The need for re-accreditation had been used by CTU leadership to restructure all study programmes to include more humanities (especially foreign language training) and increase opportunities for students to take optional courses. However, the CRE reviewers 'did not meet with much proof of radical changes of curriculum content[5] or didactics to adapt to the new [market society] requirements — nor of mechanisms to keep track of such needs' except in two faculties. Most of the academics appeared to be completely 'convinced of the high level of quality that the CTU ha[d] to maintain and of the appropriateness of their traditional ways to do so'.[6,7] These visions of quality interacted with the tendency to enrol large numbers of students because of government funding. The changed composition of the enlarged student body led to high student drop out. Moreover, after 1989, engineering ceased to be a main career channel; the best students no longer applied for places at technical universities, rather, they shifted to business studies, economics and law programmes.

Students on the whole did not protest about drop out or traditional didactics and curricula (of course, the CRE reviewers only met those who had not dropped out).

The legal rearrangements of autonomy in the wake of the 1990 higher education law at CTU did not lead to much restructuring of faculties (rectorial plans to introduce e.g. a faculty of management were blocked by faculties), but did result in 'a confusing number of decision-making bodies', leading to 'too many people deciding about important things and too many

---

[5] Admittedly, engineering curricula did not need to be so completely revamped as economics courses at the WSE, because the influence on them of Marxism-Leninism had been much more limited.

[6] Needless to say, 'quality' means academic quality, not social quality (for this distinction, see Van der Meulen & Rip 1997).

[7] Traditional teaching methods in Central Europe meant, *inter alia*, a high proportion of lectures where students were supposed to take extensive notes (textbooks being scarce), and examinations that stressed rote learning of facts.

decision levels, without a clear structure among them'. Efforts to adapt to new legal and societal requirements apparently had been incremental.

4.2   Slovak Technical University in Bratislava

The Slovak Technical University (STU), founded in 1938, is the largest technical university in Slovakia. In the late 1990s, it was an 'unusual, confederate university'. Its faculties gained such independence that university-wide decision-making almost ceased to exist. Partly, this resulted from the Czechoslovak higher education law of 1990 mentioned above, which was inherited by the Slovak Republic when it split off in 1993. Other technical universities in Slovakia, however, did not disintegrate to the same extent as STU,[8] so that not everything can be blamed on external circumstances. STU was characterised by 'petrified university operation', little flexibility and 'particular' inefficient use of 'human, financial and infrastructural resources'.[9] In university decision-making structures, students 'do not play an essential role as stakeholders'.

Students complained about aged professors, the slow upgrading of teaching methods and content, shortage of textbooks, aged and scarce equipment. Students' mobility within STU was limited; in practice they were bound to study programmes within a single faculty, which in some cases duplicated or even triplicated course units in other faculties. Faculties controlled entrance examinations, hence enrolment figures, as in the Czech Republic.

At the same time, the attitude of academics at STU was to maintain quality at the old-time levels, neither recognising the changed student-to-staff ratio of the quickly expanding higher education system nor the changed student body (hence changed teaching needs) as a result of the expansion.

Funding depended mainly on the state (almost 90%) and was too low to pay competitive salaries, leading, as in CTU, to brain drain of younger and more dynamic academics. Additional income, it seems, could only be gained through attracting foreign students or through R&D contracts with private industry, neither of which were large sources, due to the slow development of Slovakia's economy.

---

[8] Authors' observation from Tempus project 'EQATU' (S JEP 11 530-96).
[9] For instance, academic appointments were in the hands of faculty deans, contrary to our previous case, CTU, where under basically the same higher education law, appointments were made by the rector.

In view of the need for more and more radical change, 'inside the university, we find a tendency to blame external changes'. The CRE reviewers seemed to say that the rectorate contained a number of reformists with good ideas, but they were a minority in STU.

4.3   Lajos Kossuth University in Debrecen

Lajos Kossuth University (KLTE), located in Debrecen in Eastern Hungary, is an example of the consequences of the fragmentation of higher education institutions affected by the communist regimes: in 1989, it contained only two faculties (in natural sciences and arts and humanities), while there were at least six other higher education institutions in Debrecen.

Soon after 1989, the Hungarian government planned to merge such fragmented higher education institutions into fully fledged universities in all academic centres in the country, but the realisation of these plans fell victim to the frequent changes of government. The higher education institutions in Debrecen formed one of two areas where the World Bank stimulated the *Universitas* project with a grant. By 1997, the project had not progressed beyond a hefty report on the *Institutional Development Plan for the Federation of the Debrecen Universities*; much would need to be done to succeed by the 2000 deadline. KLTE academics favoured the *Universitas*; indeed, they expected this project to solve many of their problems. However, many apparently did not know how they could contribute to its realisation: their support was mainly symbolic.

Actual support for the *Universitas* project seemed to be less forthcoming, especially from the other higher education institutions in Debrecen. They might well have seen this as a takeover by KLTE which already accommodated more than half of all tertiary students in the region. As a signal, the steering committee for the *Universitas* elected a president for only one year. This president was not one of the rectors or other leading figures of the constituent institutions. Nevertheless, by 1995, one of the six other higher education institutions in Debrecen (a three-year engineering college) had merged with KLTE to form a new faculty of engineering.

Besides the *Universitas* project, KLTE was trying to adapt to the new societal demands after 1989 by introducing new areas of education, notably in the popular areas of economics and law, in the form of two new 'mini faculties'. Adding new, very small faculties was symptomatic of a university with a very fragmented and slow decision-making structure that was biased towards maintaining the status quo. As an example of fragmentation, there were six 'cost centres' (chairs or institutes) in a department with 19 academics. In the six years since 1989, apparently little had been done to change the communist 'divide and rule' strategy in higher education.

The main source of problems in the eyes of KLTE leadership was the low governmental funding, with the concomitant problems of low salaries, brain drain, etc. Further funding was largely earmarked, so that there could be only limited internal flexibility. The use of student fees as a recurrent additional source of income had been impossible in Hungary; the university did not seem to be very eager to prepare to exploit this source when it would become available, in September 1997.

There apparently existed a wish 'in parts of the university' to focus as much as possible on the masters level programmes and research, and to get rid of the bachelors level programmes. This, together with the very limited market activity, would seem to signal a conservative academic attitude, more concerned with gaining academic reputation than with serving immediate social needs or with the economic survival of the higher education institution.

With respect to education, KLTE staff viewed a 'European level graduate' as their norm, but there was not much concrete implementation of this abstract idea. Moreover, 'teaching and learning styles seem to be based, still, on the traditional styles, which include a high proportion of frontal teaching and rote learning'. New programmes had been started especially by adding two new faculties, as we mentioned, and in some cases by 'upgrading' from bachelors to masters level. Also, education had been changed especially in the arts and humanities faculty immediately after 1989 to get rid of Marxist-Leninist courses and to replace most Russian language training with English.

4.4   József Attila University in Szeged

Szeged and Debrecen compete for the title of the second-largest city in Hungary. Accordingly, the situation of József Attila University (JATE) in Szeged was quite comparable to KLTE's in Debrecen. In Szeged, JATE was the largest higher education institution in a city with about six others. They, too, were moving towards a *Universitas*. JATE comprised three faculties (in sciences, law and arts).

JATE's institutional context, in other words, was almost the same as KLTE's. The CRE review team, which visited JATE in 1996, saw it operate under three main constraints. First, the communist regime had not been conducive to a 'culture of autonomy' and had led to chronic under-investment in higher education infrastructure. Second, the Hungarian government had only put a higher education law into effect after much discussion in 1993 and, in 1995–96, once again there were discussions about changing it. This, amongst other reasons, led to 'an uncertain framework within which to operate'. Finally, the financial constraints were seen as 'a constant (and at times) obsessive' worry.[10]

In the decision-making structures at JATE, 'fragmentation [was] the key feature'; departments had spontaneously regrouped into (informal) institutes, and functioned either independently or through the institutes within faculties. All these units seemed to operate as 'relays of opinions' and as 'instruments of self-government' rather than as 'partners in a bigger, collective game'. Plans had been developed at JATE to restructure itself into nine or ten faculties, but these had not reached implementation stage.

In the local *Universitas* merger project, JATE had clearly taken the lead. Thus, for instance, JATE's rector chaired the Board of Directors of the *Universitas* Association. JATE leadership saw the *Universitas* as an opportunity to reverse the process of 'erosion of both infrastructure and identity'. But, as in KLTE, it seemed that the distant opportunities of the *Universitas* took attention away from immediately needed reforms within JATE.

As far as relations with the market were concerned, those with local and regional authorities were good 'but links with industry [were] extremely limited'.

At least two of JATE's faculties had radically redefined their education after 1989. In arts, the necessary changes had been seized as an opportunity 'to introduce more than changes in personnel': new majors were taught, some of them on an interfaculty basis. Similar developments had taken place in law. 'The challenge posed by the new financial conditions and the new relation

---

[10] The CRE review team noted that from 1990 to 1995, the balance of research in comparison to education in the university's budget had changed in favour of research, notwithstanding the growth in student numbers: 'reality is on the whole less terrible than its perception'.

between education and research' had also affected 'the mind' at the faculty of sciences.

The opportunities which opened after 1989 to introduce bachelors level programmes in universities had been seized in some fields (fields with an urgent societal need e.g. languages and computer science). Also, study programmes had been made more flexible (i.e. more optional courses, wider choice of subjects taught). There even was an experiment to introduce two-year tertiary education.

Quality of education as well as quality of research tended to be seen at JATE (as in the other three cases mentioned in this section) in terms of usually, externally controlled qualifications of academic staff, such as numbers of full professors, (higher) doctorates and membership of the Academy of Sciences. Such a view of quality left only 'a very limited role' for the institution itself for human resource management and other quality management.

5.   RUNNING THE SAME NEVER-TO-BE-FINISHED RACE: SOME COMPARISONS AND CONTRASTS

Our findings in the cases of Hungary and the Czech and Slovak Republics can now be integrated with those in the two Polish case studies. Briefly, they can be summarised as in table 1.

Table 1: Themes of change

Institution	Responses to new autonomy	Responses to the market		
		Curriculum	Degrees	Personnel
WSE **Warsaw**	Radical change from faculty structure to *studia, kolegia* Decision-making power shifted to new actors	Many new programmes and courses quickly introduced Fee-paying courses introduced early	Degree structure widened to include 3-year degrees and MBA	Majority of staff hold other jobs; 'boundary roles' enhance curricular change; little brain drain
AEW **Wrocław**	No change in faculties Decision-making at rectorial/faculty level Change in actors comes over time	Introduction of new programmes and courses varies according to progressiveness of faculty Tuition programmes introduced after 1993	Degree structure widened to include 3-year degrees, MBA, certificates	Majority of staff hold other jobs but with more regional than international contacts; little brain drain
CTU **Prague**	Same faculties, plans for new ones blocked Faculties highly autonomous	Adaptations, some new programmes	Little enthusiasm to develop bachelors programmes	Majority of staff hold other jobs
STU **Bratislava**	Same faculties Faculties almost independent	Adaptations, some new programmes	Little enthusiasm to develop bachelors programmes	Majority of staff hold other jobs

Table 1: Continued

Institution	Responses to new autonomy	Responses to the market		
		Curriculum	Degrees	Personnel
KLTE Debrecen	New faculties added *Universitas* merger expected and wanted	Adaptations, significant new programmes	Little enthusiasm to develop bachelors programmes (even abolishing some)	Majority of staff hold other jobs but with more regional than international contacts
JATE Szeged	Same faculties *Universitas* merger expected and wanted	Adaptations, significant new programmes, some at bachelors level	Degree structure widened to include 2- and 3-year degrees	Majority of staff hold other jobs

The responses of the Central European systems considered here to the challenges posed by the democratic and market-oriented reforms of 1989 have much in common. Changes in decision-making and degree structures and in curricula, as well as some unforeseen changes in personnel, have occurred across the board. But the specifics of these changes and their mechanisms are what contribute to the further development of tenable hypotheses of change in higher education institutions.

Our cases indicate that the distinctive way each institution embraced change has been a function of opportunity and need. Opportunity here appears to be strongly related to the legal borders within which institutions operate, while need can be measured by the strength of market forces prevailing on them.

Thus, in Poland, opportunities were created through swift legislation, with power devolved to the institutional level, which has generally been interpreted to mean the academic senate. Both the rector and faculties gained decision-making power formerly held at the national level. In the case of the institutions presented here, the need to change curricula was expedient since the pre-1989 economics courses were woefully inadequate for preparing students for the new economy. Similarly, the new economy demonstrated a need for specialists with qualifications that could be best gained under a flexible degree structure. As has been shown, the two academies responded to these opportunities and needs in quite different ways and at a different pace.

The opportunities were practically the same for the Czech and Slovak institutions presented here, since in what then was Czechoslovakia a new higher education law was introduced even more swiftly than in Poland. In the Czechoslovak law, however, much more decision-making power was devolved to the faculties, making it harder for a determined group of reformists to take control of the university as happened at WSE. Furthermore, for engineering studies the need to change curricula was less than for economics, which may help to explain the slower rate of change at the two technical universities. At the same time, although the need in the, by 1996, booming Czech economy for bachelors level specialists was high, CTU did not move quickly to change its degree structure. Perhaps they underestimated the need; perhaps the institutional culture was less conducive to change (an issue we return to below).

In Hungary, the long delay in altering the legal context made opportunities for change less auspicious. In an uncertain atmosphere, institutions were inclined to wait or initiate short-term experiments. Moreover, the universities considered here, comprising a range of disciplines from science to social science to the humanities, were not markedly susceptible to the need to change in the new economy. From our data, it seems that the University of Szeged took up the challenge somewhat more proactively than the one in Debrecen, offering more new study lines and programmes of shorter duration than the traditional five-year masters programmes.

What explains the different rates of change in higher education institutions, given the same opportunities and challenges, remains an intriguing question. We can rule out disciplinary bias: WSE reacted in a much more radical way than its Wrocław counterpart. Similarly, cosmopolitan context does not always make a difference: the Hungarian institutions exhibited a different pace of internal change, yet the degree of cosmopolitanism would be more or less equal in both. (Szeged and Debrecen compete for the title of the 'largest city after Budapest' and both are at comparable distances from that metropolis.) Also, the cosmopolitan contexts of Warsaw and Prague were very similar, but CTU reacted clearly less radically than WSE. However, in the sociological interpretation of cosmopolitanism as an attitude, WSE may have been in a better position to engender such an attitude among its staff members, because connections with Western higher education were more developed before 1989 in Poland than in Czechoslovakia.

It appears we are left with the idiosyncrasies of the institution: its history, culture and inhabitants at the time of change. At WSE, the reform committee (institutionally linked to the Solidarity movement, which had set developments in Poland apart from those in other Central European countries since 1980) may have played a crucial role in this respect. But the broader institutional history appears just as significant. As Clark (1983: 82) explained, in some higher education institutions one finds 'extreme examples of institutional culture' characterised by 'the working up of an intensive and integrated self-belief' such that 'a good share of the faculty, students, administration, and alumni [come] to hold a credible story of uncommon achievement'.

Of our cases, WSE and CTU have life spans conducive, in Clark's term, to a 'saga-enriched culture'. CTU's saga includes the loss of one of its main faculties — the chemical engineering faculty was split off in the 1950s to become a separate technical university. Located partly in the same building as CTU's rectorate, its existence was a daily reminder of the 'disintegration' of CTU's self-belief. In CTU's post-1989 plans, reunification of the two has been a constant but utopian theme. WSE, on the contrary, has remained intact even under communist rule. New students at orientation come to share in the saga as they view a video of WSE's history; the important parts of its saga are repeated to outsiders: at least one half of the ministers of any government, before 1989 as well as afterwards, graduated from WSE. The fact that WSE considered itself, and was considered by the West, an elite institution may very well have generated the internal energy and the external assistance to expedite change.

How people on a bridge in a storm perceive the need and opportunity to move appears to have as much to do with what they bring to that encounter as with the conditions of the storm itself.

References

Amsterdamski, S. and A. Rhodes (1993), Perceptions of dilemmas of reform: remarks and interpretations concerning a study by the Vienna Institute for Human Sciences, *European Journal of Education*, vol. 28, pp. 379–402.

Beksiak, J., E. Chmielecka and U. Grzelońska (1991), *Higher Economic Education in Poland: its present state and proposals for immediate change*, Warsaw: Stefan Batory Foundation.

Clark, B.R. (1983), *The Higher Education System: academic organisation in cross-national perspective*, Berkeley: University of California Press.

CRE 1996a, Audit Report Czech Technical University, Prague. Geneva, CRE.

CRE 1996b, Institutional Audit of the Jozsef Attila University of Szeged. Geneva, CRE.

CRE 1997, Review Report of Lajos Kossuth University, Debrecen. Geneva, CRE.

CRE 1998, Institutional Review of the Slovak University of Technology (Bratislava). Geneva, CRE.

Garton-Ash, T. (1999), *History of the Present: essays, sketches and dispatches from Europe in the 1990s*, London: Allen Lane.

March, J.G. and J.P. Olsen (1989), *Rediscovering institutions*, New York: The Free Press.

Meulen, B.R. van der and A. Rip (1997), *Maatschappelijke kwaliteit van onderzoek tussen verantwoordelijkheid en management: Een inventarisatie van beoordelingspraktijken [Social quality of research between responsibility and management: an inventory of evaluation practices]*, mimeo, Enschede: University of Twente.

Sorensen, K. (1997), *Polish Higher Education En Route to the Market: institutional change and autonomy at two economic academies*, Stockholm: Stockholm University Institute of International Education.

Chapter 3

Academic staff between threat and opportunity
Changing employment and conditions of service

EGBERT DE WEERT AND LIETEKE VAN VUCHT TIJSSEN

Key words: decentralisation; human resource management; tenure

1.   INTRODUCTION

Academic staff constitute the core of higher education institutions. They are engaged in teaching and/or research and vary in rank from the highest rank of full professor to the lowest of instructor or research assistant. There are clear indications that staff are experiencing increased pressures to meet a wide range of obligations. Recent studies show that there is dissatisfaction among staff with the conditions in which their tasks — teaching, research and public service — have to be performed, with deteriorating effects on the motivation and quality of their work (UNESCO 1992). According to the OECD study on staffing higher education, the morale of academic staff is generally thought to be lower than in previous generations (Kogan *et al.* 1994). Factors given for this dissatisfaction are, amongst others, pay and conditions of service, and lack of research time. These changing conditions appear to threaten the traditional position of academic staff.

On the other hand, institutions are confronted with internal and external pressures prompting them to pursue staff policies in a proactive way. One is the demographic factor, as academic staff are predominantly male and ageing. Another is the economic factor that becomes apparent in the growing proportion of temporary appointments. In essence, employment relationships are moving away from the patterns of relationships associated with the public sector, to a more hybrid form incorporating private sector elements.

At the same time, there is a growing awareness that much of the quality of education and research is dependent on the capabilities of the academic staff. It becomes increasingly important for institutions to develop human resource management.

This chapter explores the changes and dilemmas with regard to the working conditions of academic staff and the endeavours of institutions to explore new ways and means of managing human resources. The aim is twofold:

– to examine the changing context of academic staff as well as their changing employment relationships; and
– to give an account of the staffing issues with which higher education institutions are increasingly confronted. These issues have been grouped under the label 'modernisation of employment relationships' and encompass terms like flexibility, mobility and employability.

The term working conditions is used here in both a narrow and a broad sense. In a narrow sense it concerns the institutional framework between employers and trade unions and the government regarding the determination of the core elements of employment. Although wage negotiations constitute an element of collective bargaining, in principle, all terms and conditions of service are included. In a broader sense, the term working conditions comprises the functioning of the academic labour market, institutional policies and management structures, as well as the context of academic work and the changing face of the student body.

Much research concerns the institutional, collective framework of labour relations and concentrates on the strategic choices of the actors involved. Rational choice theory, which starts from the view that the actor's behaviour is predominantly to be analysed in terms of strategic, economic rationality, has become a dominant approach. The emphasis on the institutional framework, though important, is limited as it neglects the various motivations, intentions and practices at the institutional level that affect working conditions. For this reason, the term employment relationship will be used here to include developments regarding the relationships between staff and management and their emerging new roles, organisational changes, as well as the specific characteristics of academic institutions. An attempt will be made to provide a broad overview of this complex range of conditions.

The scope of this chapter is limited in two respects. First, although international developments will be taken into account, these are primarily discussed from the Dutch perspective. Second, the term academic staff will be used in a rather general sense. Clearly, academics are divided by discipline and field and, as Clark (1987) has pointed out, these identities are powerful in shaping attitudes and values. The scope of this chapter does not allow a detailed discussion of the disciplinary cultures of academic staff.

2. THE CHANGING CONTEXT OF ACADEMIC STAFF

One of the main conclusions that can be drawn from Clark's (1987) classical study on the academic profession is that the profession is shaped by many national, disciplinary and institutional settings. Prominent among them is the national context. The profession in Britain is relatively unitary, with a professional self-consciousness unmatched in mainland Europe. In most European countries, academics are civil servants falling within the framework of public employment and until recently often appointed by the Crown. Academics do not constitute a profession in the strict sense but, as Neave and Rhoades (1987: 213) have put it, 'academia is an estate, whose power, privileges, and conditions of employment are protected by constitutional or administrative law'.

A more universal element attributed to academics is the notion of academic freedom. This is understood as the freedom of the individual academic in his/her teaching and research to pursue truth wherever it seems to lead without fear of punishment or termination of employment. In exchange for this freedom, academics are subjected to a particular discipline which safeguards them against external censorship. In European countries, this has been assured through the status of the civil servant, in Anglo-Saxon countries, through the system of tenure. From this stems the ideal of the collegiate organisation, according to which academics are self-governing bodies — academic oligarchies — that preserve the maximum freedom in teaching and research.

The method of recruiting new members within a particular discipline is reminiscent of the medieval guild system. Academics derive their privileges, reputation and rewards through the recognition bestowed upon them by this system. The collegiate structure was exemplified in the traditional universities where deans were normally elected for a fixed period and were *primus inter pares*. Historically, the collegiate ideal has been phrased very neatly by Whitehead who wrote in 1928 that 'the faculty should be a band of scholars, stimulating each other, and freely determining their various activities' (cited in Whitehead 1962). Apart from the question of whether academics ever formed a coherent band as Whitehead's normative statement wants us to believe, the collegiate model in its purest form is outdated, albeit the sediments of it can still be found in modern universities.

The rapidly evolving environment for higher education institutions and the implications for the traditional features of academic staff have been the subject of extensive research in the last decade. Several studies that consider the changes from the perspective of staff have been carried out, both in a national context and on a large comparative, international scale. The international Carnegie survey on the academic profession tested the hypothesis of a monomorphous profession and examined its responses to external pressures, structural change and changing working conditions (Altbach 1996; Enders and Teichler 1997). Another recent study reviewed developments in higher education policy in fifteen selected countries and examined their impact on the academic profession (Farnham 1999). Other studies in a national context concentrate on the demography of the profession, work and career characteristics (Finkelstein *et al*. 1998), faculty motivation (Blackburn and Lawrence 1995) and the declining social status of academic staff (Halsey 1992). These and several other studies underscore the proposition that for academic staff this has not been the best of times.

The pressures that affect the working conditions of academic staff originate from various sources that in a way are interrelated. Without pretending to be exhaustive, the following seem the most notable.

Massification
Higher education in most countries is moving towards open, mass systems of provision and enrolments have increased tremendously. Generally, the rising enrolments have not been matched by the willingness of governments to fund this growth. Rather, institutions have had to do more with fewer resources while meeting ever increasing demands, such as provisions for non-traditional students which entail extra costs. In some natural sciences the student-staff ratios are quite small, whereas other subject areas and sectors have quite large student numbers. The UK is perhaps the leading example of a system under stress. This is exemplified by a recent independent Review Committee that faced not only a disgruntled staff, but also a government demanding ever more from the sector. The Bett Committee (1999) stressed

the underfunded expansion in British higher education and argued for significant increase in public funding.[1]

Accountability and the quality imperative

The quality assessment movement, launched with vigour during the last decade, signals to the academic staff that they are to be held accountable for what they do and for the results of their efforts. There is much pressure on staff to meet the demands of quality evaluations, deliver the curriculum, and compete for resources. This reflects the demands of society at large (government, students, parents, employers) for more quality and cost effectiveness than before. The link with performance funding issues is apparent as the mechanisms move away from funding on the basis of enrolments towards the number of diplomas delivered. Assessing the performance of higher education in terms of the number of diplomas, however, is risky as long as the interested institutions provide the diplomas themselves. Critics have argued that this provokes managerial pressure on academic staff to increase the success rates (Lorenz 1993; Mertens 1999), although staff may apply different definitions of academic quality.

Changes in teaching and research

The traditional view of lecturing is gradually changing and there is continuous pressure for innovative curricular strategies. In the near past this was flexible learning or modularisation, problem-based learning and so on. Now, the principal concepts are breadth of learning through forcing students to take one or more courses in each of the main divisions of the university, the internationalisation of higher education systems incorporating the Anglo-Saxon system of bachelors and masters degrees, and multiculturalism.

In addition, an idea is being advocated where students themselves are more active in their own learning process. The electronic environment is playing an increasingly crucial role in this process, with on-line courses and less direct contact with the students. Whatever can be said of these developments, especially regarding information and communication technology (ICT), it is clear that teaching staff can no longer rely on traditional approaches to the planning and organisation of the curricula.

---

[1] It should be added, though, that the Bett Committee did not find evidence of reduced quality of higher education. A similar observation can be made for Dutch higher education on the basis of reports by visiting committees. Also, the research output in terms of number of publications or external grants per capita have been increasing steadily (Ministry of Education, Culture and Science 1999).

In the field of research, scientists are not protected from external pressure especially as university research is increasingly dependent on research contracts. Köbben and Tromp (1999), for example, illustrate in several cases pressures resulting from research outcomes not matching the expectations or the interests of the principal client. They sketch how easily the scientific freedom of researchers is compromised if clients cannot use the results or if the results contradict the viewpoints of the clients. In particular, when publication of results is frustrated by clients, this is interpreted by some staff as an assault on academic freedom and integrity. In most cases researchers opt for a middle course, asking themselves how far they can go without violating academic principles (Köbben and Tromp 1999).

3.   TWO NOTABLE DEVELOPMENTS

3.1   The changing composition of academic staff

Due to budget cuts, fluctuations in student enrolments and reorganisations, institutions have been driven to offset financial risks by employing temporary staff. Not only are research staff recruited on short-term contracts to carry out contract work for outside bodies, which universities increasingly need to attract, but also teaching staff are deployed on a contract basis to fill any temporary gaps.

In the USA, the deployment of academic staff has been undergoing a dramatic shift as the number of part-time and off-track full-time appointments appear to be expanding rapidly relative to that of traditional full-time, tenured appointments. Moreover, the appointments of full-time faculty are often made outside the traditional tenured or tenure-track realm (Finkelstein *et al.* 1998). In other countries the proportion of academic staff on a non-permanent basis is between a fifth to a half of all academic staff with a median of about a third (Farnham 1999). These changes in employment structures give rise to what Farnham calls the emerging 'flexi-university': a core group of permanently employed, secure, relatively well-paid academic staff, supported by an 'invisible faculty', consisting of peripheral groups of casually employed, insecure, poorly paid staff — many of whom are female — doing routine teaching, instruction and research tasks (Farnham 1999: 28). Generally the division within the academic profession, in particular between tenured staff and staff employed on a temporary contract, leads to a segmentation within the academic profession. An underclass seems to emerge, an 'invisible faculty', with limited prospects for advancement or employment stability, creating tensions between the 'have' and 'have-not' groups (Kogan *et al.* 1994).

Another development concerns the tendency to separate teaching from research. In the Netherlands this has become manifest through the emergence of research schools and research institutes as separate organisational units with their own budget and employment responsibilities. Research schools accommodate doctoral students who work as research trainees. Virtually all of them are on a temporary, four-year contract and have relatively low salaries. The majority have few future career prospects within the university. The development of research institutes and schools, which increasingly have to compete for resources from science foundations, industry and government, has led to a concentration of university research.

A further fragmentation of the academic profession is reinforced by appointing professors not on the basis of academic qualifications, but on other merits. In the Netherlands the number of endowed professors has expanded considerably in the last few years, especially those sponsored by industry. For industry it is a means to gain societal recognition, but within the university it has a connotation of *frères ennemis* and raises questions among traditional academic staff. The standard requirements to become a professor encompass lengthy periods of training and scientific work, whereas for endowed professors these qualifications apparently do not count. As they do not stand out scientifically, the proliferation of endowed professors may violate the scientific quality of the university and lead to a further 'diluting' of the academic profession (Lorenz 1993; Boot 1998).

3.2 Changing authority in the management of institutions

Demands for greater accountability, global competition and effectiveness have called for the reduction of the power of departments in favour of more managerial modes of decision-making. In most countries it was government who pushed strongly for managerial accountability, resulting in the extensive growth of administration and management within the institution. This growth may undermine the traditional notion of collegiality and the principle of shared governance. Several studies, especially in the Anglo-Saxon world where this managerialism has penetrated most, point to widening breaches between academic staff and administrators (Blackburn and Lawrence 1995; Kogan *et al.* 1994; Henkel 1997).

In Dutch higher education similar signs can be seen. The demands from management have increased considerably, causing teaching staff to experience increased workload pressure and the curtailment of professional autonomy (Blokhuizen and van Montfort 1998). But, in this respect it is important to indicate the difference between the university and the non-university sector. In the latter sector the style of control traditionally has not been based on a collegial structure, but has always been bureaucratic and hierarchical. Heads of departments were administrative positions rather than academic, and staff had a clear definition of their role as teachers. But this is changing. Teaching staff in the non-university sector are having to develop their own identity and professional roles.

For Dutch universities, the recent bill on modernising university governance (Ministry of Education, Culture and Science 1995), the so-called MUB, can be interpreted as a shift from the collegiate model towards a managerial model. The purpose of this bill has been to invest deans and the university executive board with clearer managerial authority. It is intended to adapt institutional structures and integrate managerial and administrative processes into a single system — an approach which is seen as a necessary condition for more decisive and efficient governance of universities. Important for the position of academic staff is the appointment of deans as professional managers, possessing budgetary responsibilities and a delegated authority for staffing issues. The departmental unit has ceased to exist as an organisational entity in an administrative sense. Instead, the dean has a central role with executive powers over research, teaching, finance and management issues. This implies that academic staff will be hired by middle-level management to contribute to the teaching and research programmes. It is too early to assess the extent to which the traditional model of collegiality succumbs to more hierarchical modes of decision-making. Yet, the new governance structure undoubtedly affects the position of academic staff within the institution and constrains their traditional freedom regarding research and teaching. There are indications that the shift in the governance structure from shared governance towards a more managerial or corporate model, can put pressure on the institution as a professional work community. Too much emphasis on decisive governance will result in lack of support for and little acceptance of new administrative relationships (Klankbordgroep 1998).

Up to this point we have discussed the changing work environment of academic staff and the different occupational roles within the academic profession. These changes do not necessarily all work out unfavourably for staff as they also provide new perspectives for the development of the profession. Several changes point to a process whereby the emphasis on a culture of academic freedom is being replaced by a culture where staff is accountable for their contribution to the quality and output of teaching and research. This will be worked out further in section 5. First we turn to the institutional framework of employment relationships and the determination of terms and conditions of service.

4. THE INSTITUTIONAL PATTERN OF EMPLOYMENT RELATIONSHIPS

4.1 From civil servant status to contract relationship

In higher education two main types of employment relationships can be distinguished: the civil or public and the private type, each with its corresponding employment status. In the former type, academic staff have the legal status of civil servant and are public officials. Their employment is a 'service' relationship, not a contractual one, and it is regulated by public law. In continental European countries this is the most common type, exemplified by the German *Beambte* or the French *fonctionnaires*. The private type prevails in most Anglo-Saxon countries where higher education institutions, even though financed for the greater part from public sources, are formally not part of the state. They preserve a non-governmental character, irrespective of whether they are public or private institutions, and academic staff have the legal status of employee and their working conditions are regulated by contracts of employment under private law.

The two types of employment relations differ in the way terms and conditions of service are determined. In the public type these are settled unilaterally and academic staff are supposed to be loyal to the state in return for job security, usually on a lifetime basis. In the contractual type, the substance of the obligations of staff is settled bilaterally between employers and employees, either on an individual basis or, as is often the case, through collective bargaining between the representative bodies. There are mixed systems such as 'model employer' which applied to the former polytechnic sector in the UK. This refers to the widely accepted view amongst public employees that employers should be seen to provide 'model' or optimal standards of employment such as implementing consistent and progressive personnel policies, negotiating and consulting with the unions, and maintaining high levels of job security and job protection (Farnham 1991).

The Dutch system is an example of a system in transition from a public to a contractual relationship. In 1988 the then Minister of Education, discussing the public character of higher education, stated that universities should not become private enterprises as they serve a general interest in the field of education and research. Because this has its effects on personnel matters, there is no room for something like a collective labour agreement (VSNU 1988: 18). In other words, employees in a labour organisation characterised by a 'service' relationship are by definition civil servants who have no rights to collective bargaining.

It is remarkable how this perspective has changed so quickly. The overall higher education policy objective has been to devolve responsibility for managerial decisions from government to the institutions, the main purpose of which is to facilitate flexibility so that higher education can respond to the rapidly changing demands of society. This trend is quite apparent in the areas of funding, housing and staffing. Budgets have been integrated to include staff costs and other costs which institutions may spend as they wish. At the same time institutions have gradually received more freedom in determining terms and conditions of service. The following three main phases can be identified (Van Vucht Tijssen 1995; De Weert 1999).

a) *Sectoralisation.* Until 1989 the central government through the Minister of Internal Affairs determined basic salaries and working conditions for all those employed in the public sector. Since 1989 two shifts occurred. First, the determination of working conditions was transformed into a bargaining process between two more or less equal parties. Second, the responsibility for those employed in the public sector has shifted away from the Minister of Internal Affairs to (as is the case for those working in the educational sector) the Minister of Education. Only the pensions and social security rights still come within the remit of the Minister of Internal Affairs.

b) *Decentralisation of secondary conditions.* In the 1990s decentralisation has taken a further step. The earlier adage that terms and conditions of staff were determined by the Minister, 'unless stated otherwise' has been reversed in the amendment of the Higher Education Law of 1994. The point of departure is that institutions are legally able to determine employment conditions of their personnel, with the exception of primary or 'protocol' issues. These include: the system of job evaluation and salary scales and increases which are decided for the educational sector as a whole; redundancy entitlements and other social security issues; and standard working hours. Secondary terms of employment refer to all remaining conditions, such as pension facilities, bonuses, teaching load, sick leave and sick pay arrangements, maternity leave, recruitment and appointments. This phase has resulted in a codification of secondary conditions which until that time were rather fragmented.

c) *Decentralisation of all terms and conditions of staff.* The last step in the process has been the Minister's decision to devolve responsibilities for the primary conditions, including salary negotiations. One of the main arguments was that this would enable institutions to facilitate their role as legal employers.

The outcome of this process is that governmental regulation has been replaced by an institutional framework in which universities and institutes of higher professional education (HBOs), being the employers (represented through their intermediary bodies VSNU and HBO-council respectively), sit at the bargaining table to negotiate with the trade unions about pay, salary increases and conditions of service. This means that the entire package of terms and conditions of service has become the subject of negotiation, resulting in a collective agreement that will be binding on all parties.[2] Universities, HBOs and research institutes have their own separate agreements, although they contain quite a few overlapping elements.

In many ways the social partners agreed on the basic philosophy of devolving responsibilities from the central government to the institutions, although in several phases there were different viewpoints on the pace of the process and the possible consequences. The Minister was reluctant to let his authority slide, but the belief that through this process institutions would be better able to cope with external constraints and utilise instruments for modern personnel management, such as the introduction of systems of individual remuneration, appeared to be decisive. Another argument was that decentralisation would contribute to the improvement of the quality of teaching and scientific research. The trade unions generally favoured this development and expressed their views that institutions were better bargaining parties as they were more sensitive to the special needs of academic staff. Trade unions regarded the institutions as partners in opposing governmental attempts to cut the higher education budget. For institutions with a lump-sum funding, collective agreements on pay impact directly on their budget. Institutions are directly responsible for the salary demands of their personnel, rather than shifting these on to the government.

---

[2] Exceptions are pensions and social security regulations regarding unemployment and illness.

Overall, however, institutions have expressed the desire to take responsibility and to act as employers. One of the most prominent advocates of this change, the late Jankarel Gevers, chairman of the Board of Governors of the University of Amsterdam, stressed on many occasions that modern employment relationships are not compatible with a 'foreign' and distant official regime, but rather with personnel management that is tuned to the special circumstances of higher education institutions. Due to these changes, personnel matters are no longer handled separately, but can be combined with other issues in an integrated management model.

4.2   An interim assessment

Negotiations did not always proceed smoothly. It was clear that both actors had to adjust to each other in their new roles. For outside observers, the question of salary increases seemed to be a major obstacle. The argument used by the unions that wages had not kept up with those in other public sectors and in the market sector remains a dominant issue. Sectoralisation means that salary settlements attained in one sector are used as a model for negotiation elsewhere. Employers in higher education have indeed turned their bargaining tactics to this end and have attempted to mitigate budgetary constraints set by the government. There is also the risk, however, that what one sector achieves, for example primary education which is politically a priority area, the other sector has to sacrifice.

The fixation on pay, however, overshadows some other important matters that have been crucial in the bargaining process; issues that have been classified under the term 'modernisation of employment relationships'. Modernisation is understood as a market-like agreement which enables employers to manage their institutions as flexible corporations. With regard to staff appointments and dismissals as well as personnel management in the context of reorganisations, flexibility appears to be a crucial factor in the bargaining process. This flexibility includes the liberalisation of the rules governing the recruitment and selection of staff, personal contracts of service and more casualisation of academic employment; a flexibility which, according to the employers, requires the abolition of the civil service status for academic staff. The trade unions, obviously, oppose the abolition of the civil servant status as staff would no longer enjoy its protection, but would be left to the whims of the market.

In this context it is important to note that under present conditions, institutions are responsible for redundancy payments. This means that the payments for all dismissed staff impact on the budgets of institutions and cannot be passed on to government. The notorious waiver clauses in the UK, signed by young staff to relinquish redundancy rights, do not occur in the Dutch context. However, some universities are evading this obligation by introducing scholarships for young researchers rather than offering them employment contracts. The abolition of civil servant status would probably relieve institutions from these payments. Apart from this direct financial concern, higher education management takes the position that if they are legally able to act as true employers — and this has essentially not been disputed — then the logical consequence would be to abandon the civil servant status and replace it with private employment status[3]. The transition towards an employer model would then be complete. A final decision has been postponed, depending on the outcome of a study focused on the effects of the change for staff.[4]

The resulting agreement has been a compromise between different issues. Apart from matters regarding pay and standard working hours, and social security issues, the agreement contains some new elements, namely:

- extra facilities for maternity leave;
- education and training facilities for staff and career development;
- temporary appointments should have a minimum of two years with a maximum of two subsequent extensions. The fourth appointment is automatically on a permanent basis;
- improvement of the salary position of research trainees;
- extension of the possibilities for dismissal when functions are discontinued or personnel made redundant.

---

[3] The formal status of the teaching body has also been debated at considerable length at European level. With regard to teachers, the European Commission suggested to remove functionary status from all public sector activities which are also carried out within the private or non-state sector. Such a measure might overcome the nationality restriction (see Neave 1992).

[4] The issue whether employees of public institutions are *by definition* public servants has recently been placed in the context of the debate in the Dutch parliament on the 'further privatisation of the universities'. According to this view, privatisation is neither a goal, as such, nor points to the question of whether public universities should be transformed into private corporations. The starting point is the public function of universities, and the juridical status of the institution is, in this context, not decisive. Public universities are not considered part of the central government but are established by law and derive from this law their legal personality (Ministry of Education, Culture & Science 1998; Noordzij 1998). This idea of 'privatisation' implies that academic staff are no longer to be considered as civil servants, but are employed by the universities as the legal employer.

4.3   National or local agreements?

The question which arises from the devolution of responsibilities for staffing issues is whether this shift will actually change the working conditions of staff and, if so, will these be for the better or for the worse, and for whom? Or is it simply a change of vocabulary and merely a storm in a teacup?

The answer depends on the balance between what has been determined in the national agreement and what has been left to local agreements at the institutional level. The covenant signed by government, employers and trade unions prescribes that negotiations at the national level include: salaries, function appraisal schemes, working hours, social security and 'all that employers and unions decide among themselves'.

If collective agreements are 'boarded up' in the sense that they cover a whole set of conditions in a very detailed way and are declared as binding on all parties, not much may change. The move from civil to contractual type of employment seems to be artificially replacing one inflexible system with another. In contemporary society, however, individualisation seems also to penetrate the domain of employment relationships. Collective bargaining is being eroded in favour of agreements at the level of individual firms or specific employment areas. This is not only visible in the private sector, but also in public services such as the health sector, where agreements are targeted to specific professional groups. In higher education, similar trends are becoming apparent at least in countries where institutions are able to employ and manage their own staff without interference from the state. For Commonwealth countries, Schofield (1997) identifies trends away from:

- uniformity in dealing with staffing issues towards devising methods and systems which allow for individual, subject or market differences;
- national salary structures applying to all institutions, towards greater institutional flexibility in determining salary and conditions of service.

Although there will always be tension between what will be decided nationally and locally, there are good reasons to leave as much as possible to be decided at the local level. Local agreements leave more freedom of action and responsiveness to external developments and tailor approaches to specific, local circumstances. At the individual level, for example, *à la carte* reward systems are being developed, whereby personal and variable contracts of employment are drawn up. Individual staff can choose from a variety of conditions such as maternity leave, pay bonuses, computers and other fringe benefits. Besides these individual differences, a central prescription of how the 'ideal' formation and work patterns should be structured and uniformly imposed across the board at all institutions restricts their autonomy.

Moreover, national agreements may restrict local policies and practices and may have counterproductive effects. The issue of maternity leave which aims at increasing the number of female staff, illustrates this dilemma. If these facilities have to be paid for through the collective agreement, employers with a high proportion of female staff will encounter higher costs. This may result in risk selection of recruitment policies and indirectly towards larger pay differences between men and women. If this happens, maternity leave should not be financed through the collective agreement, but rather, through some form of collective assurance system whereby costs are spread over all employees. As a current research project at Utrecht University shows, initiatives like maternity leave should not be considered in an isolated way, but should fit into a broader package of emancipation policies located at the local (faculty) level (Emmerik *et al.* 1998).

It is clear that collective agreements have seen better days, but it would be an oversimplification to adopt the view that personnel policies are a matter entirely within the area of responsibility of the individual institution. On the contrary, there are good reasons to argue that collective agreements continue to play an important part in determining working conditions. As Willke (1998) argues, remuneration is not an objective quantity, but will always be based on a negotiating process. It is possible to negotiate on an individual basis, but in that case the transaction costs would be extremely high, not only because of the high number of staff, but also because of the socially sensitive character of remuneration. Therefore, collective negotiations with recognised trade unions about salaries and conditions of employment will be very efficient, whereby economies of scale can be attained. Moreover, through collective negotiations there is a more efficient response to signals from the market (see Willke 1998).

Additionally, the national agreement should not be limited to wages, but cover a set of broader issues. A multidimensional agenda would facilitate an acceptable agreement for both parties in their respective priority areas. For example, employers have stressed the importance of more flexibility in employment relations whereas trade unions see wages as one of their priority areas. It is not a zero-sum game, but a compromise between a few central issues. However, the tendency of parties to have an extensive agenda should be discouraged as national agreements should function as a general framework, in which employment issues can be determined and refined at the institutional level.

5.   ORGANISATIONAL CHANGES AND HUMAN RESOURCE MANAGEMENT

The devolution of the responsibilities for staffing issues from government to institutions can be considered as a lever for change at the institutional level. Traditionally, personnel management at the local level is concerned with administering staff appointment systems and other personnel activities including the application of job evaluation schemes, salaries, and the like. This has a bureaucratic character ensuring that institutions meet their legal obligations. If institutions take responsibility for their staff, they cannot merely leave this to their personnel offices; they need to integrate personnel issues into the overall strategic management of the institution. The complexity of the utilisation of human resources, the recruitment, deployment, retention and reward systems all require strategic thinking at every management level.

The new Dutch bill on university governance, as mentioned above, implies a shift from the collegiate structure towards an integrated management model where the distinction between personnel administration on the one hand and educational and research policy on the other hand will be removed. The philosophy is to tilt the university towards a more product-oriented, professional organisation with a greater emphasis on the achievement of institutional and departmental aims and objectives. An important element of this change is to assign clear and tailor-made responsibilities for teaching and research to deans and directors of research and teaching institutes. They are the 'problem owners' (Fruytier and Timmerhuis 1995; Timmerhuis 1997) who have personal responsibility for results at all levels and for the quality of the academic staff, their teaching and research. The responsibility for human resource management appears to be a central element in this change. Academic staff are the capital for institutions and attention to and feedback from them are of crucial importance. At the same time, researchers and teaching staff should not merely pursue their own goals, but keep in mind the goals of their own unit in relation to the larger organisation.

The culture of individual members of staff by and large is to provide their tasks with a highly personal interpretation. There is no tradition of evaluation of their functioning and the way they perform their tasks, as this would entail an enormous intrusion into their presumed integrity and authority. The flexibility of the organisation has been pursued through the number of temporary appointments and not in terms of the flexibility and mobility of the total staff, a policy which has some consequences:

- a tenured staff of considerable size, which in the case of low mobility becomes more expensive over the years. In due time, all cohorts approach the maximum remuneration level as automatic salary increases are made according to seniority;
- a rapidly changing category of young, temporary staff who have little opportunity of finding a permanent job;
- an increasing average age of staff. The proportion of academic staff at Dutch universities aged 50 years or over rose from 20.5% in 1990 to 32.9% in 1997. This may lead to serious recruitment difficulties in the future;
- a low proportion of female staff, especially in the higher ranks. The Netherlands is amongst the European countries with the lowest proportion of female professors (5% in 1998), whereas many other countries approach 10%. Apart from the mechanisms behind gender disparities, explanations are sought through organisational factors (Portegrijs 1998). A governmental bill obliges institutions to set targets on the number of women in higher ranks and to develop strategies for equal opportunity practices. These targets are difficult to achieve within the context of the prevailing staff structure.

From an organisational perspective it is important to challenge some persistent practices in higher education and create more 'breathing' space to pursue human resource policies. Some practices will be discussed here at length: first, the issue of tenure, a term interchangeably used with lifetime or permanent appointments emanating from the civil servant status; next, the issue of flexibility and mobility in the academic labour market.

5.1 Tenure: necessity or anachronism?

The system of tenure has become increasingly a source of controversy during the last few years. Tenure means different things in different national contexts and, as Tierney and Bensimon (1996) point out, there exists an enormous variety of tenure processes at different institutions, within institutions, or even within departments. Tenure is commonly understood as a lifetime job guaranteed by the institution. Under this scheme, a departmental reorganisation or a budget reduction does not constitute legal grounds for dismissing staff and the institution is obliged to offer such staff new jobs. Dismissals in case of financial exigency incur substantial costs due to compensation payments. Because of these rigidities and the legal implications, the system of tenure has come under attack. In the UK, the Education Reform Act in 1988 brought a statutory halt to academic tenure and gave universities the right to dismiss academic staff because of redundancy. Also in the USA the tenure system is coming under scrutiny from both internal and external critics, and alternatives to the tenure system are being considered.

The debate on tenure is part and parcel of the current argument concerning the entrepreneurial, market-responsive educational institutions. One such view, recently expressed by Pieter Winsemius (at the annual VSNU-conference, 1999), is that universities should abolish permanent appointments and only offer temporary contracts. As compensation, professors should be better paid, especially if they teach a useful, profitable course. Critics of the tenure system argue that professors who received tenure a long time ago may lose interest or may not be willing or able to invest in new developments. If tenure occurs around 30 years of age, there is still a long career path of 35 years ahead. As requirements change, institutions confronted with financial and technological developments find that the rigidities imposed by a tenure system demand a high price. Under a term contract system it is much easier to dismiss incompetent or unproductive professors. Moreover, if the tenure system does not recognise mandatory retirement, institutions are legally in a difficult position to pension off older staff.

In the debate about tenure, the question as to why tenure has persisted for such a long time should be asked. From a historical point of view the case for retaining the tenure system has been justified as a means of guaranteeing academic freedom. Attacks on professors during the McCarthy era, the civil rights movement and the 'political correctness' movement gave much ammunition for defending free inquiry and speech, standards of ethics and morality. Machlup, in his classical essay from 1964, defended tenure on the grounds of protecting the rights of faculty to pursue their research and teaching. Machlup wanted the professor 'to be uninhibited in criticising, and in advocating changes' (Machlup cited in Finkin 1996: 23). In order to attract and sustain the intellectually curious, the university must offer protection.

In addition to the argument about academic freedom, it can be questioned whether the rigidities imposed by tenure really are as inefficient as critics maintain. Economists have cast doubt on the claim of the ineffectiveness of the tenure system. McPherson and Schapiro (1999) argue that the highly specialised nature of academic production gives rise to the need for long-term job security. Those who wish to invest their time and effort in new and original areas of inquiry have to concentrate over the long-term in a specialised field. This is quite risky for those on temporary contracts. This is most evident in the natural sciences. But also in the social sciences theories may attract strong objections from society in the short-term, but prove to be of long-term value. Here, tenure functions as an incentive for academics to invest in long-term and speculative research and teaching projects.

A strong efficiency basis for tenure is given by Carmichael (1988) who argues that the justification for tenure rests on information and incentive problems. The university administration is dependent to a considerable degree on incumbent academics to judge the quality of junior staff. If academics thought they were vulnerable to being replaced by more highly skilled outsiders, they would be less likely to encourage the promotion of able junior academics. Especially if budget cuts are being made, academics would be expected to protect themselves by excluding quality newcomers from academic life and to dominate senior academic posts. On the other hand, tenure creates an incentive for academics to reveal truthfully their judgments about the abilities of junior staff and to hire the best candidates available (see also Bomhoff 1999).

Some of these efficiency claims are hard to test, such as the investment of academics in long-term projects or faculty infighting. Dnes and Seaton (1998), however, found no empirical evidence in the UK data in favour of the Carmichael hypothesis. The 1988 Reform Act on academic tenure did not cause incumbent academics to consolidate their hold on senior posts after the reform. Neither has it hindered the importance of academic performance, nor the promotion of younger, less established academics (Dnes and Seaton 1998).

The opposite point of view in the tenure discussion, its abolition in favour of temporary contracts only, has some consequences. It may be more expensive as institutions have to offer attractive conditions both in terms of salaries and conditions of service as compensation for giving up tenure. Institutions with high quality standards are able to attract well-qualified staff on this basis as it is attractive for the individual member to work at such an institution. A disadvantage of having predominantly temporary appointments is that the continuity of the organisation is too much dependent on the existing staff. Experiences from some specific sectors (health and arts) suggest that temporary staff are less inclined to build a corporate identity and identify with institutional and departmental objectives. Personnel management in those institutions is predominantly concerned with recruitment, selection and dismissal, with insufficient attention paid to staff evaluation, assessment and development.

The approach advocated here is that the arguments for and against tenure should go beyond thinking about tenure as an all-or-nothing proposition. That is, tenure is either valuable for all forms of employment relationships in higher education or it is inefficient and costly. Alternatives could be explored which maintain the beneficial elements of tenure while leaving more institutional flexibility.

One option is to let faculty choose between tenure and term appointments coupled with the benefits normally associated with tenured faculty such as travel funds, sabbatical leave, and so on. This option might be attractive for the top faculty whose labour market chances are very favourable and need no protection through tenure. Another strategy is to link tenure to some form of assessment procedure. Several American states, for example, have introduced systems of post-tenure review. In such a system, faculty are evaluated every six years whereby one or two subsequent substandard evaluations may result in a set of specific goals, which, if unmet, could eventually lead to dismissal (McPherson and Schapiro 1999). Although there are many doubts about setting up procedures that would result in such a severe sanction, it should be made clear to staff that they are, in principle, not immune to a regular check on their actual performances in the field of education and research. Moreover, institutions should discuss with all staff who have long employment status, whether they are still the right person for the job.

5.2   Mobility and flexibility in the academic labour market

In current human resource policies, mobility and flexibility constitute major components. Mobility aims at enhancing the employability of academic staff over a range of jobs and locations both within the institution and on the external academic labour market. A common distinction is between vertical mobility whereby the academic career develops from junior staff to higher ranks in the hierarchical academic order, and horizontal mobility, that is, a change of research direction or a move to another type of work or employment field. Geographical mobility indicates a change of work environment, but within the same discipline. Apart from differential reward systems and a contractually flexible labour force, flexibility refers to a variety of job types and work tasks. Mobility and flexibility are two sides of the same coin: the more flexibility in functional categories and forms of employment, the more chances for staff to move on to other jobs.

Critics have argued that flexibility and mobility policies are pursued under the guise of getting rid of personnel who are redundant or show poor performance. Although this critique makes sense, mobility can also be directed in ways that are mutually beneficial to the individual academic and the organisation. Studies in the field of the sociology of science have shown the positive effects of mobility, when scientists move from one institution to another both nationally and internationally. Although academics remain in the same field of research, they take with them their own ways of tackling scientific issues and past experiences which may find receptive ground in the new environment. Also staff who get tired of their job, or see their career chances blocked, may benefit from a move.

As far as geographical mobility is concerned, the academic worker is extremely mobile. The classical image of academics as locals and cosmopolitans, having loyalty to their own institution while at the same time being part of an international community of scholars through publications, conferences and joint research projects persists. The advancement of knowledge entails an enormous dynamic activity crossing institutional and national boundaries. These network activities have been reinforced through modern electronic communications which make academics less restricted to a specific location. The cosmopolitans, however, are found mainly among top researchers and less among the larger part of academic staff who in some countries show a relatively low mobility. In the Netherlands there exists a strong tendency for students to graduate at a certain university, do their postgraduate studies there, and subsequently apply for a position at the same institution and achieve internal promotion. This contrasts with the situation in Germany where it is virtually impossible to climb the academic ladder within the same university as that studied at. Countries where mobility is also low are Spain, where more than 91 per cent of tenured posts are awarded to local candidates, and Sweden (see Farnham 1999). Questions arise whether such 'inbreeding' may harm the vitality and quality of the composition of staff.

Although the positive effects of mobility are obvious, its possibilities are easily overestimated. As far as horizontal mobility is concerned, universities are focused on developing and maintaining specialist fields. Academic careers require lengthy periods of specialist training which reduce the possibilities to switch to other scientific areas or types of jobs. Academics are easily caught in a kind of 'employment trap' which makes it hard for them to switch easily from one research domain to another, let alone find employment outside higher education. The possibilities for vertical mobility within the same field in the prevailing career structure is also rather limited. Academic ranks are not well distinguished in terms of different tasks or work content.

An alternative is not to hold to specific functional levels arranged vertically based on skills and expertise, but to create horizontal 'task packages' and personal development plans which encompass a broader domain than teaching and research. Teaching staff, for example, can be charged with different kinds of tasks such as curricular development, organisation of project groups, contract activities, student counselling, developing and implementation of ICT, maintaining contact with the professional world and internships. Research staff may function as the manager of one project and at the same time be involved in carrying out another project or participate in interdisciplinary projects.

An illustration of horizontal mobility policies can be found in the model designed by Utrecht University on Rules and Regulations on Functions, Careers and Rating (WP-FLOW). This model aims to create more possibilities for a differentiated career within teaching and/or research. The basic idea is that teaching tasks and research tasks are equivalent for the attainment of the institutional objectives and that these task components feature in different proportions in the functions for academic staff and the workload of a single member of staff. It becomes possible for a member of staff to concentrate exclusively on teaching or research for the duration of a previously arranged period. The distinction between these functions lies exclusively in the relative volume and thus the nature of the tasks, but there are overlapping areas which facilitate the mobility from teaching to research or vice versa within a single level.

An important element in this model is the link with basic qualifications for teaching (Van Vucht Tijssen 1998). At the introduction of WP-FLOW, academic staff were consulted about their qualifications and performances in the fields of research and teaching. Agreements were made about tasks for the following two years. The model partially replaces promotion according to seniority with promotion based on proven qualities. The model gives an impetus to human resource management where agreements concerning task assignments and results, staff assessments and appraisal schemes as well as merit pay constitute the core components. Such a differentiation of academic tasks may facilitate the employability of academics over a broad range of tasks and this enables them to develop their professional qualifications. This reinforces the need to enhance training and staff development linked to institutional priorities. The present collective agreement provides facilities for career development through further education and training.

6.   IN CONCLUSION

Academic staff have experienced a marked change over the past decade in the institutional climate in which they work. The determination of terms and conditions of service has been devolved and institutions need to take responsibility for staffing issues. Collective national labour agreements continue to play a role as far as economies of scale are concerned and function as a framework for regulations which can be tailored to specific, local circumstances.

One notable development we mentioned is the increase in temporary appointments, with all the negative consequences. This increase may be connected with too stringent regulations governing dismissal. Employers appear reluctant to recruit staff on a permanent basis. A relaxation of regulations might result in a substantial increase in permanent appointments. These are no lifetime appointments, but employment has to be earned through effective performance and assessment of competencies on a continuous basis.

Whether this development is a threat for academic staff depends on the extent to which they experience their privileged status as a contrast to ordinary working people in contemporary society. For institutions that increasingly have to operate in a dynamic environment, it is important to create more flexibility with regard to personnel policies and to reduce the sharp distinction between classical lifetime appointments and temporary contract appointments. At the same time, it should be recognised that it is crucial to attract and keep well-qualified and well-motivated staff. Terms and conditions of employment including career prospects should be such that higher education institutions can compete with other employment sectors for labour.

To establish new policies in the area of personnel management is not a short-term process. It requires time and energy and leadership at all levels within the institution. Academic staff are professionals in their discipline, with expertise in research and teaching. Their knowledge and commitment are necessary for the development of new objectives as well as for the realisation of institutional and departmental aims and objectives. The general move from an individual culture to a task-based one, with implications for the organisation of work is evident. Academic leadership encompasses the reduction of the distance between those who manage and those who are at the core business of higher education, namely good researchers and good teachers. Perceived in this way, the changing employment relationships create new opportunities for those working in higher education.

References

Altbach, P.G. (1996), *The International Academic Profession*, The Carnegie Foundation for the Advancement of Teaching, San Fransisco: Jossey-Bass.

Bett Committee (1999), Is there life after Bett? *Times Higher Education Supplement*, June 25.

Blackburn, R.T. & J.H. Lawrence (1995), *Faculty at Work*. Baltimore: Johns Hopkins University Press.

Blokhuizen, C. & F. van Montfort (1998), *Ingenieurs, Scholing en Onderwijscultuur*, Tilburg: Tilburg University Press.

Bomhoff, E.J. (1999), Toga's bij het uitzendbureau, *NRC Handelsblad*, April 24.

Boot, A. (1998), Groei bijzondere leerstoelen. *Folia* (October): Universiteit van Amsterdam.

Carmichael. H.L. (1988), Incentives in academics: Why is there tenure? *Journal of Political Economy*, 96 (3), 453-472.

Clark, B.R. (1987), *The Academic Profession: national, disciplinary and institutional settings*, Berkeley: University of California Press.

Dnes, A.W. and J.S. Seaton (1998), The reform of academic tenure in the United Kingdom, *International Review of Law and Economics*, vol. 18, 491–509.

Emmerik, H., M.E.G. van der Velde and P.L.J. Hermkens (1998), Ouderschapsverlof, L&E Working Paper no. 13.

Enders, J. and U. Teichler (1997), A victim of their own success? Employment and working conditions of academic staff in comparative perspective, *Higher Education*, vol. 34, 347–73.

Farnham, D. (1991), From model employer to private sector model: the PCFC sector. *Higher Education Review*, 23 (2), 7-33.

Farnham, D. (ed.) (1999), *Managing Academic Staff in Changing University Systems: international trends and comparisons*, Buckingham: SHRE and Open University Press.

Finkelstein, M.J., R.K. Seal and J.H. Schuster (1998), *The New Academic Generation*, Baltimore: Johns Hopkins University Press.

Finkin, M.W. (ed.) (1996), *The Case for Tenure*, Ithaca: Cornell University Press.

Fruytier, B. & V. Timmerhuis (1995), *Mensen in onderzoek. Het mobiliseren van human resources in wetenschapsorganisaties*, Assen: Van Gorcum.

Halsey, A. (1992), *Decline of the Donnish Dominium*, Oxford: Clarendon.

Henkel, M. (1997), Academic values and the university as corporate enterprise. *Higher Education Quarterly*, 51 (2), 134-143.

Klankbordgroep Invoering MUB (1998), *De kanteling in het universitair bestuur*. SDU: Den Haag.

Köbben, A.J.F. and H. Tromp (1999), *De onwelkome boodschap, of: hoe de vrijheid van wetenschap bedreigd wordt*, Amsterdam: Jan Mets.

Kogan, M., I. Moses and E. El-Khawas (1994), *Staffing Higher Education: meeting new challenges*, London: Jessica Kingsley.

Lorenz, C. (1993), *Van het universitaire front geen nieuws*, Baarn: Ambo.

McPherson, M.S. and M.O. Schapiro (1999), Tenure issues in higher education, *Journal of Economic Perspectives*, vol. 13, no. 1, 85–98.

Mertens, F.J.H. (1999), Kwaliteitsbewaking in het Nederlands hoger onderwijs: enkele persistente problemen van het Nederlands Hoger Onderwijs. *Tijdschrift voor Hoger Onderwijs*, 17 (1), 40-55.

Ministry of Education, Culture and Science (1995), *Wetsvoorstel Modernisering Universitaire Bestuursstructuur (MUB)*, Zoetermeer.

Ministry of Education, Culture and Science (1998), *Hoger Onderwijs en Onderzoek Plan (HOOP)*, Den Haag: Sdu.

Ministry of Education, Culture and Science (1999), *Wetenschappelijke verslagen 1997*. Zoetermeer.

Neave, G. and G. Rhoades (1987), The academic estate in Western Europe, in: B.R. Clark (ed.), *The Academic Profession: national, disciplinary and institutional settings*, Berkeley: University of California Press, 211–71.

Neave, G. (1992), *The Teaching Nation: prospects for teachers in the European Community*. Oxford: Pergamon Press.

Noordzij C.J., (1998), *Naar een nieuw arbeidsrechtelijk regiem voor de Nederlandse universiteiten*, Utrecht: VSNU.

Portegrijs, W. (1998), Eerdaags evenredig? Universiteit Leiden: vakgroep Vrouwenstudies.

Schofield, A. (1997), Developments in human resource management in Commonwealth universities, CHEMS Paper no. 4.

Tierney, W.G. and E.M. Bensimon (1996), *Promotion and Tenure: community and socialization in academe*, Albany: State University of New York Press.

Timmerhuis, V. (1997), *Wetenschapsorganisaties in verandering: keuzen in organisatieontwikkeling en personeelbeleid.* Tilburg: Tilburg University Press.

UNESCO (1992), *Improving the managerial effectiveness of higher education institutions: state of the art.* UNESCO: International Institute for Educational Planning.

VSNU (1988), *Van Regelrecht naar Doelgericht, Arbeidsvoorwaardenbeleid Nederlandse Universiteiten.* Utrecht: VSNU.

Vucht Tijssen, B.E. van (1995), Personeels- en arbeidsvoorwaardenbeleid aan de Nederlandse universiteiten vanaf 1960. In: De Groof, J. (ed.), *Personeelsbeleid aan de Vlaamse universiteiten*, Deurne: Kluwer Rechtswetenschappen België , 63-77.

Vucht Tijssen, B.E. van (1998), *Organisatieverandering, Academisch Leiderschap en HRM*, Utrecht: Utrecht University.

Weert, E. de (1999), The Netherlands: reshaping the employment relationship, in: D. Farnham, *Managing academic staff in changing university systems*, Buckingham: SRHE, 158-174.

Willke, M. (1998), Is er toekomst voor collectieve arbeidsvoorwaarden?, in: B. v. Riel (ed.), *Het Kapitalisme sinds de jaren '70*, Tilburg: Tilburg University Press, 55-74.

Whitehead, A.N. (1962), *The Aims of Education*. London: Benn.

Chapter 4

Internationalisation as a cause for innovation in higher education
A comparison between European cooperation and the Dutch cross-border cooperation programme

MARIJK VAN DER WENDE, ERIC BEERKENS AND ULRICH
TEICHLER

Key words: innovation; institutionalisation; internationalisation

1.   INTRODUCTION

1.1   Defining internationalisation

While internationalism has always been an inherent feature of higher education — students and scholars have travelled since the middle ages; research has never been completely bounded by national borders; and some disciplines and knowledge are universal in nature — it is today gaining even more in importance. International mobility of the workforce, the globalisation of the economy and the use of information and communication technology (ICT) are among the most important factors that give rise to the internationalisation of education. In response, active policies for internationalisation have been developed at supra-national, national and institutional levels. As a result, three trends can be observed.

First, international mobility of individual students and scholars has shifted from being an activity of a limited, elite group to one that is in principle

65

open to the masses, independent of financial position or social status. In Europe, for instance, the European Action Scheme for the Mobility of University Students (the ERASMUS programme), which was founded by the European Commission in 1987, grew in less than ten years to more than 100,000 mobile students per year (Teichler 1998). Also, the number of institutions sending their students abroad has expanded: in 1997, almost 1,600 institutions applied for funding under the new version of the programme (Barblan & Teichler 1998).

Second, the concept of internationalisation has been broadened. From its initial and almost exclusive focus on student exchange, it has developed into a concept including curricular reform, improvement of quality in education and research and institution-wide strategic development (Kälvermark & Van der Wende 1997). Recent studies on the internationalisation of higher education report on the development of internationalised curricula (Van der Wende 1996), on the relationship between internationalisation and quality (Van der Wende 1999), and on the broad range of strategies to support institution-wide internationalisation (De Wit 1995). The studies demonstrate that internationalisation is seen more and more as a process related to the strategic orientation of higher education institutions and to the strengthening of the quality of higher education and research.

Third, supra-national decision-making is increasingly affecting higher education. Schemes, conventions and directives regarding the transfer of credits, and the recognition of academic and professional qualifications are influencing curricular structures and content. Even further, proposals such as the Sorbonne Declaration[1] on the harmonisation of the architecture of European higher education, potentially affect higher education at the system level.

In order to define internationalisation more precisely, a differentiation should be made between the various policies and strategies which are covered by the term.

---

[1]   *Joint declaration on the harmonisation of the architecture of the European higher education system*, Ministers in charge of France, Germany, Italy and the United Kingdom, Paris, The Sorbonne, May 25th, 1998.

Internationalisation of higher education, in terms of the outcome of intended policies
This type of internationalisation appears as a result of governmental or supra-national policies aimed at making the higher education system more international. An international dimension is integrated into the teaching, research and service functions by introducing international cooperation, student and staff exchange, recognition measures, internationalised curricula, etc. This type of internationalisation leaves unchanged the national basis of higher education in terms of governmental steering, funding, regulation, evaluation, etc. The initiatives are based on agreements between countries, with full respect of the sovereignty of the nation state in the governance of higher education. In the case of the European Union programmes, this is reflected in Article 126.1 of the Maastricht Treaty and is known as the 'subsidiarity principle'.[2] It seems that higher education institutions tend to respond in a re-active manner to these policies, following the criteria for eligible actions quite closely in order to be awarded extra funds to carry them out.

De-nationalisation of higher education
This type of internationalisation refers to a number of processes causing or facilitating the expansion of higher education systems across borders. First of all we should note the changing balance in the control of higher education systems. As introduced by Clark (1983) in his triangle of coordination in higher education, the forces of academic oligarchy, state authority and market demand interact with each other to give shape and direction to academic work in national systems of higher education. In many countries, governments have introduced deregulation policies in favour of more institutional autonomy and stronger market influences (Dill & Sporn 1995; Goedegebuure *et al.* 1994). This deregulation and increased competition, in combination with globalisation and decreasing national funding for higher education, ensure that higher education institutions are motivated to expand their activities across the borders of the nation state. Another factor contributing to this type of internationalisation concerns ICT which enables institutions to deliver their programmes and services internationally and on a large scale to a virtual and borderless world. In this context, higher education institutions generally behave in a more pro-active fashion, since there are no prescribed policies or frameworks to follow. It becomes entrepreneurial and even risk-taking. Many examples of internationally entrepreneurial

---

[2]   The principal of subsidiarity means that in the areas which do not belong to the exclusive competence of the community, communal policy will be developed only where national policy-making does not suffice (Article 3b of the Maastricht Treaty).

68   *Chapter 4*

universities can be found in countries like the USA, the United Kingdom, Australia and New Zealand. These universities not only attract many fee-paying foreign students, they also generate international income through overseas or branch campuses, distance learning and franchised programmes, etc. According to Teichler (1998), the European Commission pursues, more or less overtly (or disguised), a de-nationalisation policy in its approaches to cooperation and mobility in higher education (see also Barblan & Teichler 1999). As well, the European Commission encourages curricular cooperation in the search for facilitating mobility and emphasising a European dimension of higher education, which is bound to conflict with curricular constraints traditionally set at national levels by governments as well as by academic and professional agencies.

Cross-border regionalisation of higher education
This term can refer to a variety of cooperative settings, which has been analysed and characterised by Race (1997). Examples concern the cooperation between the Nordic countries or between the border regions of France and Germany. In this type of cooperation, the focus is regional instead of international and activities are based on the development of the region as a socio-economic and political entity. The activities are meant to make institutions benefit from each other's vicinity in spite of a national border separating them. The cross-border cooperation between the Netherlands, Belgium and Germany, for instance, is aimed at making the systems on both sides of the borders more responsive to the needs of the regional labour market and at enhancing mutual access and complementarity of study programmes. Cross-border mergers of institutions or the creation of bi-national institutions are not ruled out in the future. It seems that this type of internationalisation can be both the result of intended governmental or supra-national policies or from de-nationalisation processes; institutions can operate in a re-active or a pro-active way.

1.2   Scope of the chapter

The massification of internationalisation, the broadening of the concept of internationalisation and the increase in supra-national decision-making, lead to a change in the perception of internationalisation. No longer is internationalisation focused just on the activities of individuals, nor are its effects expected to contribute to their individual development only. Rather, internationalisation is now seen as a process with an impact on the curriculum, at the institutional and system levels. In this respect, it is important to analyse how this process is taking place, how it is affecting these levels, what types of changes it is actually creating and to what extent the changes will persist. Within the institution, such changes may concern, for instance: new content, objectives, structures, delivery sites and modes for curricular development; change in teaching and learning processes, the language of instruction, the introduction of new types of students and staff, new roles and communication patterns; change in qualification structures and in procedures for grading, credit allocation, recognition and quality assurance; a new orientation in research programmes and practices; the creation of new positions and roles, organisational structures and units; and new procedures for decision-making (including involving foreign partners).

Innovation theory provides a useful framework for this type of analysis. Studies in innovation and the adoption and diffusion of innovations emerged in the 1960s and focused mainly on innovations in the fields of rural sociology, marketing, communication and organisation (Rogers 1983). According to several organisational studies (e.g. Mann & Neff 1961; Hage & Aiken 1970; Havelock 1969), the process of innovation follows a series of predictable sequential stages. We will focus on the final stage of the innovation process, often referred to as the institutionalisation phase (Levine 1980), the routinisation phase (Hage & Aiken 1970) or the stabilisation phase (Mann & Neff 1961). The general and guiding questions for such an analysis would be:

– in what way (internal/external; re-active/pro-active) and to what extent does internationalisation lead to innovation in higher education?
– what type of innovation and to what extent can such innovation(s) be expected to persist?

Below, a theoretical framework for studying innovation in higher education is introduced. This will be used to analyse and compare two examples of internationalisation. Both concern internationalisation as the outcome of deliberate (governmental or supra-national) policies. We will compare a European programme (i.e. the ERASMUS programme) with a regional cooperation programme (i.e. the programme for cross-border cooperation between the Netherlands, Belgium and Germany) in terms of the institutional responses to these policies. We will analyse the responses from the point of view of the innovations that they are likely to cause within the institutions.

2.   THEORETICAL FRAMEWORK: AN INNOVATION PERSPECTIVE ON INTERNATIONALISATION OF HIGHER EDUCATION

Several studies have been undertaken on innovation processes in organisations (see e.g. Havelock 1969, 1974; Rogers 1983). In this study, we will treat the term innovation from the viewpoint of the adopting unit. Therefore we use Rogers' (1983: 11) definition of an innovation because it stresses the perspective of the adopter, by defining innovation as 'an idea, practice or object that is perceived as new by an individual or other unit of adoption' (see also Jenniskens 1997; Bartelse 1998; and in this volume Jenniskens & Morphew, chapter 5, and Bartelse & Goedegebuure, chapter 11). Since higher education institutions are the types of organisations where professionals have a high level of autonomy, the adoption by the individual will be very meaningful indeed. At the same time, these individuals are organised in different units and structures, often on the basis of knowledge areas as an organisational principle. This implies that the various units may differ in their adoption of the same innovation. Furthermore, this definition allows for the fact that what is seen as new by one actor or unit, may not be perceived as such by another actor or unit, even within the same organisation. Moreover, an innovation can come from both various levels within the institution and an external actor (e.g. a government). Consequently, an institution may act in a re-active or pro-active way.

A specific source on innovation in higher education is the work of Arthur Levine. In his book *Why Innovation Fails* (1980) the emphasis is on the last stage of the innovation process which is most often neglected but, in effect, is the most important: institutionalisation. Levine (1980: 7) describes this phase as the institutionalisation or termination of the new operating plan, which is either routinised and integrated into the organisation or it is ended. The term institutionalisation was conceptualised by Broome and Selznick (1955: 238) as 'the emergence of orderly, stable, socially integrating patterns out of unstable, loosely organised activities'. The application of Levine's innovation theory to the process of internationalisation will provide an insight into the factors that define whether or not the internationalisation strategies and efforts will result in a sustainable and enduring change in higher education institutions.

2.1   Types of innovation

Levine (1980: 4) distinguishes between five basic types of innovation, each of which has its own advantages and disadvantages as well as its own rationale. This typology can be used to analyse and characterise the type of innovation(s) that may occur as a result of an internationalisation process.

The establishment of new organisations
The establishment of new colleges is, according to Levine, the easiest way to establish a non-traditional institutional mission. Although internationalisation is quite often programme-based and many internationalisation strategies aim to diffuse the international dimension throughout entire institutions and their various programmes, this model can definitely be observed. Examples are the colleges or schools that are established as separate institutional structures in order to accommodate international (and often also interdisciplinary) programmes. The creation of such a new structure avoids the effort that would be needed to change the existing structures within the university and to reorient its faculty and students to the international dimension. Moreover, legal obstacles to international programmes, for instance related to the fact that they are taught in a different language or that they are leading to an international degree, are also evaded in this way. However, the creation of new colleges is expensive and (too) high expectations can be imposed. Furthermore, it can be inefficient, especially when over- or under-capacity cannot be compensated for due to separate organisational structures and administrative mechanisms between the college and the parent organisation. In the case of internationalisation, another disadvantage emerges if the new organisation is meant exclusively for foreign students. In that case, opportunities for integration with domestic students and for mutual, cross-cultural learning are not exploited. Also, other forms of synergy between faculty and programmes may become more difficult when the innovation takes place outside the existing institutional context.

Innovative enclaves within existing organisations
Another way to introduce an innovation is to set aside a specific location, unit or experimental programme within the institution in which the innovation is to be implemented. This seems to be a quite popular way of introducing the international dimension into higher education. A special programme or unit within the institution is created in order to accommodate international courses for international groups of students, sometimes

involving international faculty as well. The advantage of this type of innovation is that room for experimenting with international activities is created in a relatively inexpensive and easy to implement way, without changing the status quo and mainstream processes of the institution. One disadvantage related to this type of innovation is that such international programmes or units may become isolated from the rest of the institution and prevent the institution from making the organisational change needed to adopt an international dimension throughout the institution. A more recent concept that seems to provide a solution to this type of disadvantage is the so-called 'matrix structure', which allows a balance of authority between the external and internal demands upon the organisation. It also enables a link between new (temporary) and flexible units and the traditional organisational structure in order to anticipate new scientific and social developments (Van Ginkel 1995). The concept of flexible units that allows the university to respond to developments in its environment can be found also in the work of Clark (1998) who describes the role of such special units as they reach across old university boundaries (disciplines) and link up with outside organisations and groups. Several such units (they may also exist for cooperation with industry, continuing education, knowledge transfer, etc.) together form what Clark calls 'the expanded developmental periphery', which constitutes one of the five characteristics of his concept of the 'entrepreneurial university'.

Holistic changes within existing organisations
Holistic change involves the adoption of a major institutional innovation with a unified and coherent purpose. In spite of the many mission statements that declare that institutions are truly international in spirit, mission and profile, and notwithstanding that many internationalisation strategies are so ambitious as to internationalise the institution's major functions (research, teaching and services), this type of innovation is very infrequently observed in the context of internationalisation. Obviously, most established higher education institutions are, in the first place, nationally based organisations, that perform international activities in addition to their national role and mission, or that integrate an international dimension into their national mission. Levine (1980) states that in general this type of innovation is the least common in higher education. It is also the most difficult to gain acceptance and the least likely to reach the institutionalisation stage. Moreover, the risks are high, as in this type of innovation the old is replaced by the new and there is thus nothing to fall back on in case the innovation does not succeed.

Piecemeal changes within existing organisations

These types of minor innovations are the most common forms of change in higher education and the easiest to implement. They do not affect the institutional mission, function or its organisational principles. Many examples of this type of innovation can indeed be observed in the case of internationalisation. Without affecting the basic structures and mission of the institution, many small and non-mainstream activities can be developed, such as exchange arrangements, international courses, excursions and intensive programmes. It is generally done at a 'grass roots' level and is quite dependent on an individual staff member responsible for it. According to Levine (1980), a series of such innovations can produce more substantial change within the institution. This is what can be observed in many European institutions. From these series of smaller international activities, the initiative to develop an institution-wide internationalisation strategy has ultimately emerged. However, it should be noted that in some cases such an institutional strategy is nothing more than a series of separate and small activities. In other words: the whole is not more than the sum of its parts.

Peripheral changes outside existing organisations

Levine (1980: 6) describes this type of innovation as 'the establishment of institutions or changes within institutions that are not traditionally associated with higher education, but that have an effect on the activities of existing colleges and universities'. He gives an early example of the establishment of degree-granting programmes by commercial corporations such as AT&T which he expects to become competitors with traditional higher education institutions. At present, this type of innovation is becoming most significant in the form of virtual universities which operate trans-nationally with great ease, as the delivery of their programmes is supported by ICT. Their quickly emerging presence and the threat they represent have an impact on present debates in higher education. It is most interesting to see how traditional higher education institutions are responding (or not) to this challenge and to speculate on what types of innovations will result from within these organisations. Examples concern institutions that introduce forms of flexible delivery (distance learning) in order to reach out to international students while seeking enhanced cooperation with other higher education institutions and/or corporate partners (Collis & Van der Wende 1999). These peripheral changes are among the most important pushes for new developments in the internationalisation area for the future.

2.2   Phases in the innovation process

Various authors have defined different stages in the innovation process
(Hage & Aiken 1970; Rogers 1962; Mann & Neff 1961). In his book, Levine
(1980) compares a number of authors' views on the various stages that are
involved in the process of innovation. He finds consistency between the
different theories and the results of his own research and proposes a process
having four fundamental steps: (i) recognising the need for change; (ii)
planning and formulating a solution; (iii) initiation and implementation of a
plan; and (iv) institutionalisation or termination (1980: 7).

Mostly, innovative efforts focus on the first three stages and in many cases it
is believed that the third stage (implementation) is the conclusion of the
innovation process, as by then the adoption of something new, which was
the aim of the innovation, has been achieved. However, institutionalisation is
the most critical phase for any innovation and the organisation adopting it.
Research has shown that during institutionalisation, innovations usually
transform or fade away. Van Vught (1989: 57) concludes that:

> *Innovations in higher education institutions may arise easily and often,*
> *but their diffusion will be difficult and will mainly take place through*
> *communication between colleagues.*

Also, in the area of internationalisation, the stage of institutionalisation is
critical, particularly due to the fact that internationalisation in many cases
has been a re-active response of institutions to external policies formulated at
the supra-national level, making them heavily dependent on external funding
and subsidies.

2.3   Factors determining institutionalisation

The outcome of the institutionalisation process is dependent on the
characteristics of the innovation. First, for institutionalisation to be
successful, the innovation has to fit the organisational context in which it has
to evolve. Secondly, the actors involved in the institutionalisation process
have to perceive the innovation as having a relative advantage, compared
with the pre-adoption stage. Levine (1980), in relation to these factors, uses

the terms compatibility and profitability.[3]

-   *Compatibility*: This is the degree to which the norms, values and goals associated with the innovation are congruent with those of the host organisation. It depends on the extent to which the innovation fits the institutional mission and goals, as well as its coherence with other policy areas. It is a measure of appropriateness of the innovation within existing organisational boundaries. Rogers (1983: 223) uses a similar definition of compatibility. Furthermore, he states that the innovation can be compatible with (a) the socio-cultural beliefs of the organisation; (b) previously introduced ideas; and (c) client needs for innovation. In general, one might say the greater the degree of compatibility of an innovation within the organisation, the lesser the degree of dissatisfaction. The compatibility factor sets in motion the two mechanisms of the institutionalisation process: when the innovation is incompatible, the innovation characteristics are adjusted to the institutional context; when the innovation is compatible, the institutional context is adjusted to the characteristics of the innovation. These mechanisms are referred to as contraction and expansion (Levine 1980; Bartelse 1998).

-   *Profitability*: This is the effectiveness of an innovation in satisfying the adopter's needs. This factor is more difficult to define, because it is subjective. What really counts is the adopter's perception of profitability, and not objective profitability. The degree of profitability may be measured in economic terms, but social prestige factors or satisfaction can also be important components. According to Rogers (1983), the rate of adoption of an innovation will be more rapid when the perceived relative advantage is greater. Furthermore, what is perceived as profitable by an individual adopter does not necessarily coincide with what is profitable for the organisation as a whole. Individual adopters within a higher education institution may differ very strongly in what they perceive as profitable!

These two factors can lead to different outcomes of the institutionalisation process (see figure 1).

---

[3] Complexity is often distinguished as a third variable (Hahn 1974; Kivlin 1960). In this study, complexity will not be regarded as a variable that determines whether institutionalisation occurs, but as a characteristic of the type of innovation that is intended.

Figure 1: Possible outcomes of institutionalisation

Compatibility

low   high

		low	high
Profitability	high	(iv) Resocialisation	(i) Diffusion
	low	(iii) Termination	(ii) Enclaving

Source: based on Levine 1980

When an innovation is compatible with the institutional context, the innovation can either spread throughout the organisation (*diffusion*) or it can assume an isolated position within the organisation (*enclaving*). In both outcomes, the mechanism of expansion is set in motion and the institutional boundaries are adjusted to the characteristics of the innovation; in other words, the innovation's characteristics are accepted by the host. Diffusion will be achieved only when the actors involved perceive the innovation as profitable. When this is not the case, institutional expansion may be explained by rule-following behaviour: actors will comply to the institutional expectations of their context as there is no explicit institutional mismatch (Bartelse 1998). This will result in the innovation being in an isolated position within the institution (*enclaving*).

When the innovation's characteristics are not compatible with the institutional context, the innovation can either be eliminated (*termination*) or forced to adjust to the acceptable norms, values and goals of the institution (*resocialisation*). In either way, contraction occurs and the non-compatible characteristics of the innovation are excluded. Termination will occur when, according to the actors involved, there is no relative advantage to be expected from the innovation; in other words, the innovation is not perceived as profitable. Resocialisation will occur when the innovation is adjusted to the institutional context, and the outcome differs from the innovation that was originally implemented.

3. METHODOLOGY

This theoretical analysis of internationalisation as an innovation process has provided an insight into potential factors that define the success of internationalisation in terms of an optimal outcome at the institutionalisation stage. The main outcomes of the theoretical elaboration are:

- internationalisation may lead to various types of innovation within higher education institutions; the most successful outcome of the innovation process is institutionalisation, optimally in terms of diffusion;

- such optimal institutionalisation will occur only when the internationalisation strategy is compatible with the overall institutional strategy and when it is perceived as profitable by the various adopters of the innovation;

- compatibility depends on the extent to which the internationalisation strategy is congruent with the institutional mission and goals, and with other policy areas within the institution;

- profitability depends on the extent to which the innovation is perceived as effective in satisfying the needs of the various adopters, which can be distinguished by units or individuals within the institution and by the institution as a whole.

On this theoretical basis, two internationalisation programmes (i.e. the SOCRATES programme and the programme for cross-border cooperation between the Netherlands, Belgium and Germany) will be analysed and compared. Since both programmes started quite recently (1997), conclusions concerning their effectiveness and eventual success in terms of institutionalisation cannot yet be drawn. Therefore, our focus will be on the initial institutional responses to both programmes, as expressed in the applications and project plans that describe the actions the institutions want to undertake in the context of these internationalisation programmes. In doing so, our aim will be twofold:

- to identify the types of innovation (as characterised by Levine) that these programmes seem to introduce into the higher education institutions concerned;

- to collect some provisional evidence on the extent to which these programmes can be expected to meet the requirements of compatibility and profitability.

In this way, some hypotheses on the eventual success of the programmes in terms of the sustainability of the innovations they introduce can be presented.

The analysis will be based on the results of two research projects: the EUROSTRAT II project[4] and a study on the cross-border cooperation projects between the Netherlands, Belgium and Germany.[5] It should be stressed that the original focus of both studies was different from the problem that we are addressing in this chapter. Consequently, secondary data analysis has been the basis of our analyses, which should be considered as exploratory only.

4. ANALYSIS OF THE INSTITUTIONAL RESPONSES TO THE SOCRATES PROGRAMME

4.1 Introduction to the programme

The SOCRATES programme was adopted in 1994. It had two predecessors: the Joint Study Programme (JSP) scheme launched in 1976 (aimed mainly at the stimulation of academic mobility within the EC) and ERASMUS (European Action Scheme for the Mobility of University Students) in 1987.

---

[4] This study, undertaken by the Association of European Universities (CRE) and the Centre for Research on Higher Education and Work (University of Kassel, Germany), analysed the European Policy Statements (1,583 in total) as part of the first round of applications for an institutional contract under SOCRATES, which were submitted in 1996 for the academic year 1997–98 (Barblan *et al.* 1998).

[5] This study is being carried out by the Centre for Higher Education Policy Studies (CHEPS), in cooperation with the Catholic University of Leuven and Hochschul Informations System in Hanover. Both an analysis of the approved projects (83 in total) and a survey on first implementation were carried out for the programme presently in force (from 1997 to 2000) (see Beerkens & Van der Wende 1999).

In 1993 Antonio Ruberti, then Commissioner responsible for education and research, stressed the need for a more coherent continuation of existing programmes. In this approach, educational policy was extended to secondary and vocational education. The new SOCRATES programme was designed to cover these various levels of education. Within this programme, ERASMUS would continue as the programme for higher education. Besides a shift in the area of support (e.g. more support for teaching staff mobility and curricular development), the managerial nature of the programme changed. The Institutional Contract (IC), a contract between the institution and the European Commission, was introduced. The application for an IC contained both a European Policy Statement and a description of all the activities for which the institution was applying for financial support from the European Commission. According to Barblan *et al.* (1998: 10), the changes in SOCRATES meant not just a shift in bureaucratic procedures, but it implicitly challenged institutions to put a stronger emphasis on the coherence of goals and activities, the strengthening of the responsibility of the central level and the development and reinforcement of strategic thinking.

The rationale for the ERASMUS programme was predominantly political and economic: stimulating the European identity and developing international competitiveness. This raises a question about the relationship between Europeanisation and internationalisation. It has been observed that:

> *Most departments involved in ERASMUS clearly emphasised an international rather than a European approach. They appreciated European support ... but neither conceptually nor pragmatically did they wish an exclusive emphasis on Europe (Teichler 1998: 93).*

In addition, it was observed that:

> *The European Commission, while talking about Europe, is a powerful actor of internationalisation, whereby Europe is actually predominantly a sub-category of less than systematic relevance. The Commission's contribution to internationalisation rests primarily on its successful challenge to national forces of curricular coordination. In its de-nationalising effect on curricula ... Europeanisation à la ERASMUS coincides with internationalisation* (Teichler 1998: 95).

4.2   Envisaged activities and types of innovation that can be expected

ERASMUS provides three different types of support for European activities: mobility grants for students and institutional grants for activities within as well as outside the IC. Activities within the IC may concern teaching staff mobility, preparatory visits, curricular development, etc. Grants to institutions outside the IC include the university cooperation projects on subjects of mutual interest, better known as the Thematic Network Projects (TNP). Cooperation within these networks is required to have a lasting and widespread impact across a range of universities within or between specific discipline areas.

According to the first round of applications for 1997–98, activities concerning student and staff mobility took priority underscoring the European institutional policy (see figure 2).

Figure 2: Policy relevance of SOCRATES activities

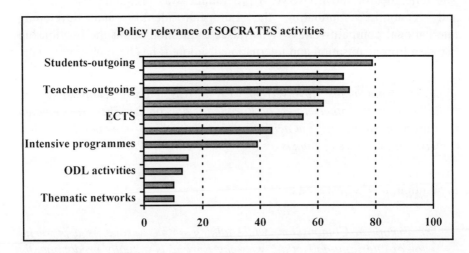

Source: Barblan *et al.* 1998

Figure 2 shows that the majority of institutions preferred to stay with the typical ERASMUS activities of *student and staff mobility*. Next, they wished to work on the development of the European Credit Transfer System (ECTS) and on curricular development (programmes with a European dimension). Much less attention was paid to preparatory visits, open and distance learning, cooperation with industry, etc. The first question now is: what type of innovation can be expected from this approach?

It could be argued that student mobility will lead to none or only little innovation within the institution, since it is a purely individual activity and because the programme provides financial aid to students without direct intervention of the institution. On the other hand, it could be said that indirectly these activities could have an institutional impact because students often turn out to be 'change agents' for host as well as home institutions. It could even be claimed that:

> *Support for student mobility was not a means in itself, but rather a means only to introduce curricular change. According to this view, the instrument of student mobility was primarily chosen because it was the only legitimate way of inducing substantial curricular change without obvious disregard of the required respect for the variety of higher education systems and for the prerogative of the national governments to shape those systems* (Teichler 1998: 91).

Staff mobility can by all means be expected to have an effect on the teaching and learning process and on the content of the curricula. Like the students, staff experience major contrasts between curricula, teaching and learning modes, administrative and institutional structures and social environment between host and home institution. This may work as an eye-opener and trigger change.

In terms of Levine's (1980) typology of innovations, these activities are most likely to lead in the first instance to piecemeal changes in the organisations only. This is because, in the first place, student and staff exchanges do not affect the basic structures and mission of the institution. And, secondly, it is because the involvement of students and staff is not systematic and substantial enough to introduce holistic change in terms of a major institutional innovation with a unified and coherent purpose. In particular cases, institutions may choose to accommodate these foreign students together in one specific international unit or class; this may lead to another type of innovation, labelled as an innovative enclave within the existing organisation. However, the general idea of ERASMUS is rather to integrate foreign students and staff into regular courses and into the domestic student and staff population.

The credit framework and curricular development activities also are likely to result, in the first instance, in piecemeal changes within the existing organisation, because they usually concern small parts of curricula and leave the basic structures and mission of the institution unaffected. The development of intensive programmes, or of joint undergraduate or postgraduate programmes, may result in 'innovative enclaves within existing organisations'. In this way, room for experimenting with new programmes is provided, without changing the status quo of the mainstream processes and curricula. The challenge in this activity would be to fully integrate the international programmes into the regular curricula. Open and distance learning activities, cooperation with industry, thematic networks, etc. could lead to substantial innovations but are not highly rated in terms of relevance (and funding).

In the longer term, the sum of the ERASMUS activities in principle could have a more profound impact and may lead to more holistic change within the institutions. About 55% of institutions actually expect the programme to cause a change in their institutional profile as a whole (Barblan & Teichler 1998). The role of students and staff as change agents, and their effect on the de-nationalisation of curricula provide an indication for this development. Besides, the IC and consequent enhanced involvement of the institutional management may add to this. Whether this will happen or not, depends on the institutions' willingness to adapt to the changes caused by the innovations. This will be dependent on the compatibility and profitability of the innovation.

4.3   Compatibility and profitability

The second question is: can we expect these innovations to be institutionalised? In order to explore this question, we will look at the extent to which innovations meet the requirements of compatibility and profitability.

First, a general observation with regard to compatibility can be made. In section 2.3, we stated that compatibility concerns the degree to which the norms, values and goals associated with the innovation are congruent with the institutional context of the host, and that the innovation can be compatible with the socio-cultural beliefs of the organisation, with previously introduced ideas and with client needs for innovation. There seems to be compatibility with the norms, values and the socio-cultural beliefs of the institutions in the sense that the importance of internationalisation of academia is in general widely subscribed to by staff as well as students. The EUROSTRAT study (Barblan & Teichler 1998) revealed that internationalisation seems to increasingly be embedded into the overall goals of the higher education institutions. A European or international dimension was found to be a central part of the mission and goals of more than a quarter of the examined institutions and played some role in another third of the cases. The compatibility of the activities with institutional goals, norms and mission is also indicated by the fact that 55% of the institutions see the activities as an instrument to change or enhance their profiles.

Second, the IC can be seen as an instrument to enhance compatibility, in terms of the fit between the innovation and the institutional mission and goals. The IC, and in particular the institution's European Policy Statement as a part of it, challenges the institutions to consider the link between their European activities and their overall institutional mission and goals and their relationship with other policy areas. It also requires institutions to clarify the relationship between their European policy and objectives and the actual activities they will be undertaking. However, the EUROSTRAT analysis revealed that the strategic reasoning that is assumed and implicitly expected from institutions in this approach, does not coincide with the fact that most of the applying institutions do not see themselves as strategic actors and are cautious when asked to commit their future to specific areas.

Third, there seems to be a certain extent of compatibility with previously introduced ideas. Considering the positive appreciation of earlier EU programmes (see e.g. Teichler & Maiworm 1997), the relatively high level of comparability of SOCRATES with previous EU programmes gives some further indication of the compatibility of the innovations introduced by this programme. Especially the student mobility part which, according to institutional representatives, has become a regular part of institutional life (Barblan & Teichler 1998: 6) and therefore one might even say that it has already been institutionalised and diffused throughout the organisation. However, this cannot be said for all parts of the programme. The EUROSTRAT study shows that traditional activities (e.g. mobility and existing inter-institutional agreements) are continued and complemented by further development of previously marginal activities (e.g. use of ECTS or curricular development). Other activities which are high on the agenda of EU higher education policy such as open and distance learning, continuing education and cooperation with industry, do not come to the fore in institutional policies and activities. It seems that these parts of the programme represent innovations that are less compatible with the current mission and goals, beliefs and needs of the institutions, although this of course may change over time.

The other factor determining the outcome of the institutionalisation process is the level of (perceived) profitability of the innovation. Diffusion of the envisaged activities is most likely when these are perceived as profitable by the actors involved. Still, the different actors in higher education may differ in what they perceive as profitable and therefore a distinction between them should be made.

Since the physical mobility of students is still regarded as the core element of SOCRATES, student perception of the activities plays a major role. Obviously, the introduction of ERASMUS in 1987 meant a profitable innovation from the students' point of view. In the new SOCRATES scheme, the financial support to individual students has declined. This is perceived as a setback for students. For the non-mobile students, however, the emphasis in the SOCRATES scheme for teaching staff mobility, intensive programmes and curricular development can be seen as a relative advantage compared to ERASMUS. Although these activities, as well as the open and distance learning projects and the thematic networks, are meant to enrich and broaden the programme, there seems to be an impression that:

> *The SOCRATES programme might become overstretched, running the risk of endangering its core activities for the sake of achieving prominent success in new areas* ... (Barblan & Teichler 1998: 8).

The EUROSTRAT study showed that, for academics, the shift of responsibility from the departmental to the institutional level has resulted in a loss of enthusiasm and sense of 'ownership'. This was enforced by the enormous discrepancy between the financial support requested and the funds actually granted and by the shift from multilateral to bilateral cooperation, leading to less frequent meetings between academics. The decrease of the administrative burden for academics, however, was much welcomed by them.

For administrators, the move from ERASMUS to SOCRATES was perceived as bringing about a substantial increase in their administrative load. The shift towards bilateral agreements, however, improved transparency in international cooperation. Another positive aspect of the shift towards bilateralism that was perceived by various institutional representatives was the expectation that the bilateral approach would increase the moral pressure for mutual reciprocity. At the same time, bilateralism was not considered a suitable approach for reinforcing curricular development or intensive programmes:

If partners place different emphases on such activities ... the activities could suffer from or even be endangered by a lack of matching interests (Barblan & Teichler 1998: 11).

In general, we can conclude that activities considered to be the core of the SOCRATES programme (i.e. activities relating to physical mobility) can be regarded as compatible with the norms, goals and mission of the institutions. Also, these activities are perceived as profitable by the actors involved, although for some actors this level of profitability is decreasing. These activities will lead basically to piecemeal changes within the organisation, although it can be argued that they could lead, indirectly and in the long run, to more substantial curricular and institutional change. One might expect these core activities to diffuse throughout the organisation. Curriculum-related activities may also lead to piecemeal change, or in some cases perhaps to innovative enclaves. Activities such as open and distance learning and continuing education have potential for innovation but they are only being undertaken on a very small scale. All these activities still raise questions about compatibility and profitability. Therefore, it is difficult to forecast at this point the outcome of their institutionalisation processes, but it cannot be excluded that some of them run the risk of being resocialised, or even terminated. Besides, for all activities the degree of dependence on external funding will be a critical factor with regard to their sustainability.

5.   ANALYSIS OF THE INSTITUTIONAL RESPONSES TO THE DUTCH PROGRAMME FOR CROSS-BORDER COOPERATION WITH BELGIUM AND GERMANY

5.1   Introduction to the programme

In 1991, the Dutch Ministry of Education, Culture and Science started the so-called Cross-border Cooperation (CBC) policy, with the aim of contributing towards an 'open higher educational space without any obstacles for mobility' (Ministerie van OC&W 1997). The 'GROS-HO programme', the first for the CBC, was aimed at educational cooperation (e.g. student and staff mobility and curricular development) and was remarkably smaller than the current programme in terms of financial support. Later, in 1996, the Ministry introduced the 'Regulation on Cross-border Cooperation in Higher Education 1997–2000'. The programme was based on the bilateral agreements between the Dutch Minister of Education and the Ministers of Education in Flanders and the German Länder of North Rhine Westphalia, Lower Saxony and Bremen. According to the programme, higher education institutions were granted financial support for this period for an institutional plan that covered activities aimed at:

– developing structural and strategic cooperation between institutions located near each other but separated by a border, in order to optimally benefit from the educational potential in the region, for example, through joint curricular and other trans-national links between institutions; and

– creating in this way an added value for education, which will result in highly qualified graduates, who will be better equipped for the regional labour market because they will have learned to deal with the cultural differences and to speak the languages of the region.

The criteria that institutional plans had to meet included aspects such as (i) a strong commitment from institutional leadership; (ii) curricular activities that demonstrated the added value of cooperation for the institutions and other partners in the region; (iii) attention to each other's languages and cultures; and (iv) a clear commitment from the partner institution. Furthermore, activities solely focused on mobility were not eligible for support.

5.2   Envisaged activities and types of innovation that can be expected

The criteria and the open character of the regulation resulted in a wide range of project activities. On the basis of an analysis of the proposals and on questionnaires sent to all project coordinators in the various countries, the following distinctions between the envisaged activities can be made (table 1).

Table 1: Envisaged activities in the CBC programme

Type of activity	Percentage of all projects (N = 83)
Educational cooperation:	
• Joint curricular development	70
• Transfer of knowledge on educational methodology	42
• Recognition and mobility	27
Focus on regional and social aspects	24
Sharing and joint use of facilities and infrastructure	14
Establishment of legal bodies to facilitate cooperation	13

Source: Beerkens & Van der Wende 1999

The projects demonstrate a remarkably strong focus on curricular issues. These activities may focus on:

– adjustment and coordination of curricula in order to make them mutually accessible to students (67%);

– making curricula which exist on only one side of the border, accessible to students from the entire cross-border region (19%);

– joint development of new curricula, which do not exist in any of the involved institutions (14%).

In this context the transfer of knowledge on educational methodology, mostly in terms of learning about each other's practices in teaching and learning processes and about specific disciplinary approaches, is often part of the pre-stage of these curricular development processes. The mutual access to study programmes across the border requires recognition measures and in some cases joint or double diplomas in order to facilitate students to move between the institutions.

Projects focusing on regional aspects (e.g. labour market demands), on the joint use of facilities and infrastructure (e.g. laboratories, research equipment) or on the establishment of specific bodies to facilitate cooperation are less frequently observed. We will now try to analyse what types of innovations can be expected from this approach.

Firstly, a general remark is necessary concerning the fact that the programme is explicitly meant to create sustainable internationalisation by means of focusing not at the individual (student) level but, rather, at the curricular and institutional levels. In this programme, there are many small scale activities concerning small parts of curricula only, thus leaving the basic structure and mission of the institution unaffected. These types of activities can be labelled as piecemeal changes. In cases where complete curricula are concerned, the emergence of innovative enclaves can be observed. Within the institutions but outside the mainstream programmes, specific programmes and/or units are created which offer curricula that accommodate students from the various partner institutions. Students, for instance, may follow parts of the curricula in their own institution and other parts in the partner institution and obtain a joint or double diploma. Within the institution, such a special programme or unit may be labelled a 'school'. Besides these two types of innovations, others may be observed. An example of the establishment of a new organisation is the Trans-national Centre for Technology, Innovation and Study that has been established by a Dutch institution and its German partner. An example of peripheral change is illustrated by an organisation which was created by regional companies, governments and higher education institutions, with the aim to create synergy between the expertise from the various partners and to enable knowledge transfer through training and applied research. Holistic change may even be expected in the case of a Flemish and a Dutch institution which are considering a cross-border merger that may result in a true trans-national university.

Another question concerns the extent to which this innovation meets the criteria of compatibility and profitability and, consequently, to what extent we can expect them to be institutionalised.

It can be said that in general the concept of cross-border cooperation, as such, which mainly has a socio-economic rationale of strengthening the regional infrastructure through coordination of higher education provisions, is not very compatible with the norms, values and goals of higher education institutions. Institutions' international interests are usually based on academic concepts like common research or educational interests and the search for excellence; these are not necessarily related to institutions within each other's geographic vicinity. This is illustrated by the fact that, from the CBC policy point of view, cooperation in courses which formerly were offered on only one side of the border, or the joint development of new courses, would be considered most profitable in terms of cost-effectiveness. However, the evaluation study shows that institutions, rather, cooperate in cases where curricula are offered on both sides of the border (67% of curricular projects) because this provides a common basis for their activities. Secondly, a regional focus may not be relevant for those institutions which recruit their students from all over the country and thus do not train them for a specific regional labour market. Third, as compatibility is a measure of appropriateness of the innovation within existing institutional boundaries, it should be mentioned that the emphasis on strategic cooperation does not match in all cases the degree of autonomy of the institutions. Depending on the degree of direct governmental steering (which is stronger in Germany and Flanders compared to the Netherlands), institutions have more or less freedom in establishing new structures or programmes, or even in adjusting programmes in the context of regional partnerships. Nevertheless, for certain institutions, the regional approach seems to coincide very well with institutional goals. For instance, for those institutions which like to expand their activities across the border in order to enhance their profile in the region, for example, in order to attract more students or to strengthen their relationships with industry, cross-border cooperation is very attractive. Real win-win situations may occur when both partners can only achieve certain institutional goals through cross-border cooperation. An example of this is the case where a single institution is too weak to establish a new study programme, but can do so in cooperation with another institution. This is where the educational offerings of the institutions are complementary to each other, or where joint efforts are required in order to make certain major investments. In some very specific cases these advantages in the future may even be an argument to consider a cross-border merger of institutions.

In terms of profitability for students it can be argued that a stay in a neighbouring country is often perceived as less attractive than a stay in a faraway country. The study indicates that students are less motivated to study abroad at an institution on the other side of the border. On the other hand, this type of cooperation provides them with a wider range of study options without travelling too much and allows them to obtain qualifications that are recognised in the neighbouring country, which may enhance their labour market opportunities.

In cases of compatible educational interests, this type of international cooperation seems to be profitable for academics since they can cooperate quite intensively thanks to the vicinity of their partners and the substantial funding of the activities. Also for administrators and the institution as a whole the size of the funding of activities is attractive. More generally, this type of cooperation is profitable since it creates possibilities for cost-effective use of limited resources and expensive infrastructure and equipment.

A further illustration of the profitability of this type of cooperation in comparison with wider internationalisation is provided in table 2. This overview shows that the belief that this type of cooperation is presenting fewer problems because of more similarity between the higher education systems and the cultural-linguistic situation at both sides of the border is only shared to a limited extent. However, the vicinity of partner institutions is seen as an advantage.

Table 2: Advantages of cross-border cooperation over wider internationalisation

Advantages of cross-border cooperation over wider internationalisation	Agree (%)
Vicinity of partner institutions	97
Cultural similarities	29
Linguistic similarities	29
Similarities in HE systems	15

Source: Beerkens & Van der Wende 1999

It can be concluded that cross-border cooperation may lead to a range of innovations and that institutionalisation will be supported by the fact that the vicinity of partners to each other and the more efficient exploitation of resources that sometimes goes with this type of cooperation, are seen as profitable factors. However, this will only occur in those cases where a regional focus is compatible with the strategic goals of the institutions concerned.

6.   CONCLUSIONS AND SOME DIRECTIONS FOR FURTHER RESEARCH

Since our theoretical framework focuses on the institutionalisation stage of the innovation process and since the two programmes have only recently started, our conclusions will be mainly tentative. First of all, it can be concluded that the innovation theory can provide a framework for the analysis of the impact of internationalisation policies on higher education institutions, as well as providing a framework for the factors that relate to the institutionalisation of these innovations. A further elaboration on the types of innovations that can be expected, could reveal more specific types of innovations that are caused by internationalisation. More research is also needed in order to gain further insights into the factors of compatibility and profitability of these innovations. This would lead to valuable knowledge for the design of internationalisation policies and programmes. Obviously, this chapter, which is based on secondary data analysis, provides only limited empirical basis for such insights. Secondly, it seems that internationalisation causes innovation in higher education indeed, although it primarily takes the form of piecemeal changes or innovative enclaves within higher education institutions. Still, some, albeit few, examples of other types of innovation could be identified. Moreover, it is arguable that these small innovations may lead in the longer term to more important changes. It would be interesting in this respect to compare the impact of internationalisation as an outcome of supra-national policy with de-nationalisation processes, since, in the latter type of internationalisation, higher education institutions seem to be more pro-active and entrepreneurial. Furthermore, questions concerning the influence of internationalisation on the role of national governments and on the use of policy instruments, for example, funding, planning, evaluation and regulation, should be addressed. Another set of research topics concerns the relationship between internationalisation and the influence of market forces on higher education. Also, the consequences for internal management of higher education institutions, for the relationship with wider institutional change and the use of new technologies is worth investigating.

References

Barblan, A., B. Kehm, S. Reichert and U. Teichler (1998), *Emerging European Policy Profiles of Higher Education Institutions*, Werkstattberichte 55, Kassel: Centre for Higher Education and Work, University of Kassel.

Barblan A. and U. Teichler (1998), *University Responsibility for European Cooperation and Mobility*, http://www.europe.eu.int/en/comm/dg22/socrates/erasmus/coop.pdf

Barblan A. and U. Teichler (1999), Internationalisation as a challenge for higher education in Europe, *Tertiary Education and Management*, vol. 5, no. 1, pp. 1–18.

Bartelse, J. (1998), *Concentrating the Minds: the institutionalisation of the graduate school innovation in Dutch and German higher education*, Utrecht: Lemma.

Beerkens H.J.J.G. and M.C. van der Wende (1999), *Grensoverschrijdende samenwerking in het hoger onderwijs: een onderzoek naar projecten uitgevoerd in het kader van de "Regeling stimulering grensoverschrijdende samenwerking hoger onderwijs 1997-2000"*. Zoetermeer: Ministerie van Onderwijs, Cultuur en Wetenschappen.

Broome, L. and P. Selznick (1955), *Sociology: a text with adapted readings*, New York: Row, Peterson.

Clark, B.R. (1983), *The Higher Education System: academic organization in cross national perspective*, Berkeley: University of California Press.

Clark, B.R. (1998), *Creating Entrepreneurial Universities: organizational pathways of transformation*, Oxford: Pergamon.

Collis, B. and M.C. van der Wende (eds) (1999), *The Use of ICT in Higher Education: an international orientation on trends and issues*, Enschede: CHEPS, University of Twente.

Dill, D.D. and B. Sporn (1995), *Emerging Patterns of Social Demand and University Reform: through a glass darkly*, Oxford: Pergamon Press.

Ginkel, H.J.A. van (1995), The challenge of institutional change, *Higher Education in Europe*, vol. 20, no. 3, pp. 8–24.

Goedegebuure, L., F. Kaiser, P. Maassen, V.L. Meek, F. van Vught and E. de Weert (eds) (1994), *Higher Education Policy: an international comparative perspective*, Oxford: Pergamon Press.

Hage, J. and M. Aiken (1970), *Social Change in Complex Organizations*, New York: Random House.

Hahn, C.L. (1974). *Relationships between potential adopters' perceptions of social studies innovations and their adoption of these innovations in Indiana, Ohio, Georgia and Florida*. Ph.D. thesis, Bloomington, Indiana University.

Havelock, R.G. (1969), *Planning for Innovation Through Dissemination and Utilization of Knowledge*, Institute for Social Research, Ann Arbor, Michigan: University of Michigan.

Havelock, R.G. (1974), *Educational Innovation in the United States, Vol II, Five Case Studies of Educational Innovation at the School District Level*, Center of Research on Utilization of Scientific Knowledge, Ann Arbor, Michigan: University of Michigan.

Jenniskens, I. (1997), *Governmental Steering and Curriculum Innovations: a comparative study on the relation between governmental steering instruments and innovations in higher education curricula*, Utrecht: Lemma.

Kälvermark, T. and M.C. van der Wende (eds) (1997), *National Policies for Internationalisation of Higher Education in Europe*, Stockholm: National Agency for Higher Education.

Kivlin, J.E. (1960), *Characteristics of farm practices associated with rate of adoption*. Ph.D. thesis, University Park, Pennsylvania State University.

Levine, A. (1980), *Why Innovation Fails: the institutionalization and termination of innovations in higher education*, New York: Albany State University of New York Press.

Mann, F. and F.W. Neff (1961), *Managing Major Change in Organizations*, Ann Arbor, Michigan: Foundation for the Research on Human Behaviour.

Ministerie van Onderwijs, Cultuur en Wetenschappen (1997), *Onbegrensd talent: internationalisering van onderwijs*. Zoetermeer: Ministerie van OC & W.

Race, J. (1997), *Regional Cooperation in Higher Education: a background and overview*. Strasbourg: Council of Europe.

Rogers, E.M. (1962), *Diffusion of Innovations*, 1st edn, New York: Free Press.

Rogers, E.M. (1983), *Diffusion of Innovations*, 3rd edn, New York: Free Press.

Teichler, U. (1998), The role of the European Union in the internationalisation of higher education, in: P. Scott (ed.), *The Globalisation of Higher Education*, Buckingham: SRHE and Open University Press.

Teichler, U. and F. Maiworm (1997), *The ERASMUS experience: major findings of the ERASMUS Evaluation Research Project*, Luxembourg: Office for Official Publications of the European Communities.

Van Vught, F.A. (ed.) (1989), *Governmental Strategies and Innovation in Higher Education*, Higher Education Policy Series no. 7, London: Jessica Kingsley Publishers.

Wende, M.C. van der (1996), *Internationalizing the curriculum in higher education: an international comparative perspective*, dissertation.

Wende, M.C. van der (1999), Quality assurance of internationalization and internationalization of quality assurance, in: *Quality and Internationalization in Higher Education*, H. de Wit and J. Knight (eds), Paris: OECD/IMHE.

Wit, H. de (ed.) (1995), *Strategies for Internationalization of Higher Education. A comparative study of Australia, Canada, Europe and the United States of America*, Amsterdam: European Association for International Education.

Chapter 5

Assessing institutional change at the level of the faculty
Examining faculty motivations and new degree programmes

INEKE JENNISKENS AND CHRISTOPHER MORPHEW

Key words: academic drift; degree programmes; isomorphism

1.   INTRODUCTION: THE NEED FOR RESEARCH AT THE FACULTY LEVEL

Since the 1970s, several industrialised countries have attempted to steer and restructure their higher education systems in the face of changing enrolments, strained budgets, and the need for better coordination and planning. Higher education policy-makers have struggled with the job of maintaining specific roles and missions for higher education institutions. In the light of these restructuring processes, both policy-makers and researchers have paid attention to the phenomenon of academic drift, a process which basically consists of lower status institutions trying to gain status by imitating higher status institutions (especially the prestigious research universities) (see e.g. Riesman 1956).

The role of individual staff members (or groups of staff members) in these imitation processes is an important one, since their actions may result in changes in the institutional profile and position on the status hierarchy. Changes in the institutional profile in terms of degree programmes offered (balanced between programmes of various levels, number of programmes, and enrolments) are the result of the introduction of new degree programmes and/or the discontinuation of other programmes. In this way, one can hypothesise that there is a relation between faculty motivations to introduce new degree programmes on the one hand and factors that are correlated to institutional and macro processes such as academic drift and dedifferentiation on the other. There is ample research that suggests that faculty are motivated by factors that would lead toward imitation and academic drift. Factors related to reward structures, prestige and professionalisation might play a role in motivating faculty to focus their efforts on areas outside their institution's historical mission. Most of the research has focused — almost exclusively — on systems of higher education and the patterns of growth at this macro level (see e.g. studies by Neave 1979; Birnbaum 1983; Riesman 1956; Meek 1991; Huisman 1995; Morphew 1996; Huisman & Morphew 1998).

However, there are examples of studies in which it is hypothesised that faculty members play an important role in the process whereby new degree programmes are added to the total supply for the primary purpose of copying 'the role and mission of the prestige institutions' (Berdahl 1985: 303) or where universities cast out 'less advanced and part-time students the better to concentrate upon full-time degree-level work' (Neave 1979: 143). Both examples illustrate how (individual and group) actions of staff members may result in instances of academic drift at the institutional level. Rhoades (1990: 191) argues that faculty members are a primary source for stability and against change in higher education:

> *... I suggest that academics are major definers and defenders of higher education images. They are the system's vested interests, and constitute an obstacle to further differentiation. Competition in higher education is for status and legitimacy, encouraging conformity to prevailing models rather than attempts by organizations to distinguish themselves from their competitors.*

Rhoades argues that the competition for status and legitimacy cuts across nations and higher education systems and that colleges of advanced technology in England, university institutes of technology in France, and normal schools in the United States are equally as susceptible to academic drift as a result.

Other researchers have pointed to the increased professionalisation and specialisation of the academic professoriate as independent variables that produce academic drift related outcomes (Riesman 1956; Metzger 1987; Birnbaum 1988; Clark 1993). According to these theories, the increased professionalisation and specialisation and the disciplinary focus of today's faculty members have created a population of 'cosmopolitan faculty' (Riesman 1956; Birnbaum 1988) or 'academic tribes' where cultural assumptions and language create divisions between faculty groups (Becher 1989; Clark 1993, 1996) and allegiance toward disciplinary norms. As a result, faculty members identify themselves as members of a discipline, adopting its definitions of what is prestigious, instead of those of their institution and department. Success for these cosmopolitan faculty members is achieved, then, primarily through behaviours and accomplishments that are recognised nationally and internationally by their peers within the discipline (Riesman 1956; Birnbaum 1988). It is because of this tendency that it is necessary to 'go to the very core of the academic organization' to study differentiation and academic drift in higher education (Clark 1995: 159).

However, a significant inadequacy in the literature on academic drift can still be observed: while researchers have theorised that faculty are involved in the process whereby academic drift occurs, they have produced little empirical evidence to justify these claims (exceptions are, for instance, the studies carried out by Karseth (1995) and Slaughter (1997)). In this chapter, we want to focus on faculty motivations to introduce new programmes and try to relate these motivations to changes occurring at the institutional level. First, we will illustrate, based on various studies, the relationship between academic drift and faculty motivations to introduce new degree programmes. From this literature overview, it can be concluded that the research and theories on faculty motivations are related to neo-institutional theory arguments. We will therefore briefly elaborate our theoretical framework, which is based on institutional theory. After a short outline of the methods and means of analysis, we will present our empirical results, ending with a discussion of the major findings and conclusions. Before delving into the literature, however, we will first specify our problem statement.

2. PROBLEM STATEMENT

As our introduction stated, research on academic drift in Europe, Australia and the United States has contended that faculty members, because of their disciplinary ties, the specialised nature of their work, and their quest for status, play an important role in the process whereby new degree programmes are added to the total supply of programmes. The argument most often put forward is that new degree programmes are not added to serve students or some predetermined need, but to serve personal, faculty interests. Yet, this same research has made little use of data at the level of the faculty member. Our chapter uses data from faculty in Europe and the United States in order to gain more insight into the relationship between the faculty and institutional levels. Our problem statement can be summarised as follows:

1. What reasons do faculty members cite as the primary reasons to introduce new degree programmes?

2. How do these factors correlate with the arguments offered by researchers of academic drift and the propositions provided by neo-institutional theory?

We will now discuss several studies on academic drift and the role of faculty members in these processes.

3.   **ACADEMIC DRIFT AND FACULTY MOTIVATIONS: AN OVERVIEW OF THE LITERATURE**

Numerous studies have documented the presence of academic drift in systems of higher education. For example, research by Birnbaum (1983) and Huisman and Morphew (1998) in the United States showed how dominant institutional forms have become even more predominant through the years. These studies illustrated how, even during periods of significant growth in resources and students (which would provide institutions more leeway in going their own way), higher education institutions were inclined to change towards those institutional forms that were perceived as being at the top end of the institutional status hierarchy. Analogously, Harman's (1977) research on Australian colleges of advanced education points out how these institutions have become more like those in the university sector as the colleges' mission has expanded to include the traditional goals of the universities. But the phenomenon of academic drift cannot only be observed between various higher education sectors but also within one sector comprising comparable institutions. Within the university sector, for instance, some universities may be higher on the status hierarchy than others, for example, because of excellence in important research areas. An illustration of this is Meek's (1991) research on the Australian system's move from a binary to a unitary framework which describes a process of drift where 'the [former] college sector began to imitate the university sector in nearly every respect: type and level of course; research aspirations; management structures; student recruitment criteria' (1991: 474).

Other research has indicated that drift occurs unrelated to demand or 'an inverse relationship exists between enrollment and vertical extension' (Schultz & Stickler 1965: 235). That is, it is not always clear that higher education institutions begin to offer advanced degree programmes because of a perceived demand for these programmes. And, because academic drift often increases an institution's focus on graduate education, it results in the neglect of undergraduate degree programmes. McConnell (1962) and Shils (1962–63) concur and argue that undergraduates are shortchanged when higher education institutions add advanced degree programmes: these expensive programmes require more faculty contact and reduce faculty-student interaction at the undergraduate level. Invariably, institutions that emphasise the new graduate programmes devalue undergraduate programmes. Shils' (1962–63) analysis of academic drift in the American higher education system, for instance, caused him to question universities' commitment to undergraduates and professional education.

Do higher education institutions add new degree programmes regardless of the demand for such programmes? Studies by Berelson (1960) and Morphew (1996) indicate that this is frequently the case. Their research showed that new degree programmes often graduate very few (even zero) students during the first ten years of their existence, suggesting that the new programme was not linked to any real demand. Similarly, Birnbaum's (1983) study of institutional diversity in eight different state systems of higher education also called into question whether new degree programmes were sparked by demand.

It has been argued that the outcomes of academic drift have a negative impact on the diversity of state and national systems of higher education and are likely to reduce these systems' ability to serve the diverse needs of students. Birnbaum (1983), among others (e.g. Clark 1976), has argued that the diversity of higher education state systems is an indicator of their quality and ability to meet changes in student population. According to this argument, the diversity of a larger system insulates the elite institutions while allowing for the colleges and less elite universities to meet the needs of society and its citizens. As labour market needs and students' needs change, diverse institutions and systems can meet the changing needs of their population, and provide comprehensive education. Academic drift, because it reduces the diversity of institutional types within a higher education system, impacts negatively upon the programmatic diversity of a system, especially with regard to level (undergraduate versus graduate), orientation (vocational versus academic) and subject matter (interdisciplinary, 'new' programmes versus established, disciplinary-based programmes). A contrary perspective, however, is that academic drift prevents the proliferation of untried programmes and dispersal of resources around small programmes.

There is disagreement regarding the proper role of governmental agencies among the more recent studies of academic drift. Several researchers have concluded that government restrictions are necessary to induce and protect differentiation (Meek 1991; Skolnik 1986; Huisman & Morphew 1998). For example, Rhoades' (1990) discussion of political competition and differentiation in higher education maintains that increased government control over mission and scope differentiation in the United States and Sweden has played a positive role in the maintained differentiation of these systems. Alternately, Rhoades claims that the relative autonomy of academics in the English and French higher education systems has resulted in dedifferentiation and academic drift. He argues that experienced faculty play an important role in the differentiation/dedifferentiation process: they serve as gatekeepers and 'constitute an obstacle to further differentiation' because their interests are tied to the maintenance of the status quo where they hold the reins of authority (1990: 191). Disciplinary 'cosmopolitans' working within central validation agencies may also constitute powerful forms of academic drift, as they act inside agencies but from outside and above individual institutions.

Contrasting evidence on the role of government intervention has also been presented. For example, Birnbaum (1983), after a comprehensive study of differentiation in eight United States higher education systems, presents findings indicating that increased governmental control over state systems has not produced greater diversity. Jenniskens (1997), on the other hand, from a comparative study of systems in the United States and Europe, indicates that there is no simple relationship between the activity/role of government and the relative rate of curricular innovation or drift. Rather, other variables related to market demand and institutions' life cycles may be involved. Some of these intervening variables are likely to be related to faculty attitudes and perceptions of disciplinary needs and interests, of students' and labour market needs, and of governmental interests.

As has been pointed out above, Riesman's (1956) and Birnbaum's (1988) descriptions of 'cosmopolitan faculty' and Becher's (1989) and Clark's (1993, 1996) discussions of academic tribes indicate the strength of extra-institutional disciplinary ties between faculty members. Moreover, research on faculty behaviour in specific institutional types and national systems indicates the potential for problems as institutional missions conflict with disciplinary forces.

On the one hand, faculty members are expected to be good teachers and value their interactions with undergraduates, but on the other hand, as institutional expectations change, the need to publish and present at national meetings is taken more seriously (see e.g. studies by Henderson & Kane 1991; Weathersby 1983; Meek 1991). These studies indicate that the tensions occurring as a result of conflicting expectations may often result in moves away from the traditional institutional mission in search of more gratifying prospects, especially when the governance structure is relatively weak at the top level (see also Neave 1979; Whitburn *et al.* 1976).

Professional associations, as well, contribute to the pressure for faculty members to publish and establish advanced degree programmes (Henderson & Kane 1991: 341; Weathersby 1983). Professional needs appear to drive institutional evaluation criteria that focus on research rather than teaching. This in turn leads to a convergence upon a single organisational form, one more closely aligned with the research university (Jencks & Riesman 1968).

Clark (1983, 1993) noted the increased professionalisation of faculty and argued that the expansion of professional associations and discipline-based bodies has had an important effect on faculty status and power in the academy. The increased specialisation of knowledge has brought increased authority to those who are specialists in those knowledge areas. Specialised knowledge is the key to authority in specialised subunits (e.g. the academic department) of the university. Clark argues that there is a positive correlation between the authority of faculty and the specialised nature of knowledge in the academy: as more journals are published, and advanced degree programmes are established, institutional authority is more likely to be vested in the faculty. That is, because of specialisation, the authority to create and maintain the academy's structure is more likely to be vested in the faculty than has been the case historically.

Fairweather (1996), in his study of what motivates faculty members, also produced findings that support the theory that faculty are rewarded for and motivated by the increased specialisation in their field. Meek's (1991) research on the Australian higher education system suggests the same. He argues that research and increased specialisation are a threat to the maintenance of diversity across institutions: 'research is clearly the most important, both in terms of the policy itself and in terms of the perceived threat to established institutional practices' (1991: 475). In agreement, Fairweather and Rhoads (1996: 88) argue that 'few faculty ... are encouraged to devote their time to teaching lower-level undergraduates in general education courses'. Instead, Fairweather's (1996) research on faculty motivation and rewards indicates that faculty in the United States — even those at non-research universities — are primarily rewarded (in terms of salary) for teaching graduate students. The situation in Europe, however, is less extreme. In most European countries, faculty rewards and salaries cannot be used as powerful material instruments for rewarding graduate teaching. Besides, not all higher education systems in Western Europe have a clear dividing line between graduate and undergraduate education (for instance France, Germany and Austria).

There is general agreement within the literature that faculty are socialised to value research over teaching (Fairweather 1996; Blackburn & Lawrence 1995; Diamond 1993). For example, Blackburn and Lawrence (1995) argue that the effects of socialisation on faculty members are recurring: graduate students are socialised during their doctoral programmes and then reintroduced to the importance of research at various points in their academic careers. Likewise, Fairweather (1996) and Diamond (1993) agree that, in order to change the socialisation process whereby faculty members come to value research over teaching, constant intervention must take place at several stages in the socialisation process. Fairweather's (1996) research suggests that institutions would be wise to hire new faculty with care: 'recruitment and selection are crucial to developing and encouraging a culture which values teaching' (1996: 86).

Summarising, we can conclude that processes of academic drift are occurring to various levels in higher education systems. The literature suggests that such drift may occur regardless of an obvious need for another institutional profile. It has been argued that the outcomes of academic drift have a negative impact on the diversity of higher education systems, but counter arguments suggest that academic drift prevents dispersal of scarce resources around small, expensive programmes. Finally, processes of academic drift are related to disciplinary ties of faculty, and the increased professionalisation and specialisation within higher education.

4.   THEORETICAL FRAMEWORK

Much research on faculty motivation is similar to neo-institutional theory arguments. Just as higher education researchers have argued that professionalisation motivates faculty to incorporate curricula and degree programmes that contribute positively to the interests and needs of the disciplinary 'community', institutional theorists have argued that 'organizations are driven to incorporate the practices and procedures defined by prevailing rationalized concepts of organizational work and institutionalized in society' (Meyer & Rowan 1977: 340). This kind of organisational, so-called isomorphic behaviour (a concept that will be explained in the section below), of course, is driven by the individuals within the organisation. For higher education institutions, faculty members play a primary role in shaping organisational behaviour and therefore must be considered when one examines what motivates higher education institutions' behaviour. Neo-institutional theory can be a useful theoretical framework for the study of faculty motivations and academic drift processes in higher education.

We will use the theoretical framework provided by neo-institutional theory, with a focus on the isomorphic roles of professionalisation and specialisation. We will examine whether forces related to professionalisation and specialisation are isomorphic forces that function to motivate faculty members to propose degree programmes that contribute to academic drift.

DiMaggio and Powell's (1991) deconstruction of neo-institutional theory into three, sometimes overlapping, mechanisms illustrates how the concepts of professionalisation and specialisation can be linked to the tenets of neo-institutional theory: isomorphism can be caused by either coercive, mimetic or normative forces. The proposition that organisations model themselves after other organisations they perceive as being more successful would constitute mimetic isomorphism. Similarly, coercive isomorphism 'results from both formal and informal pressures exerted on organizations by other organizations ... and by cultural expectations in the society within which the organizations function' (1991: 67). Finally, normative isomorphic results from increased professionalisation in an occupational field and creates an environment where isomorphism is rewarded.

Each of these isomorphic mechanisms can be linked to the forces of professionalisation and specialisation. As a result, we can see how neo-institutional forces resulting from increased professionalisation or specialisation in the faculty play a role in the processes of academic drift. As indicated earlier, numerous studies (Halsey 1981; Neave 1979; Whitburn *et al*. 1976; Henderson & Kane 1991; Weathersby 1983; Meek 1991; Harman 1977) provide examples where academic drift is linked to the actions of faculty. These studies illustrate the tension between the expectations of faculty members and the mission of their institutions. This tension exists as a product of the pressures exerted upon faculty by their membership of a discipline-based, specialised academic society. Coercive forces play a role: faculty membership in an academic society has created a cultural expectation of disciplinary specialisation. Normative forces can be seen: the increased professionalisation and focus on the academic discipline leads to faculty being more inclined to teach in departments offering advanced degrees in specialised areas. Mimetic forces are also evident: the increased interaction between faculty as a result of increased professionalisation reinforces the weight of prestige associated with the more successful departments.

We will pay attention to all three isomorphic forces in the analysis of our empirical data. Before presenting these findings, we will briefly describe how we collected our data.

5. RESEARCH METHODS

Our analysis is based on data derived from interviews with faculty members of higher education institutions in Europe and the United States. We have tried to discover common findings among the systems studied; findings that explain why faculty introduced new degree programmes. We are investigating how faculty behaviour and motivation are tied to academic drift. Interviewing faculty is a valid means of examining what goes on at the basic unit level of the institution, the level at which research and teaching activities take place.

The data examined resulted from interviews with 58 faculty members in three European higher education systems (England, France and the Netherlands) and one United States system (Pennsylvania), a research project undertaken by Jenniskens, and from interviews with 39 faculty members in five United States state higher education systems (Michigan, Nebraska, Iowa, Oklahoma and Kansas). The latter interviews have been conducted by Morphew. Interviewees were (academic) key actors in the process who had first-hand knowledge of how a new degree programme or specialisation had been added to the total list of institutional offerings. Most of the interviewees were senior lecturers or (associate/full) professors. The interviews were conducted during 1995–97. In each interview, faculty members were asked, amongst various other questions, to identify the reasons why new degree programmes or specialisations were introduced within their institution. All of the faculty members interviewed worked within comprehensive universities where a broad range of degree programmes existed (though not necessarily doctoral degree programmes). In total, 78 cases of new degree programmes were studied, all of which were implemented during the period 1971–93.

Responses to the (semi-structured) questionnaire used by Jenniskens were categorised according to key terms associated with the effects of professionalisation, specialisation and other forces operating as impetuses for the new degree programme. Direct quotes from interviews conducted by Morphew with faculty in the United States system are used to provide a 'thicker' description of the relationship between a new degree programme and the factors identified by the faculty members. The faculty interviewed for this study represent a variety of institutional types and systems, disciplines and programme areas. Disciplinary differences will not be provided by this study.

6.   FINDINGS

The data produced by our study illustrate that faculty are as likely to cite reasons related to professionalisation and specialisation as they are to cite reasons unrelated to these factors when asked about why a new degree programme was created. Moreover, the responses from faculty were complex: often, faculty cited several reasons, only some of which would be predicted by research on academic drift. Contrary to the picture painted by much of the research on academic drift, the data illustrate that faculty believe that new degree programmes are often added in response to (a) students' needs; and (b) external demands.[1]

6.1   Professionalisation, specialisation and curricular innovation

Faculty in each of the four systems studied (France, the Netherlands, Pennsylvania and England) cited factors that can be tied to the increased

---

[1] One might wonder if the reasons provided by our respondents reveal the 'real' motivations or are, to a greater or smaller extent, strategic and/or socially desirable answers. In the interviews we could not test for this. Analysis of documents (e.g. proposals for department boards or faculty committees) is of no help either because the initiator(s) may enumerate other reasons than the ones by which they were really motivated. The semi-structured questionnaire (used by Jenniskens in her study) included a long list of possible reasons, to which all respondents had to react. This procedure might reduce the chance that the respondents only mentioned the socially desirable or political ones. Besides, the interviews were to be confidential and referred to processes that were finished already, since the new degree programme had been successfully introduced. These circumstances might also increase the likelihood of having detected the 'real' motivations of the faculty members interviewed.

specialisation and professionalisation among contemporary academics. As described above, it has been theorised that these factors may motivate faculty to add new degree programmes or specialisations. Table 1 below describes the factors linked to professionalisation and specialisation that faculty cited when asked about the reasons for introducing a new programme or specialisation.

Table 1: Factors linked to professionalisation and specialisation and cited as reasons to introduce new programme or specialisation (in %)

Reasons	FR (N=9)	NL (N=16)	PA (N=13)	Engl (N=20)	Total (N=58)
New knowledge	22	44	39	15	29
Shifting faculty interests	67	50	46	30	45
New (ideas on) teaching methods	0	13	31	25	19
Raise the image, prestige or profile of discipline or department	11	25	39	5	19
New research methods	0	13	0	5	5
New approaches within discipline	33	13	23	20	21

Note: FR: France; NL: The Netherlands; PA: Pennsylvania (USA); Engl: England.

As table 1 illustrates, factors related to 'shifting faculty interests' (45%) and 'new knowledge' (29%) were cited most often across the four systems studied by Jenniskens. With the exception of the English system, faculty cited 'shifting faculty interests' approximately 50% of the time when asked why a new degree programme or specialisation was begun.

Faculty members were also asked to indicate which of the reasons that had played a role in the process had been the most important. Of the reasons displayed in table 1, only three attracted significant attention: new knowledge (that necessitated faculty to adjust the programme or add a new programme to the total number of programmes offered), the need to raise the image or prestige of the discipline and/or of the department (internally and/or externally), and shifting faculty interests.

Table 2: Factors linked to professionalisation and specialisation and cited as the most important reason to introduce new programme or specialisation (in %)

Reasons	FR (N=9)	NL (N=16)	PA (N=13)	Engl (N=20)	Total (N=58)
New knowledge	0	25	0	10	10
Shifting faculty interests	11	19	15	25	19
New (ideas on) teaching methods	0	0	0	0	0
Raise the image, prestige or profile of discipline or department	11	19	31	5	16
New research methods	0	6	0	0	2
New approaches within discipline	11	6	15	10	10

Note: FR: France; NL: The Netherlands; PA: Pennsylvania (USA); Engl: England.

Interviews with faculty in the United States helped to clarify the findings displayed in tables 1 and 2. Often those interviewed pointed out that new degree programmes were begun to match faculty interests and expertise.

At the time it came about, the composition at the faculty at [the university] was all experimental except for one clinician (me), and the chair asked me to design a programme that would suit the expertise of the department and it was decided that we would propose a programme in general psychology which would be geared toward preparing students in the basic areas of psychology (faculty member describing a new masters degree programme).

In other cases, the addition of a new degree programme made sense in terms of faculty training and seemed a natural consequence of bringing in faculty members from other research universities where a given specialisation already existed.

Many of the faculty in the programme have PhDs in linguistics. If a faculty does not have a PhD in linguistics, they have come from a university where linguistics is offered or they have a [masters] in linguistics in support of their PhD (faculty member describing undergraduate degree programme in linguistics).

Alternatively, faculty members also reported that they established new
degree programmes to bring in graduate students with interests similar to
their own. Respondents indicated that having students with research skills
and interests that matched their own made their work with students more
enjoyable and rewarding.

> *It was kind of the need for faculty to have more intellectual interaction
> with students that were at a higher level than undergraduates. The
> feeling that serving on thesis committees that they did have in their
> experience as faculty was missed by some and so this gave them an
> opportunity to teach at the graduate level, to chair a thesis, to co-present
> papers at regional and national conferences with students, to have some
> assistance in their labs where undergraduates have formerly been used*
> (faculty member describing a new masters degree programme).

Faculty members interviewed also discussed the prestige and marketability a
new graduate degree programme would bring to their department, school and
even their university. Respondents indicated that attracting good faculty was
much easier if a department offered an advanced degree programme. Such
degree programmes were often used, then, as a recruiting tool for new
students *and* new faculty members.

> *But I think it was also a concern about attracting high-quality faculty to
> a university that didn't have some type of graduate programme in
> psychology. Psychologists, for example, probably look first to doctoral
> institutions. I think there is a lot of truth in that ... whether you do or
> don't have a graduate programme and your ability to recruit competitive
> persons. That was one motive ... the feeling that their research activities
> would be stimulated and challenged* (faculty member describing a new
> masters degree programme).

Respondents indicated that department and school level administrators
pushed the implementation of a graduate level degree programme as a means
of building the profile or stature of the school and department. This occurred
significantly more often in the less comprehensive public universities that
had evolved from normal schools or regional colleges or universities. For
example, several respondents at one university indicated that the majority of
the graduate programmes had been started with the goal of helping the
former college attain university status.

The programmes in the sciences were begun for the purpose of helping the college become [a university]: there are rules and regulations about how many graduate degrees you must offer before you can become a university and the masters in sciences was needed for that part. At the same time, the entire university was reorganised [by schools] so that it could become a university (faculty member describing a masters degree programme).

Faculty members argued that administrators played an important role in the process where advanced degree programmes were added. This often occurred when a new university or school level administrator advocated the addition of new degree programmes and a greater focus on graduate education and research.

Both [the dean and the provost] were very supportive of our graduate programme. ... Now, we are doctoral granting 1 institution and we would like to be a research 2 university. These are Carnegie Classifications. We are also working on a new PhD programme and some other masters programme. So, all this is a result of his activities. [The university] was traditionally an undergraduate institution until about the mid-80s but then we started adding graduate programmes. We also had good support from the state in terms of funding, getting the funds we needed for this programme; but at the state-level, you have to compete with all the universities. At the top, there are five major universities ... we are competing with them. We are competing with some major schools (faculty member describing a masters degree programme).

6.2   Student considerations and curricular innovation

Professionalisation and specialisation were not the only reasons mentioned by the faculty interviewed. The interviews revealed that also the demand for a new degree programme or specialisation was a powerful motivator cited by faculty members within all four systems studied. Faculty members described the interests and changing needs of students as an important and valid reason to start a new degree programme. Often the new degree programme or specialisation was a formal reflection of the informal changes students had made in the curriculum; an example of this follows.

... a number of students had designed an 'individual major' in linguistics where they took the courses offered by a cohort of [linguistics] faculty ... and, with the assistance of an advisor 'designed' their own linguistics major (faculty member describing an undergraduate programme in linguistics).

Table 3 illustrates the important role student preferences and needs played in the decision to implement a new degree programme or specialisation across the four systems of higher education studied.

Table 3: Factors linked to students and cited as reasons to introduce new programme or specialisation (in %)

Reasons	FR (N=9)	NL (N=16)	PA (N=13)	Engl (N=20)	Total (N=58)
Changing students' preferences	56	19	62	55	47
Changing student population: older and part-time students	33	0	23	5	12
Improving student performance	44	19	15	10	19
Necessity to attract more students	33	13	62	90	53
Declining student numbers	0	13	46	50	31
Changes in curriculum of secondary education	33	6	8	30	19
Make programme more attractive for students	67	13	31	35	33

Note: FR: France; NL: The Netherlands; PA: Pennsylvania (USA); Engl: England.

Faculty in the four systems cited 'changing students' preferences' and 'attracting more students' to the programme in question approximately half the time when asked about the reasons a new programme or specialisation was introduced. Factors linked to 'declining student numbers' and making the 'programme more attractive for students' reflect faculty members' acknowledgment of the importance of attracting students and providing skills that will serve students well outside the university.

Reasons related to student issues were also among the ones that were seen as the most important motivations. There are differences among the four systems studied (see table 4); the French and English faculty members were more often motivated by student related reasons than their Dutch and American (i.e. Pennsylvanian) colleagues.

Table 4: Factors linked to students and cited as the most important reason to introduce new programme or specialisation (in %)

Most important reasons	FR (N=9)	NL (N=16)	PA (N=13)	Engl (N=20)	Total (N=58)
Changing students' preferences	33	0	15	10	12
Changing student population: older and part-time students	0	0	0	0	0
Improving student performance	0	0	0	0	0
Necessity to attract more students	22	6	0	50	22
Declining student numbers	0	13	8	20	12
Changes in curriculum of secondary education	0	0	0	10	3
Make programme more attractive for students	67	6	8	20	21

Note: FR: France; NL: The Netherlands; PA: Pennsylvania (USA); Engl: England.

In interviews with faculty members from the United States, it was clear that they wanted to establish programmes that would improve the marketability of their students. Faculty talked about making their students more 'competitive' with students from other universities and similar degrees.

> *Earlier we already had a BA programme in geology ... so the thought was that a BS programme would make our graduates more competitive, they would probably get more offers for graduate assistantships. So we did some surveys to see what was the difference between BA degrees and BS degrees nationally and found that usually a BS degree required more coursework in science and more mathematics supporting it* (faculty member describing an undergraduate programme in geology).

The interviews revealed that faculty were also attuned to the job market and the success of their former students. As a result, they knew what kinds of skills and coursework would pay off for future graduates. In some cases, they made curricular changes that benefited students' competitiveness even before being asked to do so by students.

> *You gotta realise that I don't believe that the students perceived any difference between aircraft engineering and aeronautical engineering at the time. So, I don't think changing the name was specifically important as they came in ... when they start thinking about a job, that's when they realise. If you truly want to design a plane, you need an aeronautical degree and you will probably get the job based on your aeronautical degree* (faculty member describing an undergraduate degree programme in aeronautical engineering).

The changing demands of students, especially non-traditional students who were working full-time, were cited as a reason to start a new degree programme or change the curricula in an existing degree programme, even in a traditional discipline. A faculty member in a physics department indicated that his department's new masters degree programme in physics was 'geared to people who work in [the state] and want to get a masters in physics while working full-time. [The programme is] for persons who want to improve themselves professionally for the purpose of improving job standing'.

Simultaneously, faculty members were becoming more aware that students had options and, as a result, they needed to improve the marketability of their programmes to attract students who might otherwise attend other universities with more marketable degree programmes. Faculty members in professional fields often cited the prospect of losing students to other universities when asked about attracting students to their programmes:

> *... I am a student, I am interested in the corporate accounting area. No problem. Come into our accounting programme. I am a student interested in commercial banking. Go to [a nearby public university], there is nothing here. I am a student interested in investment banking, brokerage business, the insurance industry, it was pretty much if I wanted to pursue those interests, I had to go somewhere else. So, we were losing some potentially talented students by not having those types of career options available to them* (faculty member describing an undergraduate degree programme in finance).

In the end, students' needs, interests and changing demographics played an important role in what degree programmes and specialisations were added and how curricula for those programmes were constructed. These motivations are not directly related to the phenomenon of academic drift. There are indications that these motivations are related in an indirect way, as faculty copy successful programmes from other institutions. Our interview data, however, are not detailed enough to justify strong conclusions in this respect.

6.3   External factors and curricular innovation

Respondents frequently cited external forces (i.e. demand, competition or governmental steering) as reasons why new degree programmes or specialisations were introduced. Except for the Netherlands, one or more reasons that are linked to external actors (like other institutions, businesses, government, accrediting agencies, professional organisations) were cited in half or more of the cases as an important reason. As indicated in table 5 below, factors related to 'increased competition' (48%) and 'demand from the business world' (24%) were most often cited within this category of responses.

Table 5: Factors linked to competition, demand or government steering and cited as reasons to introduce new programme or specialisation (in %)

Most important reasons	FR (N=9)	NL (N=16)	PA (N=13)	Engl (N=20)	Total (N=58)
Increased competition	67	19	39	70	48
Obliged by government regulation	33	0	0	0	5
Demand from business world	22	31	46	5	24
Stimulated by external actor	22	13	31	5	16

Note: FR: France; NL: The Netherlands; PA: Pennsylvania (USA); Engl: England.

Table 5 indicates that faculty members are aware of and responsive to the demands of external constituents, including businesses and competition from other post-secondary institutions. On the other hand, the data indicate that curricular innovations did not occur as a direct result of government regulation: the obligation of government intervention was only mentioned in France (a system known for its intensive and centralised regulation by the state).

When asked about the impetus for the implementation of new degree programmes, faculty often referred to the needs of the surrounding communities and businesses. Sometimes, the demand for degree programmes fitted with the interests of the faculty and together the two factors pushed forward the curricular innovation.

> *It was kind of the convergence of two things. One was a faculty member who wanted to develop a programme in public relations and the trends that we were seeing in communications and journalism of students wanting that speciality. So, the faculty member got interested and there was student demand and those two things came together* (faculty member describing an undergraduate programme in public relations).

Faculty and administrators cited local or regional studies that showed the need for the new programme. The following citation illustrates this.

> *The programme was proposed because of a health manpower study. In the '70s, there was a real concern about managing health care and part of it was determining health needs. So, they surveyed all the hospitals and various places and determined not only the need for medical technologists, but MDs, DOs, podiatrists, lots of things. Anyway, they came up with all this information by county that established that there was quite a shortage, if not a shortage, a maldistribution of health care professionals in the state. And so, for every group, some of the counties in Kansas did not even have one certified medical technologist, some of them had one. This study was very important in establishing the need for medical technologists* (faculty member describing an undergraduate programme in medical technology).

Faculty that cited similar 'demand' studies argued that such studies were important because they provided more objective information for the administration as well as state coordinating or regulatory agencies involved in the programme approval process. Moreover, such studies provided insight with regard to what kinds of skills would be needed by programme graduates. In some cases, companies approached faculty with a description of the kinds of graduates and skills they were looking for; faculty responded to these demands with proposals for new degree programmes.

> *We had many companies around here. Close by, if you go forty miles ... there is the second largest city in [the state]. So there are some*

companies, some audience so to speak [there]. We have Whirlpool, we also have Zenith, a maker of computers and electronics. So there are some companies around here that very much needed some graduate level education for their employees, so that was why we started the MS programme ten years ago. The masters programme, in its peak enrolment, had 50 students. We started basically from zero in 1987, in 1991–92, we had an enrolment of 50 students, then we had some changes, we had some students who were asking — because of changes in electrical engineering — for a computer engineering programme (faculty describing masters degree programme in electrical engineering).

For programmes that began as emphases in other majors (e.g. a mathematics degree with an emphasis in computer science), faculty described a process of attaining critical mass before a new degree programme was offered.

It was a demand, we had lots of students and ... we were very comparable to the number of students in the math programme. And so we felt that we should have a programme. That demand was evident in terms of the numbers involved in computer science emphasis within the department at the time. And also we had a couple of instructors at that time that were pushing it and wanted it to be a major (faculty member describing undergraduate computer science degree programme).

In these cases where student demand increased to the point where a new degree programme seemed warranted, the external demand for graduates was often linked to the rise in student numbers. For new programmes such as computer science (i.e. programmes in newly created disciplines or professional fields), this was almost always the case: external demand for graduates caused more students to obtain an emphasis in this area, which in turn provoked the faculty to enlarge the emphasis into a fully fledged degree programme.

In the end, then, faculty described a process where demand often precipitated a programme's creation, rather than the opposite: demand increased, student numbers increased and a new degree programme was created to cope with this demand. This process occurred slowly at times but, where real demand existed, faculty were willing to provide a supply of graduates.

There were a lot of people in the area who were doing computer work and had to get masters degrees in computer science. We had a lot of external demand like that. I was hired in the math department and at that point, we ran programmes in mathematics and people could get a math degree with an emphasis in computer science and it wasn't an official degree programme, it was math. And, over the next five years, between 1973 and 1978, we phased in real programmes that gave them an official degree in computer science (faculty member describing masters degree programme in computer science).

7.   DISCUSSION AND CONCLUSIONS

The data provided above do not give a 'neat' explanation of the link between faculty motivators and the addition of new degree programmes. This is most likely because there are always primary and secondary factors involved in the process whereby an institution adds a new degree programme or specialisation. Academic disciplines and subject matters change, faculty interests evolve, students' needs change, and the external environment shifts as well. Nonetheless, several important points can be gleaned from the data presented in this study. Perhaps most importantly, the data suggest that faculty behaviour is not easily characterised by claims of professionalisation and specialisation, even within comprehensive higher education institutions where the addition of an advanced degree programme is an achievable reality. Instead, the data imply that faculty propose and support new degree programmes for a variety of reasons, including several that have their foundation in increased professionalisation and specialisation within the academy, but cite other reasons as well that are related to external demands and forces.

Earlier in this chapter, Rhoades' (1990) claims, regarding the role of the faculty in higher education, were presented in support of those who have argued that faculty members are motivated to behave in a manner that is inconsistent with institutional dedifferentiation. The data presented above seem inconsistent with Rhoades' claims that faculty members are 'an obstacle to further differentiation'. That may or may not be true: it is not clear that the attitudes of faculty members represented above will result in greater or lesser institutional and programmatic differentiation. It is also not clear as to whether the faculty interviewed were 'local' or 'cosmopolitan' in their perspective (Riesman 1956). Their responses indicated a willingness to acknowledge their localities and institutional needs and supporters, even as they still cited their interests and the need to keep up with changes in their disciplines or professional fields. Still, the data do support an image of the faculty member that is inconsistent with some of the literature on academic drift and institutional differentiation. That literature paints a picture of the faculty member as relatively obsessed with disciplinary-based innovations, whether curricular or theoretical. In contrast, the faculty members interviewed for this study seemed as likely to cite the interests of students and the needs of the businesses in their regions as they were to cite the changing thoughts of their discipline. It can be concluded that in our cases, all three types of isomorphic forces (normative, mimetic and coercive) were, to a smaller or greater extent, present. Besides the normative forces displayed in the increased professionalisation and focus on the academic discipline, mimetic (imitating) behaviour could be observed, as well as the effects of coercive forces exerted by external bodies such as accrediting agencies, governmental bodies and professional associations.

The data presented above might seem puzzling to policy-makers. That is, there is not a clear pattern presented as to what kinds of things motivate faculty members. Yet, the findings do show that faculty members are aware of what is going on outside the academy and in their communities and their classrooms. Faculty are at least cognisant of the demands being placed on their institutions by internal and external constituents. That said, policy-makers might consider taking advantage of this awareness with policies that entice faculty members to become more aware of trends in the professional needs of their communities and students. For example, policies that promote institutional attentiveness to local, regional or national needs might produce outcomes that are mutually satisfying. The data do indicate that degree programmes are more likely to be created in response to a need, rather than an obligation. Policy-makers would be wise to consider the policy 'carrot' when working on plans that include the goal of institutional differentiation.

Finally, while the data do not appear to support the conclusions that have been hypothesised in other research on this subject, they do indicate that new degree programmes are added as a result of shifting faculty interests and new knowledge or disciplinary approaches to discovering knowledge. The question remains as to whether this kind of curricular innovation is a positive sign of change in higher education institutions. Certainly the addition of some degree programmes that are the result of innovative thinking in professional fields or disciplines is to be expected and viewed positively: many of today's productive interdisciplinary fields are likely products of changing perspectives within traditional fields of study. Programmes merging the applied and physical sciences (e.g. biomedical engineering) and the humanities and the social sciences (e.g. women's studies) are positive products of innovation that have been implemented on many campuses as a result of 'shifting faculty interests' or 'new approaches within the discipline'.

In the end, the data presented within this chapter illuminate worthy questions about how institutions grow and academic drift might occur in higher education. For example, while it may be true that degree programmes are created in response to external demand as well as disciplinary-based innovations, are some kinds of institutions more susceptible to one force rather than the other? And, what kinds of policies — at the system level — can be most effective in providing the incentive for faculty to respond to internal and external constituents' needs, as quickly and effectively as possible? These questions will become more important over time as nations, states and higher education systems struggle with change, and how to recognise and adapt to that change.

References

Becher, T. (1989), *Academic Tribes and Territories: intellectual enquiry and the cultures of disciplines*, Milton Keynes: Society for Research into Higher Education & Open University Press.

Berdahl, R.O. (1985), Strategy and government: US state systems and institutional role and mission, *International Journal of Institutional Management in Higher Education,* vol. 9, no. 3, pp. 301–7.

Berelson, B. (1960). *Graduate Education in the United States.* New York: McGraw-Hill.

Birnbaum, R. (1983), *Maintaining Diversity in Higher Education,* San Francisco: Jossey-Bass.

Birnbaum, R. (1988), *How Colleges Work: the cybernetics of academic organization and leadership,* San Francisco: Jossey-Bass.

Blackburn, R.T. & J.H. Lawrence (1995), *Faculty at Work: motivation, expectation, satisfaction,* Baltimore: Johns Hopkins.

Clark, B.R. (1976), The benefits of disorder, *Change,* October, pp. 31–7.

Clark, B.R. (1983), *The Higher Education System: academic organization in cross-national perspective,* Berkeley: University of California Press.

Clark, B.R. (1993), The problem of complexity in modern higher education, in: S. Rothblatt & B. Wittrock (eds), *The European and American University Since 1800,* Cambridge: Cambridge University Press, pp. 263–79.

Clark, B.R. (1995), Complexity and differentiation: the deepening problem of university integration, in: D.D. Dill & B. Sporn (eds), *Emerging Patterns of Social Demand and University Reform: through a glass darkly,* Tarrytown, NY: Elsevier Science/IAU, pp. 159–69.

Clark, B.R. (1996), Substantive growth and innovative organization: new categories for higher education research, *Higher Education,* vol. 32, pp. 417–30.

Diamond, R.M. (1993), Changing priorities and the faculty reward system, in: R.M. Diamond & B.E. Adam (eds), *Recognizing Faculty Work: reward systems for the year 2000,* New Directions in Higher Education, 81, San Francisco: Jossey-Bass.

Fairweather, J.S. (1996), *Faculty Work and Public Trust: restoring the value of teaching and public service in American academic life*, Boston: Allyn & Bacon.

Fairweather, J.S. & R.A. Rhoads (1996), Other factors influencing faculty teaching, in: J.S. Fairweather (ed.), *Faculty Work and Public Trust: restoring the value of teaching and public service in American academic life,* Boston: Allyn & Bacon.

Halsey, A.H. (1981), *Higher education in Britain: a study of university and polytechnic teachers, report to the Social Science Research Council*, mimeo, New York.

Harman, G. (1977), Academic staff and academic drift in Australian colleges of advanced education, *Higher Education,* vol. 6, pp. 313–35.

Henderson, B.B. & W.D. Kane (1991), Caught in the middle: faculty and institutional status and quality in state comprehensive universities, *Higher Education,* vol. 22, pp. 339–50.

Huisman, J. (1995), *Differentiation, Diversity and Decentralization in Higher Education,* Utrecht: Lemma.

Huisman, J. & C.C. Morphew (1998), Centralization and diversity: evaluating the effects of government policies in US and Dutch higher education, *Higher Education Policy*, vol. 11, no. 1, pp. 3–13.

Jencks, C. & Riesman, D. (1968). The Academic Revolution. Garden City, NY: Doubleday.

Jenniskens, I. (1997), *Governmental Steering and Curriculum Innovations. A comparative study of the relation between governmental steering instruments and innovations in higher education curricula*, Utrecht: Lemma.

Karseth, B. (1995), The emergence of new educational programs in the university', *Review of Higher Education,* vol. 18, no. 2, pp. 195–216.

McConnell, T.R. (1962) *A General Pattern for American Public Higher Education.* New York: McGraw-Hill.

Meek, V.L. (1991), The transformation of Australian higher education from binary to unitary system, *Higher Education,* vol. 21, pp. 464–94.

Metzger, W.P. (1987), The academic profession in the United States, in: B.R. Clark, (ed.), *The Academic Profession: national, disciplinary, and institutional settings*, Berkeley and Los Angeles: University of California Press, pp. 123–208.

Meyer, J. & B. Rowan (1977), Institutionalized organizations: formal structure as myth and ceremony, *American Journal of Sociology*, vol. 89, pp. 340–63.

Morphew, C.C. (1996), *Statewide governing boards: a longitudinal study of seven public systems of higher education, dissertation*, Stanford University, San Francisco, CA.

Neave, G. (1979), Academic drift: some views from Europe, *Studies in Higher Education,* vol. 4, no. 2, pp. 143–59.

Powell, W.W. and DiMaggio, P.J. (eds.) (1991*). The New Institutionalism in Organizational Analysis.* Chicago: University of Chicago Press.

Rhoades, G. (1990), Political competition and differentiation in higher education, in: J.C. Alexander & P. Colomy (eds), *Differentiation Theory and Social Change*, New York: Columbia University Press, pp. 187–221.

Riesman, D. (1956), *Constraint and Variety in American Education*, Lincoln: University of Nebraska Press.

Schultz, R.E. and Stickler, W.H. (1965) Vertical Extension of Academic Programs in Institutions of Higher Education, in: *Educational Record* (Summer 1965), 231-241.

Shils, E. (1962–63), Observations on the American University, in: *Universities Quarterly*, 17, 182-193.

Skolnik, M.L. (1986), Diversity in higher education: the Canadian case, *Higher Education in Europe*, vol. 11, pp. 19–32.

Slaughter, S. (1997), Class, race and gender and the construction of post-secondary curricula in the United States: social movement, professionalization and political economic theories of curricular change, *Journal of Curriculum Studies* 29(1), pp. 1-30.

Weathersby, G.B. (1983), State colleges in transition, in: J. Froomkin (ed.), *The Crisis in Higher Education*, New York: Academy of Political Science.

Whitburn, J., M. Mealing and C. Cox (1976), *People in Polytechnics: a survey of polytechnic staff and students, 1972–73*, Guildford: Society for Research into Higher Education.

Chapter 6

New study programmes at universities
Strategic adaptation versus institutional adjustment

JEROEN HUISMAN AND LYNN MEEK

Key words: institutionalism; organisational change; strategic choice

1.   INTRODUCTION

This chapter focuses on the 'behaviour' of higher education institutions with respect to curricular innovations. We are interested in exploring to what extent this behaviour can be typified as strategic adaptation to changes in the environment or as 'reactive' institutional adjustment. In fact, these two types of behaviour can be seen as two opposing views of organisational behaviour.

Several studies have focused on the emergence of new study programmes, programmatic diversity and curricular innovations in higher education (see e.g. Huisman 1995, 1997; Jenniskens 1997; Karseth 1995; Huisman & Morphew 1998; Slaughter 1997; Jenniskens & Morphew in this volume). Many of these studies on curricular change in higher education have been focused at the system level, trying to assess the impact of governmental regulation on the establishment of new programmes or the relationship between governmental steering and innovation (Huisman & Jenniskens 1994; Jenniskens 1997). Hypotheses concerning the impact of specific steering instruments on programmatic innovation and the question whether government regulations inhibit the emergence of new programmes were tested empirically. The results were mixed: there was support for some of the expectations, whereas in a number of other studies the results were contrary to the theoretical suppositions.

Generally, the expectations were based on two different perspectives of organisational behaviour. One perspective stresses the adaptive capabilities of organisations: they monitor their environments and adjust their behaviour according to changes in these environments (e.g. strategic choice theory, resource dependency theory, contingency theory). The other perspective, largely based on institutional theory (Scott 1995; Powell & DiMaggio 1991), stresses the taken-for-grantedness of organisational action and posits that cultural elements (normative beliefs, cognitive systems, symbols) play a crucial role in organisational processes.

In this chapter, the challenge is to combine the perspectives and assess the explanatory power of this combination. In this, we build partly upon previous CHEPS studies as the object of research, the emergence of new study programmes, is an important type of organisational change in one of the core domains of higher education: teaching and learning. We 'deviate' in two important respects. A combination of the two theoretical perspectives is used (see also Gornitzka & Maassen 1998) instead of one particular theoretical view on organisations. In addition, we test the framework by comparing higher education organisations through time. Some previous CHEPS studies were also longitudinal, but they were mainly at the system level.

The structure of this chapter is as follows. First, we describe the two perspectives, including the common elements and differences. Then we summarise the findings of the empirical research using the different perspectives. Next, we explore whether the framework stands the test of a confrontation with data on study programmes that were introduced by two Dutch universities during the period 1968–93. We stress that the data presently available do not permit a full-blown rigid test. Our efforts should be regarded as preliminary. The final section discusses the results of the study and focuses especially on the consequences for higher education management at the institutional level and policy-making at the national level.

1.1   The two perspectives on organisations and organisational change

For the study of programme innovations, we first describe the two perspectives on organisational change — institutional theory and strategic choice theory — separately. Then, using Oliver's (1991) work, we highlight the main similarities and differences of the two perspectives.

Institutional theory encompasses a broad range of perspectives. Within this range the differences are sometimes greater than the similarities (Scott 1987, 1995). We follow the perspective that is rooted in organisational sociology (Meyer & Rowan 1977; Meyer & Scott 1983; DiMaggio & Powell 1983). Zucker (1987: 444) outlines the two defining elements of institutionalisation in organisations as a rule-based organised pattern of action, and an embedding in formal structures. In general, this perspective assumes that the institutional environment constrains the organisation and determines its internal structure and, consequently, the behaviour of the actors in the organisation (see also Bartelse & Goedegebuure in this volume). In contrast to other theories that focus on the technical demands of the environment (e.g. an efficient flow of resources, information exchange and efficient production), organisations are 'rewarded' for developing internal structures that take into account external pressures. These external pressures are, for instance, governmental legislation, rules and procedures, formal pressures from other organisations, normative standards, etc. A central notion is that because of the pressures of the institutional environment, organisations show a trend towards conformity (coined by the term isomorphism). The image of an organisation is that the institutional environment inhibits the organisation to change; deviation from the expectations of the institutional environment threatens the legitimacy (and therefore the chances of survival) of the organisation. Organisations, from the institutional perspective, conform to collective norms and beliefs, and adhere to rules. Behaviour is often taken-for-granted or ritual, without rational reflection (Meyer & Rowan 1977). March (1981: 221–6) speaks in this respect of obligatory action: once certain actors do things in a particular way, others will take that way for granted.

The resource dependency perspective (as well as the strategic choice perspective), in contrast, focuses on the adaptive behaviour of organisations. It is not so much that the institutional environment is stressed, but more that attention is paid to the task or technical environment. Exchange relations with organisations in the environment and resource flows and power positions in networks of interrelated organisations are of central concern. Explicitly, the strategies of actors at central positions in the organisation — coping with and reducing uncertainty, managing resource flows, handling interdependencies — are stressed (Pfeffer & Salancik 1978; Aldrich 1979; Benson 1975; Child & Kieser 1981; Pfeffer 1981).

Above, the differences between the perspectives have been stressed. However, they also have important similarities. Following Oliver (1991: 147), strategic choice/resource dependency theory and institutional theory have in common that (a) organisational choice is constrained by multiple external pressures; (b) organisational environments are collective and interconnected; (c) organisational survival depends on responsiveness to external demands and expectations; (d) organisations seek stability, predictability, legitimacy; and (e) organisations are interest driven. Despite the similarities, the foci are different. Table 1 (adapted from Oliver 1991) provides an overview of the distinctive features.

Table 1: Differences between institutional and resource dependency perspectives

	Institutional perspective	Resource dependency perspective
Context of organisational behaviour	Constraints by institutional environment	Constraints by task environment
	Non-choice behaviour	Active choice behaviour
	Conforming to collective norms and beliefs	Coping with interdependencies
	Invisible pressures	Visible pressures
	Isomorphism	Adaptation
	Adherence to norms and rules	Management of scarce resources
	Organisational persistence	Reduction of uncertainty
	Habit and convention	Power and influence
Motives of organisational behaviour	Social worthiness	Resource mobilisation
	Conformity to external criteria	Control of external criteria
	Interests are institutionally defined	Interests are political and calculative
	Compliance self-serving	Non-compliance self-serving

The criticisms of one camp by the other are predictable. Institutionalists maintain that adherents of the strategic choice perspective overemphasise the leeway of organisational action and neglect the impact of rules, norms and values that places a limit on the scope of organisational behaviour. On the other hand, resource dependency supporters criticise institutionalists for their description of organisations as overtly passive and their lack of attention to processes of power and agency.

In the last decade, a debate on organisational sociology that concerns the relationship between the two perspectives has been raging (see e.g. Oliver 1988, 1991; Ginsberg & Buchholtz 1990; Zajac & Kraatz 1993; Greening & Gray 1994; Kraatz & Zajac 1996; Huisman & Beerkens forthcoming). Some authors argue that the perspectives are incommensurable, while others maintain that the perspectives are complementary. The former prefers to confront the perspectives or test them separately, while the latter tries to integrate the views and hopes to reach a more comprehensive understanding of organisational behaviour. Both perspectives seem to have some explanatory power of innovation processes in higher education but, so far, researchers have not taken up the challenge of integrating the perspectives. The integrative attempts of Kraatz and Zajac (1996) and Oliver (1991) offer us some interesting tools to take up that challenge.

1.2   The two perspectives in studies in higher education

Zajac and Kraatz (1993) investigated the impact of change in the organisational environment resulting from the restructuring of higher education institutions — more than 600 American private liberal art colleges — over a fifteen-year period. By taking a highly institutionalised or structurated (i.e. where given structures and functions are taken for granted) field like higher education (see e.g. Meyer & Rowan 1977), the authors assumed that restructuring — adding business programmes to the portfolio, including graduate programmes, and changing from single-sex to coeducational education — would be exceptional instead of regular. The assumption was not only based on institutional theory, but also referred to ecological theory (Hannan & Freeman 1977, 1989). The data proved that such restructuring indeed took place significantly, suggesting some support for strategic choice and resource dependency theory. Furthermore, the changing environmental conditions and organisational characteristics (low endowments, high debts, geographic location, age, size and reputation for premium quality) had an impact on the organisations in the predicted way. Also, the effects of the restructuring on the performance of the institutions were taken into account. The changes had a positive impact on organisational performance, implying that change increased the likelihood of survival. In sum, contrary to the ecological and institutional expectation, technical and market-based forces — resource dependency elements — predicted the forms of restructuring.

Kraatz and Zajac (1996) used a similar design to explore the limits of institutional theory, using the same data set as in their 1993 study. The focus was on illegitimate action of the organisations, the impact of the technical environment, increasing homogenisation of the organisational field, early versus late adoption of professional programmes, and imitative behaviour (towards resembling prestigious colleges). Again, the institutional perspective was unable to explain the observed behaviour and performance of the institutions. The technical environments appeared to have a much more substantive impact on the organisations' restructuring activities, implying that institutional theory 'may underestimate the power of traditional adaptation-based explanations in organizational sociology' (Kraatz & Zajac 1996: 812).

Huisman and Morphew (1998) tested some institutional hypotheses concerning growing homogeneity in American state systems of higher education and the Dutch university sector. Despite the institutional expectation that higher education institutions would become more similar over time, the data using time spans of almost twenty years indicated the opposite development: the institutional diversity (in terms of the programmes offered) increased. However, in the patterns of programme acquisition some isomorphic patterns are recognisable, hinting at the existence of institutional behaviour. American higher education institutions seem to emulate institutions presumed to be of high status; in the Dutch case, patterns of imitative behaviour also can be detected.

Huisman (1995) developed a model based on resource dependency and social exchange theory and applied the framework to the introduction of new study programmes and specialisations within study programmes in the Dutch university sector. Dependency relationships in this sector were significantly determined by enrolment rates: the more first-year enrolments, the higher the budget for the unit providing the programme. It was expected therefore that those units within universities that were confronted with decreasing or strongly fluctuating enrolments were more inclined to introduce new programmes or specialisations than units not confronted with enrolment variations. A loglinear model applied to data on study programmes offered in the period 1975–93 showed that indeed enrolment decreases and oscillations, in combination, were good predictors of programmatic innovations.

Huisman (forthcoming) and Huisman and Beerkens (forthcoming) followed Tolbert and Zucker's (1983) analysis of conditions under which first and late adopters implemented programmatic innovations. The innovations studied were new study programmes. Institutional theory and strategic choice theory would both predict that early adopters rationally scan their environments, consider the pros and cons of the intended innovation and consequently carry through the implementation. The perspectives differ when predicting the behaviour of the followers. Institutional theory (DiMaggio & Powell 1983) posits that the followers imitate the first adopter without careful 'rational' reflection on the advantages/disadvantages of the innovation. Strategic choice theory, however, maintains that, in principle, followers are no different from early adopters in their behaviour. The followers also would analyse their environment, and features of this environment affect the choice of whether or not to implement the innovation. It was hypothesised that differences in behaviour, institutional versus strategic, would become manifest in the consequences of the behaviour. If the institutional argument were true, the study programmes of late adopters would be less successful (in terms of enrolments). They would be of relatively poor quality, and thus would experience more difficulties in surviving. Applying the hypothesis to seven chains of innovations (including a first adopter and a set of two to five followers, all being similar study programmes), the tests showed that there was no consistent pattern of followers being worse off than initiators. The empirical data seem to point to the effects of both strategic adaptation and institutional behaviour.

In sum, the literature suggests that, for both perspectives, empirical support can be found. Strategic choice explanations seem to be slightly superior to institutional explanations, indicating that higher education organisations are not simply the languid subject of the institutional environment. Quite to the contrary, strategic choice and adaptive behaviour seem to encapsulate the conduct of the organisations more adequately. However, the institutional model should not be rejected; there are signs that to some extent institutional behaviour is apparent too. A further test will now be proposed to combine the institutional model and the strategic choice model, drawing on the work of Oliver (1991).

1.3   A typology of strategic responses

Oliver (1991) has developed a typology of organisational responses, ranging from acquiescence to manipulation, indicating a range of behavioural replies to pressures from the environment. Oliver accepts that organisations are affected by their institutional environments, but at the same time organisations are considered capable of making strategic choices. These choices can be contrary to the institutional theory expectations and — of equal importance — organisations are able to influence their environments. What is lacking in the debate on environmental pressure up to now is discussion on when and how organisations adjust to the institutional pressure and expectations, and when self-interest and active agency dominate (two exceptions are Meek & Goedegebuure 1989; Meek 1991). The typology of responses consists of five general types (each subdivided into three types, termed tactics) of behaviour ranging from passive conformity to institutional pressures to active agency and resistance to such pressures. Table 2 provides an overview of general types and tactics (Oliver 1991: 152).

Table 2: A typology of strategic responses

Strategy	Tactic	Example
Acquiescence	Habit	Following taken-for-granted norms
	Imitate	Mimicking institutional models
	Comply	Obeying rules and accepting norms
Compromise	Balance	Balancing the expectations of mutual constituents
	Pacify	Accommodating institutional elements
	Bargain	Negotiating with institutional stakeholders
Avoid	Conceal	Disguising nonconformity
	Buffer	Loosening institutional attachments
	Escape	Changing goals, activities or domains
Defy	Dismiss	Ignoring explicit norms and values
	Challenge	Contesting rules and requirements
	Attack	Assaulting the sources of institutional pressure
Manipulate	Co-opt	Importing influential constituents
	Influence	Shaping values and criteria
	Control	Dominating institutional constituents and processes

The integration of the perspectives does not make sense if it does not increase our understanding of the processes and factors that lead to specific behaviour (either strategic or institutional). Therefore, in addition to the typology, Oliver (1991) puts forward a set of hypotheses predicting organisational responses dependent on why the pressures are exerted (cause), who is exerting the pressures (constituents), what the pressures are (content), how or by what means the pressures are exerted (control), and where they occur (context).

One challenge is to test such hypotheses in the area of the introduction of new study programmes in the university sector, for this would answer important questions regarding under which conditions institutional and/or strategic choice behaviour can be expected. However, the data available from our studies do not allow for a rigid test. A large-scale effort would be necessary to collect the data. Therefore, a less ambitious path is taken. First, we will investigate whether Oliver's typology is empirically applicable to the behaviour of organisations that seek to establish new study programmes in the Dutch university sector. The aim is to investigate whether and how the implementation of new study programmes can be typified in terms of the strategies and tactics outlined above, thereby answering the question: do Dutch universities comply with the institutional expectations or do they actively manipulate their environment? We try to answer this question by looking at programme acquisition at two of the thirteen Dutch universities. Second, we will explore whether organisational and environmental characteristics have different effects on the behaviour of the two universities investigated. Do the two universities (a relatively young university and a more traditional old university) differ in their behaviour and do specific policies or other environmental influences have an impact on the type of behaviour? We will use descriptions of curricular innovations collected from yearbooks, anniversary books, historical overviews, etc. to reach our conclusions.

Before we actually present the empirical findings, a critical comment on Oliver's typology is necessary. Although the detailed categorisation of tactics is constructive, it is often difficult to make such fine-grained empirical distinctions between the tactics, especially given the fact that in this research we are dependent on readily available empirical data. Therefore, we refer mainly to the five types of strategies, and only make reference to tactics where feasible.

1.4 The institutional context of Dutch university education

To be able to explore the strategies, we take the regulations and governmental policies and intentions as a point of departure. Both resource dependency and institutional theory would maintain that the Dutch government, being the main provider of resources, can be regarded as the main source of organisational legitimacy. Organisational survival is dependent on the responsiveness to governmental demands and expectations. Therefore, it can be assumed that the governmental regulations and policies to a considerable extent are guiding the universities' behaviour.

The 1960 regulations (Act on Scientific Education) did not change significantly until 1993 as far as the establishment of new study programmes is concerned. Under this law, the government only funded three types of programmes. The first type is a programme taken up in the Academic Statute, which implies that an academic programme is offered at least at one Dutch university. To be able to offer such a programme, the organisation's governing board had to submit a proposal to the Minister. Taking into account the spread of opportunities for development for all universities, the

Minister decided on approval/disapproval of the university's proposal. The second type of programme involved the university being given the opportunity to supply a so-called experimental programme. Such a programme would be funded for a period of up to ten years. Within this period inclusion in the Academic Statute should be realised, otherwise the university would not be funded for the programme and the students in the programme would no longer be entitled to student support. In practice, this implies that the programme would be discontinued. The proposal had to be submitted to and decided upon by the Minister, who was informed of the opinions of other universities, mediated by the Academic Council (later the VSNU, the Association of Universities in the Netherlands) and the Educational Council. The third option for a university was to provide a 'free' study programme, which only needed the approval of the organisation's internal decision-making bodies. A free study programme was based on an existing *kandidaat* and, from 1982, an existing first-year programme. The explanatory memorandum of the Academic Statute clarifies that the regulations set out above constitute an uncomplicated procedure to stimulate institutions to develop initiatives for educational innovation.

In the 1960s and early 1970s, universities were confident of obtaining approval for such initiatives. In economically prosperous times and growth in student enrolments, an extension of the provision of study programmes was in general considered unproblematic. In the late 1970s, however, it became clear that the Minister desired a reallocation of tasks across the universities: the budget for higher education more and more became a burden on the state budget. This implied that a proposal to copy an existing programme (by definition an academic programme) would be judged critically. In the 1980s, the objective of reallocation was pursued in a more rigorous way. In the first retrenchment operation (1983), universities realised a severe cutback of almost seven per cent of their budgets by closing down programmes, establishing regional co-operation and exchanging tasks. Another, similar retrenchment operation took place in 1986.

The growth in the number of programmes in both the higher professional education and the university sector that took place in the 1980s — despite the retrenchment operations — induced the government to develop new instruments to control curricular innovation. Despite the promises to follow the recommendations set out in the 1985 policy paper *Higher Education Autonomy and Quality* (implying considerable leeway for the institutions to establish new programmes within sectors or disciplines allocated to the organisations), a more rigid instrument was introduced. From 1993, any proposal for a new programme had to be submitted to an advisory committee

(ACO), whose members are appointed by the Minister. The decision of the committee to add a new programme to the Central Register (the successor to the Academic Statute) would be based on guidelines provided by the Minister. One of the guidelines concerns the issue of programme duplication: the supply of programmes should be efficient at the system level.

In our longitudinal analysis of additional programmes at the universities of Rotterdam (*Erasmus universiteit Rotterdam*, EUR) and Groningen (*Rijksuniversiteit Groningen*, RUG), we will stress to what extent the new programmes 'deviate' (in terms of content or structure) from existing regulations and practices. We will summarise the process of preparation and implementation of the new programmes and analyse this process in terms of Oliver's classification. It may be the case that such a process, because of its complexity, cannot be categorised by one strategy or tactic. If necessary, we will typify an action by using more than one strategy or tactic. As has been mentioned, the analyses will be based mainly on existing documents. Davids and van Herwaarden (1993) on the EUR and Henssen (1989) on the RUG provided relevant information.

2.   EMPIRICAL RESULTS

Below, we present the empirical results. For the large majority of the new programmes the available data allowed for a typification of the strategy and tactic. We present a short description of the higher education institutions and give a few examples of the 32 cases we studied. The cases are in philosophy, political science, social history, and arts and cultural sciences (Rotterdam) and chemistry, human movement science, philosophy and society, and statistics (Groningen). The available space does not allow us to discuss in detail all the new programmes at the two organisations.

2.1   Erasmus Universiteit Rotterdam (EUR)

The EUR started officially as a university in 1973, after a merger of the faculty of medicine (founded 1966) and the *Nederlandse Economische Hogeschool* (1913). Rotterdam — one of the largest cities in the Netherlands — had long campaigned for a university. The growth of the Dutch student population and consequently the wish to extend the number of universities led to the upgrading of the former *hogeschool*. In 1973, the EUR consisted of four faculties: medicine, law, economics, and social sciences and the inter-university interfaculty business administration. Being a relatively young and small university, the extension of the number of programmes offered remained an important topic during its first twenty-five years of existence. In total, two new faculties and eight new programmes were established by the EUR during the period 1974–93. We will discuss four of these chronologically.

Philosophy (1974)
According to government regulations, a university should contain a so-called central interfaculty, in which at least philosophy was taught. The academic programme in philosophy was developed in 1973–74 in co-operation with staff members of existing faculties and was introduced in September 1974. The programme differed somewhat from other philosophy programmes, by focusing on systematic philosophy (one of the three major specialisations mentioned in the Academic Statute: systematic philosophy, history of philosophy, and analytical philosophy). Later, other specialisations were developed, although the stress on the former remained visible. We typify the introduction of philosophy as 'acquiescence' (compliance to the norm of what a university should be).

Political science (1978)
The faculty of social sciences was confronted with decreasing student numbers at the beginning of the 1970s. Ideas to develop a part-time programme, offering post-initial courses and programmes or specialisations in educational sociology and the sociology of international relations were suggested. Partly because of the success of the public administration and public policy programme at the University of Twente (1976), a faculty committee suggested introducing a programme in political science with a focus on policy and governance. At the same time, a subdivision in the sociology programme was suggested, one specialisation aiming at policy and sociology and another aiming at general sociology (theory and empirical research). The 1977 proposal of the committee for a four- to five-year political science programme with an emphasis on public policy was reconsidered in 1978. With the support of the Academic Council and the approval of the Minister, a more 'traditional' political science programme was established, allowing for specialisation in empirical political science, normative political science, Dutch politics, and comparative and international politics. This innovation is typified as 'compromise' (bargaining with internal and external stakeholders to come to a satisfying solution).

Social history (1978)
As early as 1971, plans were developed for a faculty of humanities. Contrary to the comprehensive faculties of most universities, the EUR faculty (according to the university itself) should focus on history, art science and general language and literature studies. The first initiative was to develop a four-year programme in history (with a stress on societal aspects) with specialisations in history and economics, history and social sciences, and history and law. The specific characteristic — focusing on societal aspects — was toned down a year later. The execution of further plans was inhibited by two factors: the Minister disapproved of the focus being solely on history and expected the university to develop plans in other areas of the humanities; and other universities (notably Universiteit Tilburg) developed similar plans in the humanities at the same time. For some time it seemed that the programme would never be realised: the Academic Council submitted negative advice to the Minister and preferred a programme at the University of Tilburg. However, the Minister eventually approved of the experimental programme in 1978. The four-year study duration — in light of the restructuring efforts of the late 1970s to shorten the nominal length of the study programmes — proved to be a decisive factor in the deliberations of the Minister. The behaviour with respect to the introduction of social history is characterised as 'acquiescence' (following the institutional model of organisational extension presented a decade ago by the then Minister) and 'deviance' (dismissing the taken-for-granted model of the Academic Statute history programme).

Arts and cultural science (1993)
The idea for a programme in arts and cultural science suggested by the Minister and an EUR committee in 1982 was influenced by the successful emergence of social history. Governmental financial support and the threat of closing down the social history programme accelerated the development of plans and decision-making within the university. A proposal for an experimental programme was submitted to the Minister. The Minister asked for advice from the VSNU, who did not object (despite the disapproval of the relevant disciplinary sections). The Educational Council was also positive, but the Minister preferred the status of it as a specialisation within the social history programme and promised additional funding for the innovation at the end of the 1980s. However, in 1993, the programme was accepted as a full programme and taken up in the Central Register. We typify the introduction of arts and cultural science as a combination of 'avoidance' (escaping the existing norms and values) and 'manipulation' (submitting the programme for introduction in the Central Register, despite ministerial disapproval).

2.2   Rijksuniversiteit Groningen (RUG)

The university was established in 1614 on the initiative of the *Statenvergadering van Stad en Ommelanden van Groningen* (a then regional council). At that time, it was the second university of the Netherlands (after Leiden, 1575). Shortly after, the universities of Amsterdam (1632) and Utrecht (1634) were founded. Together, these four universities are considered the 'classical' universities in the Netherlands, offering a broad range of programmes in most disciplines. The university started with six professors in four faculties: theology, law, medicine and philosophy. At present, the university has ten faculties. All disciplines, except agriculture are represented at the RUG.

Chemistry (1971)
This 'free' programme was started on the basis of the needs expressed by students. Dissatisfaction with the existing chemistry curriculum at the end of the 1960s led to a publication by students: 'Chemistry: a narrow-minded academic programme'. The publication should be seen in the perspective of student agitation in that period. The students maintained that the curriculum did not pay attention to the effects of chemical research on society. The department developed a programme in 1971, leaving room for the students to select courses, especially from the faculty of behavioural and social sciences. 'Energy' became the central theme of the programme. The programme merged with the Environmental Study Centre Groningen to form the interfaculty department of energy and environmental studies (*Interfacultaire Vakgroep Energie en Milieukunde*, IVEM) in 1984. The behaviour related to the introduction of the new programme is typified as 'compromising' (finding consensus between wishes of the students and requirements of a programme focusing on chemistry).

Human movement science (1984)
An interfaculty workgroup (members of faculties and higher professional education, HBOs) was established to provide the 'free' programme at the beginning of the 1980s. An experimental programme was not possible, because the Minister rejected it. Therefore, the RUG sought to circumvent ministerial interference by proposing a 'free' programme. However, the Minister also disapproved of the free programme, because of the cutback operations at the beginning of the 1980s. It is doubtful that the RUG followed the rules by changing the original experimental programme into a free programme. Students who entered the programme between 1984 and 1986 were allowed to finish the programme (up until September 1991). At about the same time, in collaboration with the faculty of medicine and the

higher professional education programme physical education (*Rijkshogeschool Groningen*), a specialisation — instead of a programme — was developed and implemented in the study programme pedagogical studies. This study programme prepared students for positions in sports, recreation, health care, revalidation and therapy. We characterise the behaviour of those involved as 'manipulation' and 'deviance' (trying to bend the rules of the game of establishing programmes).

Philosophy and society (1984)
A department within the faculty of behavioural and social sciences established the 'free' programme in 1984. The programme could be seen not only as a result of a struggle between different social science movements but also as a reaction to the closing down of the programme in cultural anthropology due to the cutback operation in the 1980s. The academic programme was replaced by a 'free' programme (allowing for specialisation in philosophy and society, and in cultural anthropology). The Minister disapproved of the programme, unless the RUG promised to focus on philosophy and society to the exclusion of cultural anthropology. The RUG agreed to this and the programme started in 1984. However, the programme was closed down in 1986. After the student numbers declined in the 1980s, the department was not viable and the faculty had to reorganise its departments and programmes. The behaviour is characterised as 'deviance' (similar to the previous case, the loss of the anthropology programme was to be compensated for by the free programme; the university to some extent tried to bend the rules).

Statistics (1992)
In the university's Development Plan 1991–95, the cooperation between the mathematics and econometrics departments to combine the specialisations (between statistics and stochastic processes and applied statistics, respectively) in statistics was mentioned. In the proposal to the University Council it was stressed that the programme would be attractive to students (either new students or students from related study programmes switching from mathematics, economics or econometrics). After approval of the University Council, the free programme started in 1992. We typify the introduction of statistics as 'compromise' (accommodating institutional elements and, to some extent, balancing the expectations of students).

3.   OVERVIEW OF THE EMPIRICAL RESULTS

Bringing the typifications of the 32 new programmes at the two universities together, the following picture emerges (table 3).

Table 3: Overview of typifications of new programmes introduced by RUG and EUR

Year	Name (and University)	Strategy: tactic
1968	Social economics (RUG)	Acquiescence: imitate
1971	Chemistry (RUG)	Compromise: bargain
1974	Philosophy (EUR)	Acquiescence: compliance
1976	Theoretical & comparative literature (RUG)	Acquiescence: habit
	Welfare policy studies (RUG)	Defy: challenge/Manipulate: influence
1982	Computer science (RUG)	Compromise: bargain
	Health care policy and management (EUR)	Defy: challenge and dismiss
1983	Educational studies (RUG)	Compromise: bargain
	Interdisciplinary studies humanities (RUG)	Compromise: balance
	Medieval studies (RUG)	Avoid: conceal
1984	General and comparative romance (RUG)	Compromise: pacify/Defy: challenge
	Human movement science (RUG)	Manipulate: influence/ Defy: challenge
	Philosophy and society (RUG)	Defy: attack
1985	Applied linguistics (RUG)	Compromise: balance
	Non-western demography (RUG)	Acquiescence: comply
	Public administration and public policy (EUR)	Acquiescence: comply
	Short-cycle Japanese studies (EUR)	Defy: dismiss
1989	Religious studies (RUG)	Compromise: balance
	Short-cycle labour studies (RUG)	Defy: dismiss
	Short-cycle East Europe studies (RUG)	Defy: dismiss
1990	Technical pharmacy (RUG)	Defy: dismiss
1991	Fiscal law (EUR)	Acquiescence: imitate
1992	Computer applications in the humanities (RUG)	Compromise
	Statistics (RUG)	Compromise: balance
1993	Environmental and infrastructure planning (RUG)	Compromise: balance
	International law (RUG)	Acquiescence: comply
	Techn. eng. & management science (RUG)	Avoid: conceal
	Arts and cultural science (EUR)	Avoid: escape/Manipulate

The overview makes clear that all types of strategic responses can be observed at the universities, ranging from 'acquiescence' to 'manipulation'. The strategies of compromise, defiance and acquiescence are omnipresent; the strategies of manipulation and avoidance are relatively scarce. In a number of cases, a further distinction could be made in tactics such as balancing, dismissing and complying.

Exploring the patterns of strategies, there seem to be no differences between the RUG and the EUR. Both universities show the full range of strategies. An expectation inspired by institutional theory, that a younger university (less permeated with the norms and values of the organisational field) like the EUR would be more inclined to apply defying and manipulative strategies than an older, more traditional university (RUG), is not supported by the data. Furthermore, a pattern across time, for example types of strategies differing from the 1960s to the 1990s, could not be detected. Even important policy initiatives, such as the budget cuts in the 1980s and the implementation of the new Act on Higher Education in 1993, do not seem to have an identical impact on the types of strategies. One could posit — from a resource dependency perspective — that when the resource flows are threatened (looming budget cuts) manipulation and defiance especially are used as strategies to cope with the emerging situation (see also Huisman 1995). However, some relevant cases observed here had to be designated as cases of acquiescence. Despite the threat, institutional — instead of strategic — responses were observed. On the other hand, there are also cases where institutional responses would have been more or less obvious. Instead of choosing the safe institutional course, the universities challenged the requirements and expectations of their constituents (especially the government), which in some cases eventually led to the demise of the innovation. In short, the exploration does not yield a clear pattern of strategies.

4.   CONCLUSIONS AND DISCUSSION

Reflecting on the applicability of Oliver's (1991) framework of strategies, a few remarks can be made. In a number of cases the denomination of tactics was disputable, therefore we remained with the general typification in terms of strategies. It is difficult to make fine-grained distinctions between the tactics, and it is questionable whether the subdivision is tenable in empirical research. However, the tactics could be seen as examples of the general strategy and in that sense they were helpful in our research. Also, in some cases it was difficult to characterise the implementation of a programme equivocally. This had to do partly with the diverging information on the cases: in some we had information on the content of the programme, in others we had information on the decision-making process, etc. In addition, some processes of innovation were difficult to label as one unique strategy. In a few cases, multiple strategies (and tactics) were identified. This mainly had to do with a lack of clarity in Oliver's framework, neglecting the variety of constituents in the institutional environment. Balancing the expectations and wishes of one constituent (e.g. the expectations of government) can lead at the same time to dismissing the expectations and needs of other constituents (e.g. those of students).

If we step aside from the fact that the research design could be improved and additional research should be carried out, the results so far (and the results of other studies on programmatic innovations in university education, e.g. Meek 1994; Meek & O'Neill 1996; Huisman 1995; Huisman & Morphew 1998; Huisman & Beerkens forthcoming) allow us to make a few remarks relevant to policy-making in higher education. In theoretical terms, both the institutional environment and the task environment of higher education organisations are created to a considerable extent by the government. If we follow the framework of our study, these environments determine to a degree the types of strategies chosen by the universities in the period 1968–93. This environment, including the regulations concerning the establishment of the different types of new programmes (academic, experimental and free), apparently allowed the universities to apply the broad range of strategies and tactics. A first reflection on the relationship between the success of the programme in terms of its attractiveness to students, the reception by the labour market, its role within the portfolio of the university, etc., and the strategy applied by the university shows that there is no clear relationship between the institutional submission and success on the one hand, and strategic resistance and failure on the other. In other words, the regulations permitted initiatives 'against the current' to become successful, as well as allowing innovations in line with the expectations to become failures. Again, it must be stressed that this must be substantiated, but at least there are clear examples of both.

This raises the question of whether the current governmental instrument to control programme innovation — submitting proposals for new programmes to the advisory committee (ACO), advising the Minister of Education, final ministerial approval of the proposal — is adequate. The instrument, in force since 1993, inhibits in all cases the emergence of new programmes that are to some extent against the current. All proposals have to fit the requirements set out by the Minister. It restricts the universities in developing — at first sight — a number of controversial innovations that might turn out to be successful initiatives and even trend-setters for other innovations.

References

Aldrich, H.E. (1979), *Organizations and Environments*, New Jersey: Prentice-Hall.

Benson, J.K. (1975), The interorganizational network as a political economy, *Administrative Science Quarterly*, vol. 20, pp. 229–49.

Child, J. and A. Kieser (1981), Development of organizations over time, in: P.C. Nystrom and W.H. Starbuck (eds), *Handbook of Organizational Design; adapting organizations to their environment*, vol. 1, New York: Oxford University Press, pp. 28–64.

Davids, M. and J. van Herwaarden (1993), *Erasmus Universiteit Rotterdam 1973–1993*, Rotterdam: Universitaire Pers.

DiMaggio, P.J. and W.W. Powell (1983), The iron cage revisited: institutional isomorphism and collective rationality in organizational fields, *American Sociological Review*, vol. 48, pp. 147–60.

Ginsberg, A. and A. Buchholtz (1990), Converting to for-profit status: corporate responsiveness to radical change, *Academy of Management Journal*, vol. 33, no. 3, pp. 445–77.

Gornitzka, Å. and P.A.M. Maassen (1998), *Governmental policies and organisational change in higher education*, paper prepared for the 11th CHER Conference, Kassel, Germany, 3–5 September.

Greening, D.W. and B. Gray (1994), Testing a model of organizational response to social and political issues, *Academy of Management Journal*, vol. 37, no. 3, pp. 467–98.

Hannan, M.T. and J. Freeman (1977), The population ecology of organizations, *American Journal of Sociology*, vol. 82, pp. 929–64.

Hannan, M.T. and J. Freeman (1989), *Organizational Ecology*, Cambridge, Mass: Harvard University Press.

Henssen, E.W.A. (1989), *Rijksuniversiteit Groningen 1964-1989*, Groningen: Wolters-Noordhoff.

Huisman, J. (1995), *Differentiation, Diversity and Dependency in Higher Education*, Utrecht: Lemma.

Huisman, J. (1997), De regulering van het opleidingenaanbod: een slingerbeweging tussen overheidsplanning en zelfregulering, *Beleidswetenschap*, vol. 11, no. 2, pp. 122–42.

Huisman, J. and I. Jenniskens (1994), Comparing governmental influence on curriculum innovations: an analysis of Denmark, Germany and the Netherlands, in: L. Goedegebuure and F. van Vught (eds), *Comparative Policy Studies in Higher Education*, Utrecht: Lemma, pp. 249–72.

Huisman, J. and C. Morphew (1998), Centralization and diversity: evaluating the effects of government policies in US and Dutch higher education, *Higher Education Policy*, vol. 11, no. 1, pp. 3–13.

Huisman, J. and E. Beerkens (forthcoming), Early and late adopters of new knowledge products: strategic or institutional behaviour? in: R. Kalleberg (ed.), *Comparative Perspectives on Universities and Production of Knowledge, Comparative Social Research*, vol. 10, Greenwich: JAI Press.

Huisman, J. (forthcoming), *Dedicated followers of fashion: programme emulation at Dutch universities*, in: H. Wagenaar (ed.).

Jenniskens, I. (1997), *Governmental steering and curriculum innovations*, Maarssen: Elsevier/De Tijdstroom.

Karseth, B. (1995), The emergence of new educational programs in the university, *Review of Higher Education*, vol. 18, no. 2, pp. 195–216.

Kraatz, M.S. and E.J. Zajac (1996), Exploring the limits of the new institutionalism: the causes and consequences of illegitimate organizational change, *American Sociological Review*, vol. 61, no. 5, pp. 812–36.

March, J.G. (1981), Footnotes to organizational change, *Administrative Science Quarterly*, vol. 26, pp. 563–77.

Meek, V.L. (1991), The transformation of Australian higher education: from binary to unitary system, *Higher Education*, vol. 21, no. 4, pp. 11–43.

Meek, V.L. (1994), Higher education policy in Australia, in: L. Goedegebuure, F. Kaiser, P. Maassen, V.L. Meek, F. van Vught and E. de Weert (eds), *Higher Education Policy: an international comparative perspective*, Oxford: Pergamon, pp. 13–48.

Meek, V.L. and L. Goedegebuure (1989), *Higher Education*: a report, Armidale: University of New England.

Meek, V.L. and A. O'Neill (1996), Diversification of Australian higher education, in: V.L. Meek, L. Goedegebuure, O. Kivinen and R. Rinne (eds), *The Mockers and Mocked: comparative perspectives on diversity, differentiation and convergence in higher education*, Oxford: Pergamon, pp. 60–78.

Meyer, J.W. and B. Rowan (1977), Institutional organizations: formal structure as myth and ceremony, *American Journal of Sociology*, vol. 80, pp. 340–63.

Meyer, J.W. and W.R. Scott (eds) (1983), *Organizational Environments: ritual and rationality*, Beverly Hills: Sage.

Oliver, C. (1988), The collective strategy framework: an application to competing predictions of isomorphism, *Administrative Science Quarterly*, vol. 33, pp. 543–61.

Oliver, C. (1991), Strategic responses to institutional processes, *Academy of Management Review*, vol. 16, no. 1, pp. 145–79.

Pfeffer, J. (1981), *Power in Organizations*, Boston: Pitman.

Pfeffer, J. and G.R. Salancik (1978), *The External Control of Organizations: a resource dependency perspective*, New York: Harper and Row.

Powell, W.W. and P.J. DiMaggio (eds) (1991), *The New Institutional Perspective in Organizational Analysis*, Chicago: University of Chicago Press.

Scott, W.R. (1987), The adolescence of institutional theory, *Administrative Science Quarterly*, vol. 32, pp. 493–511.

Scott, W.R. (1995), *Institutions and Organisations*, Thousand Oaks: Sage.

Slaughter, S. (1997), Class, race and gender and the construction of post-secondary curricula in the United States: social movement, professionalization and political economic theories of curricular change, *Journal of Curriculum Studies*, vol. 29, no. 1, pp. 1–30.

Tolbert, P.S. and L.G. Zucker (1983), Institutional sources of change in the formal structure of organizations: the diffusion of civil service reforms, 1880–1935, *Administrative Science Quarterly*, vol. 23, pp. 22–39.

Zajac, E.J. and M.S. Kraatz (1993), A diametric forces model of strategic change: assessing the antecedents and consequences of restructuring in the higher education industry, *Strategic Management Journal*, vol. 14, pp. 83–102.

Zucker, L.G. (1987), Institutional theories of organization, *Annual Review of Sociology*, vol. 13, pp. 443–64.

Chapter 7

Budgeting at the institutional level
Responding to internal pressures and external opportunities

BEN JONGBLOED AND HAN VAN DER KNOOP

Key words: resource allocation; responsibility centre budgeting; management control

1.   INTRODUCTION

Just like any organisation in a private enterprise economy, universities and other institutions of higher education have to obtain a certain share of the GDP in order to survive. By exchanging educational and research services for resources from the rest of the community, these organisations earn their income. This income takes on several forms: block grants from the government, specific government grants, revenues from investments, sale of educational and research services, and income from charity (OECD 1990: 10). Here a first (superficial) comparison with profit-oriented business organisations would end, since in most countries income earned directly from the market does not play a dominant role in university funding. Most higher education institutions depend substantially upon contributions from public funds, that is, upon the share of tax revenues allocated to them by government. One could maintain, however, that universities and colleges in this respect compete for public money with each other, and with other fields of expenditure, and operate, too, upon a *market* in which representatives of the general public spend funds on academic services. Hence, universities and colleges are in a position that does not differ substantially from that of autonomous business organisations in a private enterprise economy. To secure their budget they have to compete and react to claims and conditions laid upon them, not just by government.

In past decades, not only the level of public funds allocated to higher education institutions underwent substantial changes, but also the criteria of allocation have constantly been subjected to reforms and policy changes executed by governments all over the world. Changes in the criteria of allocation at the systems level have been executed for many reasons. Two important trends in this respect are the emergence of *performance-based budgeting* and the introduction of *market-type mechanisms*.[1] Both are aimed at stimulating productivity, cost awareness, innovativeness, and responsiveness in the higher education sector, and are accompanied by deregulation and decentralisation policies. A question that arises is, if budgeting systems change at the systems level, do similar changes always take place at the institutional level? Does it follow that, because systems change takes place, institutional change mechanically follows?

The purpose of this chapter is to look at the principles of resource allocation at the institutional level. First of all, we discuss the specific context of institutional budgeting in a university setting (section 2), moving on to a particularly relevant form of budgeting, namely *responsibility centre budgeting* (section 3), a form of budgeting frequently encountered in divisionalised organisations. As we progress, we will comment on some conditions that have to be fulfilled by the budgeting model. These conditions are partly derived from the *health cost insurance sector* (section 4). After presenting our, more or less, theoretical reflections, we will look at resource allocation reforms that have taken place in two Dutch universities, namely the University of Amsterdam and the University of Twente (section 5). Both universities have adjusted their internal allocation schemes as well as the related managerial responsibilities, in order to change the culture of their staff and to improve the efficiency and responsiveness of their organisation and its sub-units. In doing so, the central management has tried to build an organisation that can adjust quickly to changing market forces and seize opportunities more easily, in other words: build an *entrepreneurial university* (van Delden *et al.* 1987; Clark 1998).

On the basis of the two case studies and on information we have on other Dutch universities as well as the argument put forward in the theoretical part of this chapter, we will draw some conclusions on internal budgetary incentives and their relationship to internal organisation and management control. Our chapter will concentrate mainly on universities, although many aspects will also be relevant for other types of higher education institutions and, perhaps, diversified non-profit organisations in general.

---

[1]   See also chapter 8 in this volume by Koelman and De Vries.

2. INSTITUTIONAL BUDGETING, DECENTRALISATION AND MANAGEMENT CONTROL

Institutional budgeting can be defined as the set of procedures and decisions relating to the resources (i.e. *budgets*) allocated by the central administration to the different departments and units of an organisation. The method of allocating funds to so-called budget units is an important part of the 'inner life' of universities because, ultimately, the organisational units of a university (the departments, schools, research institutes, service units, etc.) and the people working in those units can realise their ambitions only insofar as they have sufficient resources. An effective budgeting process therefore is essential to the success of any organisation: it translates policies into tasks and related funds, it reflects the overall strategy and mission of the university, as well as the financial incentives (the 'carrots and sticks') used by the central administration in making the units work towards realising that mission and adopt policies which the central administration wishes to encourage. In short, the internal resource allocation method is an instrument for encouraging departments to embrace change.

In the budgeting process, objectives and means coincide, the interests of different constituencies are in conflict, and aspirations are balanced with reality. Therefore, many potential tensions will emerge during the budgeting process, as budget units will all be competing for 'a piece of the cake'. Crucial in all of this is finding the right balance between centralised policy-making and decentralised decision-making, or university-wide objectives and departmental objectives (Ehrenberg 1999). It can be argued that the same kinds of problems exist also at the systems level, where the funding authorities (usually the Ministry of Education or, in some cases, a funding council acting as an intermediary) have to balance the national (i.e. collective) perspective with the institutional perspective.

Internal resource allocation methods are part of the structures and mechanisms that aid the central management (the *administration*) of the higher education institution to attain its overall strategic goals for the institution. This is not to say that strategic goals and university-wide priorities are wholly determined by the administration. Decision-making at universities takes place in a complex process of negotiating between administration and academia — a process which some authors have typified by the term 'garbage can model of organisational choice' or 'organised anarchy' (see e.g. Cohen & March 1974; Cohen *et al.* 1988). Whatever the degree of truth in such a qualification may be for a particular organisation, the idea of institutional budgeting is to impose some kind of order and coordination in the university. The budgeting process implies a kind of accountability relationship between the administration and the budget holders. The administration is delegating authority for the use of resources to the budget holders and, in return for this, is holding them accountable for their performance.

The character of internal budgeting schemes therefore is dependent on issues of internal organisation and management control. If the division of responsibilities within the organisation is characterised by a strong degree of decentralisation, we would expect this to have consequences for the internal budgeting scheme. Universities, and indeed many other non-profit institutions, are multi-layered organisations from the administration (Board of Governors) down to the chair holders and their subordinates. The origins of this structure lie in the diversity of activities carried out and the high degree of specialisation of the academics working in this type of organisation. Academia is where the creativity, originality, unconventional wisdom, insight and sustained wrestling with problems and concepts rest. This justifies appropriately specified levels of decision-making authority (i.e. *autonomy*) for the professionals 'on the working floor'. Budget holders and departmental heads who stand close to the professionals on the working floor will know best how to employ the resources available to them for instruction and research. The best a university's administration can do is 'steer from a distance' and provide the regulatory framework for the budget units and let them know, in broad terms, what is expected of them and how their performance is measured.

Delegation of authority will immediately make some observers point at potential *principal-agent problems* that will become manifest because the central administrative offices will have incomplete information about the university's departments or its individual institutes. In economic terminology: the administration (the *principal*) is unaware of the *technology*, that is, about how the lower-level *agents* carry out their tasks, and what effort they exert. Because of this asymmetric information distribution, the problems of moral hazard, free-rider behaviour, and incomplete contracts will be manifest. However, it is impossible for the administration to learn exactly what is going on at the various levels. In fact, administration may not want to know and, instead, may want to rely on trust and professional norms (codes of conduct, peer review, competition and judgments from colleagues working in the same disciplinary sub-fields) to guide academic behaviour.

Turning again to the role of the central management in institutional budgeting, we conclude that the challenge lies in enhancing the likelihood of departments meeting or exceeding the performance goals negotiated with them by the use of appropriate incentives, both in terms of how performance is measured and assessed and the methods used to reward good performance (or penalise poor performance). Regular reporting of performance is crucial to this as is the internal budgeting scheme which clearly underpins the process. In designing internal allocation mechanisms or internal reward systems, the central management will have to *motivate* the professionals at the base without monitoring them excessively. Part of the motivation derives from the financial incentives contained in the allocation mechanism. To put it differently, the incentives in the allocation mechanism should 'appeal' to the professionals at the base. If there is a conflict between the objectives of the professionals and the fundamentals of the budgeting scheme, the motivation will almost certainly be less than optimal. Massy (1994) refers to this as the 'value incongruity problem'. Internal budgeting should also motivate managers to perform in line with the organisational objectives; it should enhance goal congruence.

Motivation is one element of *management control* (Anthony & Young 1984). The other element is *coordination* (Milgrom & Roberts 1992). The central administrative offices will have to ensure that the decisions of relatively autonomous units have a common element in the sense that they all contribute to the carrying out of university-wide objectives. Coordination can be achieved by means of contracts, agreements and budgets. The policies implemented for achieving motivation and coordination among professional decision-makers constitute different solutions to the problem of management control. The internal allocation model is one of the policy instruments for exerting management control.[2] Its role is multi-faceted, ranging from planning and coordination to motivation and evaluation. Motivation cannot simply be seen in terms of the cash nexus. There are other types of motivation in academia besides the pay cheque or the bonus. There is self-esteem, desire for honour, for consideration amongst those whose opinion one values, intellectual excitement, curiosity, reputation and standing. All of these are literally beyond price. Therefore, the internal allocation model is certainly not the only element in contributing to the motivation of academics. However, we would argue that, at least, it is an important condition in shaping the collective outcome of academic behaviour.

---

[2] Elements of human resources management (recruitment, reward, appraisal, training of staff) will also have important implications for the motivation of staff (see the chapter by De Weert & Van Vucht Tijssen in this volume). For the moment, however, we will concentrate on budgeting policies.

3.   RESPONSIBILITY CENTRE BUDGETING

Budgeting models come in different shapes. Research on internal budgeting schemes can be found in the work by US authors such as Bill Massy (Massy 1990, 1996), Edward Whalen (1991) and Robert Zemsky (Massy & Zemsky 1994). In Europe, especially continental Europe, the literature on the subject of internal budgeting is relatively scarce. Exceptions from the Netherlands are studies by Otten (1996), Verheyen (1998) and Goudriaan *et al.* (1998) which contain discussions of allocation mechanisms as used in Dutch universities and higher vocational institutions. Studies carried out in Great Britain are Shattock and Rigby (1983), Williams (1992) and Brown and Wolf (1993), while other examples from the British Isles are included in a book edited by Berry (1994). Examples from Australia are included in Anderson *et al.* (1996). Hoenack, however, writes (1994: 155): '... there has been much less study of internal budgeting practices and their effects on incentives and resource allocation', and, pointing at (US) exceptions, like Pfeffer and Salancik (1974), James (1978, 1991) and Getz and Siegfried (1991), he states that the development of improved budgetary incentives within universities may benefit from research on '... factors influencing universities' internal budgeting methods and cross-subsidisation practices (for instance, between teaching and research) ...' (1994: 160).

In this section, we would like to discuss a particular type of budgeting that can be chosen from many different options for internal resource allocation in university settings. In doing this we make use of the theory of *cost accounting* (see e.g. Drury 1995: 435). First of all, we recall that internal budgeting should be undertaken within any organisation in order to coordinate individual managerial decisions. Detailed plans (referred to as budgets) should prevent, for example, the marketing department of a business organisation introducing a promotional campaign that increases sales to a level beyond that which the production department can handle cost efficiently. In addition to some other functions, internal budgeting should also encourage departmental heads and professionals to perform in line with university-wide objectives.

Within universities, too, it can be argued that budgets should be set up for so-called *responsibility centres*, segments of the organisation where an individual manager (or managing body) can be held responsible for the segment's performance (see e.g. Whalen 1991). Three types of such centres can be distinguished (Drury 1995: 35):

1. in a *cost* centre, managers are accountable for the expenses that are under their control;
2. in a *profit* centre, managers are accountable for sales revenues and expenses;
3. in an *investment* centre, managers are normally accountable for sales revenues and expenses, but in addition they are responsible for some capital investment decisions.

Which responsibility centres can be identified in universities? While universities possess first of all many of the elements of professional organisations (Mintzberg 1994: 188, 268), almost all of them also exhibit the characteristics of a *divisionalised* organisational structure. The university's sub-units — faculties or departments — produce educational and research services in separate fields of scientific specialisation. In many countries (e.g. in the Netherlands), such divisions are governed by individual managers, the *deans*. In most cases the division management is held responsible for certain operations relating to its educational and research service products, notably also for the inflow of new students.

The divisions of a university can be considered therefore as *profit* centres (Drury 1995: 729) or, rather, as *pseudo-divisionalised* profit centres (Drury 1995: 731). Here, the main revenues, the core funds for teaching and research received from central administration, are paid out in many cases as an unidentifiable part of the block grant allocated by the central government to the university, without any reference to individual faculties. On the other hand, the revenues from research council funds (competitive funds awarded to specific research projects) as well as the revenues from contract activities (the sale of educational and research services to the general public, that is, the private and public sector) are clearly attributable to individual faculties, and are very often administered exclusively within these sub-units.[3] With regard to the former income flows (both deriving from contract work), faculties can be seen as real profit centres, and the managers involved have profit responsibility, that is, they are responsible for generating a non-negative balance of revenues and expenses that does not deviate too much from zero.[4]

---

[3] Using the Dutch terminology, research council funds are known as *second flow of funds*, while income from contract activities is called *third flow of funds*. The *first flow of funds* (currently some 72% of university revenues) consists of the block funding from the central government, supplemented with tuition fees paid by students. The second flow of funds amounts to 5% and the third constitutes the remaining 24% (figures for 1996).

[4] It is assumed here that a university does not strive for maximum profit, but cannot afford, in the long run, systemic financial losses. It is assumed also that a university produces at the lowest possible costs or, at least, tries to do so. For comparison we refer to the

For completeness' sake, however, it must be noted that activities such as those conducted by general administration or certain types of support services may remain centrally structured on a functional basis, that is, with all activities of a similar type organised into a separate unit with its own budget and responsibility for providing services to all divisions (Drury 1995: 730). Here one would speak, instead, of *cost* centres. Rather than discuss support units now, we will look at the *academic* departments and, furthermore, concentrate on *Dutch universities*.

A proper internal budgeting process starts, at least conceptually, with the main factor that restricts the performance of the organisation for the planning period. In most private enterprises this factor is sales demand. The sales budget (based upon estimates of demand volume and price) is therefore generally the foundation of all other budgets (for production costs, and for selling, distribution and administrative expenses) since all expenditure is in most cases ultimately dependent on the volume of sales (Drury 1995: 449). The main factor that underlies and restricts almost all operations of Dutch universities is the *first flow of funds*, that is, the lump sum (*block grant*) received from the central government, augmented with income from tuition fees. Hence, the budgeted amount of this flow should be, and is in fact generally used as, the budget from which all other budgets are derived, or, at least, to which all other budgets are brought into harmony.

In a divisionalised private enterprise, internal budgeting starts with the budget for the sales of the *division*. This requires estimates of volume and price for the division's sales demand. From this a budgeted profit and loss account for each individual profit centre can be derived. Analogously, for the divisions of a university, a proper internal budgeting system that gives correct motivational incentives should start with separate budgets for the first flow of funds revenues that can be placed on the account of (i.e. attributed to) the individual faculties.

However, as was indicated above, in the Netherlands (as in the United Kingdom) the first flow of funds is assigned to the universities as a block grant, a *lump sum*, without any reference to the faculties within the higher education institutions. These block grants are based, to some extent but not completely, upon production characteristics of each university, and upon fixed — that is, for the universities, exogenously determined — money prices corresponding to these characteristics (Hazeu & Lourens 1993). The problem then is according to which allocation system will the university's

---

    objective function specified by Garvin (1980) in his classical work on university
    behaviour.

budget for the first flow of funds be distributed *within* the university over the relevant profit centres.

To shed some light upon this problem we return to the *profit* responsibility of the individual faculties. As stated above, this responsibility is assumed to imply that the faculty management as well as the overall university management pursue the objective of a non-negative balance of income and outlays that does not deviate too much from zero in the long run. Although it is not maximum profit relating to the first flow of funds that is aimed at, nevertheless, the internal budgeting system with its corresponding motivational incentives should be such that for each individual profit centre (e.g. faculty), the allocated revenues from the first flow of funds in general just covers costs. It is noted here that costs are to be understood as being 'netted', that is, as (gross) operational costs less revenues from the second and third flow of funds for the divisions.

At this level of generality we cannot reach further conclusions without entering the classic domain of *marginal costing*. Allocative efficiency might suggest, then, that in a proper allocation system the production level for educational and research services of a faculty should be such that the budget revenues per whatever unit it is upon which the internal allocation system is based, equal the marginal costs of the faculty per the same unit. If, for instance, in a faculty marginal costs would be higher than the budget revenues, a marginal increment of educational or research services would require more resources[5] than the institution is prepared to provide through its internal budgeting system. Hence, resources should be withdrawn from this particular field and allocated to a faculty in which the balance between marginal costs and revenues is negative.[6]

We enter here the interesting fields of public utility pricing (Halm 1970: 208-15; or Coase 1970: 113-28) and transfer pricing (Drury 1995: 758–92). It is well-known that the above formulated rule per se cannot prevent a *loss* with a division if fixed costs within the faculty are large in proportion to variable costs, or if variable costs are decreasing — in which cases marginal costs are less than average costs. Drury (1995: 771) advocates, therefore, *two-part transfer pricing*. For a university budgeting system this would imply a fixed fee from which the faculty can recover its fixed costs, and a sum per unit of production that equals its marginal costs. Note that such a

---

[5] Recall that resources are already netted with the revenues from the second and third flow of funds.

[6] Or the revenues from the second or third flow of funds should be increased.

structure is commonly found with the pricing of public utilities such as electricity or telephone services. Revenues precisely cover all costs.

In any case, then, with a proper internal budgeting system a university that reaches its target will operate at a financial break-even point. This also holds for each individual faculty. It means that the distributional system for the first flow of funds within the university should be such as to warrant the *continuity* of each division, that is, the division's continuous existence with a reserve position that does not fall structurally below zero.[7] In the long run, then, each faculty raises from the internal budgeting system a sum of money per unit that equals its average costs. Hence, the allocation system should take into account in some way the systematic variations between faculties in the costs of producing educational and research services. Here parallels exist with other budgeting systems, such as, in the Netherlands the allocation models for the general payments from the central government to municipalities, or for the payments for social aid to municipalities (NEI 1998).

4.   SOME PRINCIPLES OF INSTITUTIONAL BUDGETING

A comparison may be made, more specifically, with the budget allocation models as proposed in health care reforms in the spirit of Enthoven's (1988) consumer-choice health plan. In the Netherlands, this approach has led to investigations into budgeting systems in which income-related premiums, paid — through taxes — by insured individuals into a central fund, are distributed among sickness insurers in the form of risk-adjusted capitation payments for their insured (Lamers 1997: 4).

In health care reform studies, extensive investigations, for example, those of Lamers, take place to identify adequate predictors of the health care costs of an insurer in order to arrive at acceptable budget formulas. From these and other comparable studies one may also derive some general requirements for an internal university budgeting model. Based upon Lamers (1997: 15) and NEI (1998: 58) one may think of:

---

[7]   Cf. footnote 5.

- *Availability*: the budgeting system should be based upon production characteristics that are obtainable without undue expenditure of time or money, and without making the administrative system unfeasible;
- *Invulnerability to manipulation*: the production characteristics used in the allocation model should not be subject to manipulation by the faculties;
- *No perverse incentives*: the budgeting system should not provide incentives for unnecessary outlays or university-wide inefficiencies;
- *Professional autonomy*: the budgeting system should respect the professional autonomy of the faculty;
- *Dynamics*: the budgeting system should allow for changing circumstances;
- *Stability*: faculties should know where they stand; large changes in budget revenues should be avoided;
- *Validity*: the internal budgeting system should take into account genuine and systematic cost differences between faculties.

The last condition warrants more attention. In health care budgeting models, the risk-adjusted capitation payments to insurers are in fact genuine insurance premiums (Gerritse & Poelert 1990: 10). They are derived from the *expected* per capita costs within the risk group to which the insured belong — according to the well-known 'Principle of Equivalence' that requires equality between premium and *expected* costs. The expected costs differ between homogeneous risk groups, that is, groups of insured with the same chance of needing health care.[8] It may be noted that the best single predictor of an individual's future health expenditure is reported to be prior utilisation of health care, or prior costs (Lamers 1997: 17). This is a rather doubtful basis for a budgeting system since it may give rise to perverse effects. Basing allocations on past experience represents, though, an approach to higher education budgeting, *line-item increment budgeting*, that has been — and still is — very common in many organisational settings. In line-item incremental budgeting, a unit's budget is the same as last year's, unless the resource recipient (the organisational unit) can persuade the resource allocator that it needs extra funds for some specific new line of expenditure (e.g. a new programme), or to combat salary (inflationary) increases (Massy 1994: 5). The incremental budgeting approach has 'disastrous implications for efficiency' (Massy 1996: 38–9), even though it has the advantage of 'keeping the peace' within the organisation because everybody is getting what they have grown accustomed to. Needless to say, incremental budgeting also scores very low on the aspect of change orientation.

---

[8] It is worth noting that this care and, therefore, the magnitude of the costs involved as well as the difference in costs between homogeneous risk groups, are completely at the discretion of the members of one profession, the physicians.

Returning to the 'validity' condition, which argues for taking into consideration systematic cost differences between budget units, it is clear that a budget can only be based on costs provided the costs, in some way or another, allow standardisation. For this, the following general classification of costs (Mol 1993: 178; Drury 1995: 492–3) into three categories can be made.

1. *Engineered costs*: variable costs that are clearly dependent upon and defined by the level of production, and to a large extent allow for objective standardisation.
2. *Committed costs*: fixed costs that are incurred in each year as a consequence of a major decision made some time ago in direct relation to production capacity, and allow equally for standardisation.
3. *Discretionary costs*: all other costs, for which management has some significant range of discretion, and for which no immediate relationship between inputs (as measured by the costs) and outputs exist, and, hence, do not have the possibility of being standardised. Examples are expenditure for research and development, for advertising, or for representation.[9]

For the production of educational and research services of faculties, the share of discretionary costs seems to be very high indeed. For research, no objective rules are available for determining the amount of money[10] that a faculty would need. In addition, the costs of many research projects are, essentially, completely at the discretion of the professionals in the relevant discipline. Some research projects in the natural sciences can be carried out only with heavy international involvement and assistance, in order to collect sufficient funding. This, for instance, is often the case in physics (e.g. research with particle accelerators). In mathematics, on the other hand, some sheets of paper will often be sufficient.

Likewise, the costs of educating students seem to be largely of a discretionary character. In medicine, students may be required to dissect a human corpse — a requirement that is not a technical necessity for the production of good physicians, but nonetheless it is a reflection of professional norms and judgment. In a language course, students write an essay — for which the marginal material costs are nil. Ideas about optimum class size and teaching methods are only gradually developing. All this is

---

[9] Note that, for expenditure like this, it may not always be clear whether these are genuine *costs* or, in fact, *consumption outlays*.
[10] Again, net of revenues from the second and third flow of funds.

due to the existence of different disciplinary fields in which, to a large extent, only the professionals themselves can judge the research and educational methods and material requirements.

Hence, cost differences between faculties seem to be determined predominantly by discretionary costs in widely different fields. This is an important difference to the allocation models in health care insurance, where the budget is to be distributed — according to the judgment of *one* profession — to a given population of insured who express a need for care. There, it makes sense to investigate the cost differences between insurers in relation to objective background characteristics of the insured. In a university that operates predominantly in the spirit of Polanyi's 'Republic of Science', internal budget allocation cannot help but reflect the discretionary and intrinsic judgments of *several* professions.

A core of objective (standardised) costs could perhaps be derived from minimum requirements necessary to produce educational and research services, such as administrative or classroom facilities within a faculty. However, leaving out this part of the cost, there seems to be no well-established, objective and value-free method to determine the appropriate amount of funds to be spent within the university on educational and research services for individual disciplinary fields.[11] In line with Drury's (1995: 493) discussion of discretionary costs, the conclusion arises therefore that an institution's internal budgeting system can only be based upon comparisons with similar organisations, that is, other universities, or upon past expenditure patterns of the institution itself. This suggests that historical cost data, expressing accepted differences in educational and research expenditure, by necessity will play an important role in the internal budgeting systems of universities. This may have the disadvantage of perpetuating inequities between faculties in funding, however, as was stated above, it avoids large disturbances in the organisation.

Due to the lack of objective data on costs, the university's administration, therefore, will partly need to rely on *subjective* judgments — not just on costs, but also on performance. And, in doing so, it will have to take into account the external environment of the university and the opportunities and signals originating from that environment. For instance, the choice of

---

[11] This may be put in different terms by stating, in line with footnote 9, that some of the faculty costs might in fact be considered as *consumption expenditure*. Here, we meet the ambiguous economic character of a public university as part of a government sector that is not primarily aiming at profitable production (Mol 1993: 19–20). Taking this point of view, internal budgeting can be regarded as maximising a *utility function* (cf. Massy 1996: 66–70).

budgeting scheme will partly reflect the features of the funding scheme operated by the Ministry of Education, even though this *external* funding scheme in many respects will not be based on objective cost data. Echoing the incentives contained in the governmental model will prevent the institution from rewarding budget units on the basis of other incentives compared to the ones that ultimately drive the budget of the institution as a whole. After all, a resource allocation model is also a channel for messages between providers and users of resources. Therefore, the central management, in answering the calls for accountability from its sponsors — the most important one still being the government — will be forced to translate these messages in its resource allocation method.

An example of the incorporation of subjective judgments in internal allocation decisions is the use of judgmentally determined *performance assessment* factors (Massy 1996: 247). Such factors will often be non-quantitative expressions of the quality of an educational programme or a research project. Assessment information can either be incorporated directly into an allocation model (e.g. if part of the budget is driven by values taken on by performance indicators) or it can be used outside the allocation mechanism, for instance, if the central administration is reserving a pool of funds for selected initiatives. The former is often used for rewarding past performance, while the latter is found in cases where faculty is encouraged to strive for results in the future. Because of its subjective nature, judgmental information can only be used effectively if there is a healthy degree of understanding and trust between centre and budget units about what results are to be delivered and how the monitoring will take place. Judgmentally driven, performance-based allocations therefore are likely to be the outcome of *dialogue* instead of a mechanical model.

The next section will sketch a few characteristics of the internal budgeting models chosen by two Dutch universities. We will try to identify in what respect the models reflect the features of budgeting models discussed so far and how the budgetary systems of the two universities have recently been reformed.

5.   THE BUDGETING MODELS OF TWO DUTCH UNIVERSITIES

We will now turn our attention to the budgeting models used by the University of Amsterdam and the University of Twente. The first (22,000 students) is a large classical university, covering all major academic fields. The second (5,700 students) is a relatively small university, oriented primarily towards engineering studies, but also offering a few social science programmes. In 1997, the University of Amsterdam was able to generate 11 per cent of its revenues from contract activities. The corresponding figure for the University of Twente was 16 per cent.

Both universities employ *funding formulas* for their internal budgeting decisions. It was suggested (in the previous section) that the internal resource allocation mechanism of a university will resemble, at least to some extent, the model used by the Ministry of Education for determining the core funds (lump sums) appropriated to the universities in the Netherlands. In a recent study by the Institute for Research on Public Expenditure and CHEPS (Goudriaan *et al.* 1998), it was concluded that in 1995 only four (out of 13) Dutch universities used a funding model that had a strong resemblance to the *HOBEK* model used (from 1993) by the Ministry of Education at that time. Therefore, the Dutch universities would indeed seem to make use of their autonomy in the construction of their allocation mechanisms. However, four other universities were still using a 'copy' of *PGM*, the predecessor of *HOBEK*, for internal resource allocation.[12] This would suggest that the external funding model is still regarded as an important force to be reckoned with in shaping the internal allocation model.

University of Amsterdam
The internal allocation model employed by the University of Amsterdam for distributing the government block grant (and tuition fees) among the different faculties was based upon, until recently, rather intricate formulas[13] that produced faculty budgets separately for education and for research facilities (inclusive of a mark-up for costs of management and administration). Both budgets were put together and made available as a lump sum to each faculty, which could spend it on education or research in ways they believed to be most effective. In 1995, the internal budgeting

---

[12] Compared to *HOBEK*, *PGM* constituted a considerably more differentiated and complicated model, as it applied three different tariffs (i.e. staff/student ratios — for humanities, social sciences, and science/medicine) to the number of enrolled students, where enrolments were forecast using projected and actual graduation rates. *PGM* produced separate allocations for personnel (academic and support staff) and material costs. *HOBEK* differentiates between two categories of students and graduates (sciences — social sciences), funding *actual* numbers on the basis of only two funding tariffs (having a ratio of 1.5 : 1). Research allocations per university, as in *PGM*, were mostly determined on a historical basis, although a small performance component can be found in the number of PhDs produced per university.

[13] Derived from *PGM*.

system was redesigned, and a new method was used for gradually moving the historically determined budgets in directions negotiated between central administration and faculty management (the deans and their teams). This represented a more 'policy-driven' way of budgeting. Choices and performance targets were laid down in *management contracts* negotiated between the university's governing board and the individual faculties. The underlying education budget was based on the number of first-year students, graduation rates, and a factor reflecting the degree of diversity in a faculty. Diversity was approximated through (1) the number of educational programmes; and (2) the number of chair holders (representing disciplinary sub-fields) in the faculty. The variable part of the research budget was dependent on the education budget, the number of PhDs, the number of researchers paid from national research council grants and the number of chairs. However, the largest, mainly non-variable, part of the research budget was a subjectively determined (i.e. policy-driven) allocation per faculty, based mainly on historical considerations.

In short, the central administration used objective information on cost and performance per faculty and combined it with subjective information and judgments on the faculty's past performance and future plans.

Still, it proved hard for the administration to really affect faculty policies and priorities, for instance, with regard to a faculty's efforts (and resources used) in teaching and research. Therefore, a new policy was introduced that ran parallel to a restructuring (i.e. regrouping) of the faculties. One has to keep in mind, however, that the University of Amsterdam already had a strong tradition in which the individual faculties are regarded as pseudo-divisionalised profit centres. The basic starting point for the most recent reform in institutional budgeting is the introduction of an *internal market* for academic labour services within each faculty. The demand for academic labour originates from the (research and education) institutes within a faculty; supply of academic manpower is provided by the so-called, professional basic units (or departments) of the faculty. In this set-up, the education institutes provide all educational services of the faculty while in research institutes the production of research services takes place. All members of the scientific and non-scientific staff belong to one of the basic units. The academic labour required by the institutes in order to perform their educational and research tasks is hired from the basic units. Basic units and institutes have to negotiate about contracts and agree on (so-called) transfer prices.

The budgets from the internal allocation system are received only by the institutes, and not by the basic units. From their budgets, the institutes have to cover *all* costs that relate to their educational and research tasks. The institutes only have a small staff. The professional basic units have to sell labour services to the institutes and so, in the way of consultancy firms, earn sufficient income in order to pay the salaries of their (academic) personnel. All other costs in the basic units should also be covered by the transfer price agreed. These other costs may relate to administrative services or, for example, to expenditure for training and development. The professional basic unit is responsible for maintaining an adequate level of professionalism in its scientific specialists.

A faculty of the University of Amsterdam may consist of several institutes and basic units. The managers of these entities are the actors on the internal market. The dean of the faculty has the ultimate and overall responsibility for the faculty. However, the dean is not supposed to interfere actively unless the internal market does not function properly. The dean should act as an arbitrator who sees to it that the rules of the game are respected and the market clears.

Through the separation of the demand for and the supply of academic labour, deficiencies and imbalances in quantitative and qualitative manpower will surface. The interests of the institute managers and of the managers of the basic unit will not always run parallel. An institute may refuse to buy certain labour services offered by the professional basic unit, because these services do not match its educational or research programme needs. In a case like this, the basic unit will not be able to cover all its salary costs, and will run a financial deficit. Here, then, the dean is supposed to interfere in order to prevent financial imbalance within the faculty. Also, a strong incentive is given to the basic unit for an active human resources management.

Finally, we stress that the separate budgets for the individual education institutes are based upon formula funding, although on a far more simple and transparent model compared to the previous one. The budgets for the individual research institutes will result from negotiations between faculty and Board of Governors. All budgets will be binding: deans are not allowed, unless in agreement with the university board, to reallocate funds between institutions. This puts a floor beneath the amounts spent on, in particular, educational services, and guarantees minimum levels of educational quality throughout the university.

The University of Twente

The University of Twente has a long history of decentralised budgeting, meaning that the central university administration has pushed decisions about costs and revenues down to individual faculties and academic units. Fully concordant with the idea of responsibility centre budgeting, faculties received a lump sum budget that was based on a transparent set of formulas that partly respected the differential cost structures of faculties. Faculties were also held responsible for the services rendered to them by other faculties and support units of the university. A system of internal charging (using transfer prices) had already been in place since 1988, making faculties aware of the costs of using office space, lecture halls, libraries, computer facilities, and material inputs of many different kinds. A prominent feature of the financial policy of Twente has always been the goal of having faculties carry out research and teaching for third parties by allowing them to keep most of the income earned in contract work. This has strongly contributed to the 'entrepreneurial' profile of Twente (Clark 1998).

Of course, over the years, and partly in reaction to outside threats, opportunities and newly established programmes, the internal allocation model was subjected to revisions. In a series of rounds it was made more simple, more oriented to outputs and made to fit in more within the means provided by the central government (Schutte & Ten Klooster 1997). Compared to the University of Amsterdam where only two different tariffs per student were used in its allocation model, the University of Twente model incorporated a more elaborate set of tariffs. Tariffs as well as fixed allocations per faculty were based (as far as the education budget was concerned) on the outcome of an exercise in which each programme was assigned a score on a five-point-scale that reflected a number of dimensions of programme costs, such as support staff, laboratory facilities, space and infrastructure, depreciation, materials and student counselling. The scores were translated into tariffs (i.e. marginal allocations per unit of output) and fixed allocations per faculty (insensitive to changes in output levels). The ratio between the highest and lowest tariff was 1.5 : 1 (the *HOBEK* ratio); for the fixed allocations it was 4 : 1. Needless to say, these ratios met with some criticism, especially from those faculties that over time were confronted with large increases or decreases in student numbers or with the need to rebuild their curriculum in response to calls for increasing the quality of teaching and learning. However, the ratios have survived many storms in this respect, even from critics who argued that, in recent years, the cost differences between disciplines have become smaller due to the emergence of problem-based, or computer-aided learning.

From the early 1990s, the university's allocation model, especially the part of it that drives the education budget, has been targeted at funding *outputs* instead of inputs. The indicators for outputs selected were: the number of first-year students, the number of diplomas awarded to those completing their first year of the programme, and, receiving the largest weight, the number of masters degrees awarded. The features of the *research* component of the faculty budget derived partly from the national funding model: an education-related part, a part driven by the number of PhDs awarded, and a part — in fact, the biggest — that was based on historical considerations. The latter was input-oriented, invariant to changes in a faculty's research performance.

In fact, the largely 'mechanical' character of the allocation decisions[14] that resulted from applying the budgeting model led the board of the university to seek instruments that would give it more discretionary power over the directions taken by individual faculties. On average, 95% of the combined faculties' budget was formula-based; some five per cent was choice-based as it constituted the central incentive funds for innovations in teaching and research. For instance, the board felt that inter-/multidisciplinary activities were hardly encouraged at the interfaculty level. It pointed at an imbalance between the university-wide strategy and the respective development plans of the faculties and called for a proper balance between devolved budgets and central budgets. This seems to be in line with the so-called coordination and 'principal-agent' problems alluded to in section 2. The decentralisation policy has created an environment that is tempting faculties to pursue their own goals at the expense of other faculties or to sacrifice long-term objectives for short-term ones. Faculties that are successful in generating contract income may also be tempted to look more after the application-oriented needs of the market instead of the curiosity-driven research questions not yet posed by the market.[15]

As a means to restore the balance, the university's central board, backed by a recently (1998) installed Board of Trustees, is working on a new internal budgeting policy. The budgeting mechanism would allow for a bigger pool of central funds to be used as a steering device by the central board.[16] For

---

[14] An external advisor, Bill Massy, called upon by the university's central administration to look at the university's budget policy, spoke of a situation in which the university was running on 'automatic pilot'.

[15] See the chapter by Koelman and de Vries in this volume for similar observations on market-oriented activities by state-funded institutions.

[16] At one point it was suggested (see footnote 14) to have a third of the means available for judgmental allocations. More recently, however, a share of 10% of the block grant received from the government was proposed (FEZ 1998: 5).

steering to work, however, it will have to be combined with a 'healthy dose' of trust between central management and the deans of the faculties. It also requires accountable faculties, strong deans, professional managers and sound administrative practices at the faculty level. The need for a new internal allocation model was also driven by the desire to react to governmental policies relating to the funding of research and the new Act[17] on the governance of universities. Internal forces, especially the wish to introduce *majors* and *minors* into the university's teaching programmes, also called for reshaping internal allocation principles.

The developments outlined above require a new organisational structure. Elements of this structure, also sketched out above for the University of Amsterdam, are *schools* within a faculty, acting as a unit where teaching services (at the undergraduate level) are located, *research centres and institutes* within a faculty or at interfaculty level, where (multidisciplinary) research is carried out, and, finally, *research schools*, where graduate training is carried out and inter-university research of high quality (as ascertained by the Royal Netherlands Academy of Arts and Sciences) is located. A more managerial governance structure, both at the central university level and at the faculty level, in which the managers responsible for the units have sufficient authority and freedom to manoeuvre, is regarded as a prerequisite for all of this to work. Like in the Amsterdam case, management contracts negotiated between the Board and the deans will be drawn up, containing agreements on strategy, goals, performance indicators and budgets, as well as on the monitoring of the contracts. It will be clear that, compared to the previous structures, education and research will be organised as separate activities.

The budgets allocated to research institutes and research schools will be put in the hands of scientific directors who will be responsible for selecting the researchers to carry out the multi-year research programme. Research budgets will be awarded on the basis of project proposals. They will need to be of a sufficient scale to satisfy a number of criteria for guaranteeing that the research is in line with the overall goal and profile of the university, and meet the standards of quality and 'social relevance'. In recent years, the condition 'relevant to society' has been gaining in importance. For the University of Twente it is translated into having the university's research contribute to solving social and technical problems — problems that increasingly are characterised by their trans-disciplinary or interdisciplinary nature. In practice, the Board believes that the university will have to select a restricted number of large-scale research groups in which it wishes to invest

---

[17]   See chapter 10 in this volume by De Boer and Denters.

over the coming years. For the future, five-year research budgets are going to be tied to programmes, and not to faculties. The bulk of research funds, therefore, will be earmarked and not available as a lump sum.

6. CONCLUSIONS

In this chapter we discussed an important aspect of the inner life of universities, viz. internal budgeting. It was shown that budgeting relates to a lot of important issues in the university, such as implementation of strategies, choice of organisational structure, human resources management and accountability towards sponsors. Trends in society also have their bearing on institutional budgeting. Most notably, the drive towards marketisation and performance-based funding affects the choice of budgeting approach and its accompanying management structure.

Many authors argue for a strong degree of decentralisation in the university organisation. The delegation of fiscal authority as reflected in the responsibility centre budgeting model is believed to have many advantages as was discussed in section 3. In any case, internal budgeting is a means of imposing some order in a professional organisation such as a university. It contributes to the goals of cost awareness, responsiveness, efficiency, motivation of staff and market orientation. However, a potential danger lies in the issue of balancing university-wide objectives with individual faculty goals. The decentralisation limits the central administration's ability to influence the behaviour of the decentralised units. Activities that would contribute to fulfilling the university's overall mission would be left mainly to the operating units. A 'nation of shopkeepers' could emerge.

Building the right incentives into the allocation model therefore is the ultimate challenge. Our knowledge of this issue is still in its infancy. It revolves around many other issues, because budgeting is affecting and is being affected by many parts and areas of the organisation. Based on the (mainly Dutch) evidence we have on changes in internal budgeting, we see a trend of the university's central management taking some steps to affect more successfully the strategies and directions chosen by individual faculties. Although it may seem that this constitutes a decrease of autonomy for the faculties, one could also argue that it represents a more managerial way of running a diversified non-profit institution. Still, the resources appropriated to organisational sub-units are tied to the performance of the units, along with a devolution of the control of the resources. However, rather than seeing themselves as providers of resources, the central administration is beginning to see itself as purchasers of products for which they are prepared to pay. This represents a more market-oriented approach to budgeting: a grant relationship is turned into an exchange relationship (cf. Harrold 1998).

The ultimate outcome of this trend towards creating internal markets and using techniques such as marginal costing, cost accounting, transfer pricing and standardisation of costs could be that, more and more, the university is becoming like a *holding company*, in which each teaching and research division is working within the context of a multi-product umbrella organisation. Research on the construction of internal allocation models in an organisation like this will be needed to shed more light on the issue of identifying the proper incentives and motivators for achieving the right balance between academic and monetary values.

References

Anderson, D., R. Johnson and B. Milligan (1996), *Performance-based Funding of Universities*, Commissioned Report no. 51, Higher Education Council, Canberra: AGPS.

Anthony, R.N. and D.W. Young (1984), *Management Control in Nonprofit Organizations*, Homewood, Illinois: Irwin.

Berry, R.H. (ed.) (1994), *Management Accounting in Universities*, London: The Chartered Institute of Management Accountants.

Brown, M.A. and D.M. Wolf (1993), Allocating budgets using performance criteria, in: P.G. Altbach and D.B. Johnstone (eds), *The Funding of Higher Education: international perspectives*, London: Garland Publishing.

Clark, B.R. (1998), *Creating Entrepreneurial Universities: organisational pathways of transformation*, Oxford: Pergamon, Elsevier.

Coase, R.H. (1970), The theory of public utility pricing and its application, *Bell Journal*, Spring, pp. 113-28.

Cohen, M.D. and J.G. March (1974), *Leadership and Ambiguity: the American college president*, New York: McGraw-Hill.

Cohen, M.D., J.G. March and J.P. Olsen (1988), A garbage can model of organizational choice, in: J.G. March (ed.), *Decisions and Organizations*, Oxford: Basil Blackwell.

Delden, A.T. van *et al.* (1987), *Naar een ondernemende universiteit*, Utrecht: NGC, Veen.

Drury, C. (1995), *Management and cost accounting* (third edition), Chapman and Hall, London.

Ehrenberg, R.G. (1999), In pursuit of university-wide objectives, *Change*, January/February, pp. 29–31.

Enthoven, A.C. (1978), Consumer-choice of health plan: a national-health-insurance proposal based on regulated competition in the private sector. New England, *Journal of Medicine*, 298, 709-720.

Enthoven, A.C. (1988), *Theory and Management of Managed Competition in Health Care Finance*, Amsterdam: North Holland.

FEZ (Dienst Financieel Economische Zaken) (1998), *Nota Hoofdlijnen Financieel Beleid. 'Naar een nieuw elan'*, Enschede: University of Twente, May.

Garvin, D.A. (1980), *The Economics of University Behavior*, New York: Academic Press.

Gerritse, J. and J.D. Poelert (1990), *Middelen op Maat: naar een verdeelsleutel voor uitkeringen aan zorgverzekeraars*, Instituut voor Onderzoek van Overheidsuitgaven, VUGA, Den Haag.

Getz, M. and J.J. Siegfried (1991), Costs and productivity in American colleges and universities, in: C.T. Clotfelter, R.G. Ehrenberg, M. Getz and J.J. Siegfried (eds), *Economic Challenges in Higher Education*, Chicago: University of Chicago Press, pp. 261–392.

Goudriaan, R., B. Jongbloed and D.C. van Ingen (1998), *Kostendeterminanten en doelmatigheid van het Nederlandse hoger onderwijs*, Ministerie van Onderwijs, Cultuur en Wetenschappen, Beleidsgerichte studies nr. 57, SDU, Den Haag.

Halm, G.N. (1970), *Economic systems, a comparative analysis*, Holt, Rinehart and Winston, London.

Harrold, R. (1998), Resource allocation, in: T. Husén, T.N. Postlethwaite, B.R. Clark and G. Neave (eds), *Education: the complete encyclopedia*, Oxford: Elsevier.

Hazeu, C.A. and P.A. Lourens (1993), Changing patterns in the funding of university education and research: the case of the Netherlands, in: P.G. Altbach and D.B. Johnstone (eds), *The Funding of Higher Education; international perspectives*, London: Garland Publishing.

Hoenack, S.A. (1994), Economics, organisations, and learning: research directions for the economics of education, *Economics of Education Review*, vol. 13, no. 2, pp. 147–62.

James, E. (1978), Product mix and cost disaggregation: a reinterpretation of the economics of higher education, *Journal of Human Resources*, vol. 13, pp. 157–86.

James, E. (1991), Decision processes and priorities in higher education, in: S.A. Hoenack and E.L. Collins (eds), *The Economics of American Universities*, Albany: SUNY Press.

Lamers, L.M. (1997), *Capitation payments to competing Dutch sickness funds based on diagnostic information from prior hospitalizations*, dissertation, Erasmus University, Rotterdam.

Massy, W.F. (1990), Budget decentralization at Stanford University, *Planning for Higher Education*, vol. 18, no. 2, pp. 39–56.

Massy, W.F. (1994), *Resource Allocation Reform in Higher Education*, Washington, DC: NACUBO.

Massy, W.F. (ed.) (1996), *Resource Allocation in Higher Education*, Ann Arbor, Michigan: University of Michigan Press.

Massy W.F. and R. Zemsky (1994), Faculty discretionary time: departments and the 'academic ratchet', *Journal of Higher Education*, vol. 65, no. 1, pp. 1–22.

Milgrom P. and J. Roberts (1992), *Economics, Organization and Management*, Englewood Cliffs, New Jersey: Prentice-Hall.

Mintzberg, H. (1994), *Mintzberg on management* (Dutch translation), Amsterdam/Antwerpen: L.J. Veen,.

Mol, N.P. (1993), *Bedrijfseconomie voor de collectieve sector*, 3rd edn, Samson H.D. Tjeenk Willink, Alphen aan den Rijn.

NEI (1998), *De bijstand in model (A model for social aid)* (in Dutch), Nederlands Economisch Instituut, Rotterdam.

OECD (1990), *Financing Higher Education: current patterns*, Paris: OECD.

Otten, C. (1996), Principles of budget allocation at the institutional level, *Higher Education Management*, vol. 8, no. 1, pp. 69–83.

Pfeffer, J. and G. Salancik (1974), Organizational decision making as a political process: the case of a university budget, *Administrative Science Quarterly*, vol. 19, pp. 135–50.

Schutte, F. and J.W. ten Klooster (1997), *The budget allocation system of the University of Twente: description, problems, analysis*, paper for the Seminar on Budget Allocation, University of Twente, Enschede, November.

Shattock, M. and G. Rigby (eds) (1983), *Resource Allocation in British Universities*, Guildford: SRHE.

Verheyen, P. (1998), The missing link in budget models of nonprofit institutions: two practical Dutch applications, *Management Science*, vol. 44, no. 6, pp. 787–800.

Whalen, E.L. (ed.) (1991), *Responsibility Center Budgeting*, Bloomington: Indiana University Press.

Williams, G. (1992), *Changing Patterns of Finance in Higher Education*, Buckingham: SRHE and Open University Press.

Chapter 8

Marketisation, hybrid organisations and accounting in higher education

JOS KOELMAN AND PIET DE VRIES

Key words: academic accounting; hybrid organisation; marketisation

1.   INTRODUCTION

The metaphor of the market and its practical application are very much in vogue in higher education policy. Privatisation and marketisation seem to be a global tendency which goes beyond education and research. Privatisation and marketisation have been introduced in sectors such as public transport, social welfare and security, health, and infrastructure, which in many countries for a very long time have belonged to the public domain. Marketisation can be defined as the introduction of market-type mechanisms, which is characterised by the OECD as 'all arrangements where at least one significant characteristic of markets is present (competition, choice, pricing, dispersed decision-making, monetary incentives, and so on). It excludes the two polar cases of traditional public delivery and complete privatisation' (OECD 1997).

The privatisation and marketisation issues might be perceived in a broader perspective of a call for change and renewal. The beginning of this redirection towards the market sector, during the eighties, can be traced back to the supply-siders' views on economic policy and public finance (Bishop *et al.* 1994). Supply-side economists redirected attention away from the Keynesian emphasis on the positive effects of government-induced demand and expenditures towards the working of markets and production processes.

From this point of view, it was claimed that public expenditures and taxes had run out of control and, together with huge budget deficits, had a pernicious impact on inflation, interest rates, employment and economic growth. Since the beginning of the eighties, retrenchment policies, budget cuts and reconstruction policies have dominated the public sector in most of the industrialised countries.

The budget cuts of the eighties were followed by a more basic reassessment of the public sector functioning. In this regard, a variety of instruments may be mentioned, such as contracting out, privatisation, renewed funding methods, and public-private partnerships. Such a reassessment also may be observed in the European higher education sector, traditionally funded primarily by the government. In this sector, market-type mechanisms (market-oriented activities) have been introduced. For instance, public higher education institutions are pushed (or pulled) from the traditional teaching and research activities into more market-oriented activities to generate additional resources. Contract research and contract teaching (providing programmes for specific customers) are the two types of market-oriented activities that are mentioned most often (Kaiser & Van der Meer 1999: 2).

It is this marketisation of higher education, constituting one of the major institutional changes in European higher education over the last fifteen years, which will be addressed in this chapter. The discussion will be confined to two issues. Firstly, the theoretical economic rationale underlying marketisation will be discussed. Secondly, we will deal with a more practical issue, namely the consequences of marketisation for the accounting systems of higher education institutions. Because of their market activities, institutions of higher education have more sources of income than they ever had before. These new flows of money have to be accounted for in a proper way. It will be shown that market-oriented activities require accounting principles which basically differ from those applied to traditionally publicly funded institutions which do not, or only to a very small extent, undertake contract activities.

The reasoning that relates the two issues at hand may be summarised as follows. It starts with the conventional wisdom that the failures of the market mechanism constitute a firm basis for government intervention and provision. Concerning higher education, the presence of external effects induces governments to intervene and provides the rationale for government funded higher education institutions. However, governments fail as well. In economics this phenomenon is elaborated in the new institutional economic theory. New institutional economics points out that informational questions such as the cost of the bureaucratic system may frustrate the attainment of an economically optimal government provision. More generally, the new institutional perspective emphasises the central role of information in organising production and consumption processes. These considerations could lead to a smaller role for the government and a policy of marketisation at the system level. This implies that institutional and organisational design become crucial aspects in the provision of public goods. For example, a specific organisational device may cause goal congruence within the different parts of the organisation, and in this manner promote efficiency and reduce the cost of monitoring. Finally, it clearly fits in this new institutional reasoning that an institutional or organisational change such as marketisation requires a reconstruction of the management information system, and its subsistent accounting principles. Our theoretical exposition of marketisation processes thus results in a discussion of its practical consequences in terms of accounting approaches. Marketisation at the system level therefore has major implications for the organisational level.

The chapter is organised as follows. In section 2, some descriptive approaches to marketisation in higher education will be given. Subsequently 'markets' in higher education will be interpreted as quasi-markets. The third section addresses the economic theoretical notions and background of the marketisation movement. It will be explained that the theoretical origins of the marketisation concept stem particularly from institutional economics instead of mainstream economic theory, that is, neoclassical economics. This point of view may be contrary to popular belief. In section 4, it will be argued that marketisation in higher education results in 'hybrid organisations'. The strong and weak points of this type of organisation will be discussed, as well as options to bring the risks arising from the weak points under control. Section 5 points out the interrelation between organisation type (hybrid organisation) and the nature of the accounting system required. It will be shown that in a market-like environment, the accounting system is an indispensable source of management information. Section 6 elaborates the most important changes in accounting practices for higher education institutions, called for as a consequence of the marketisation. It will be argued that the application of commercial accounting principles will lead to problems, because the information products of commercial accounting are more or less meaningless in a hybrid setting. In the final section, some conclusions will be inferred.

2.   MARKETISATION AND QUASI-MARKETS IN HIGHER EDUCATION

In economics, the market metaphor and its accompanying marketisation processes stem from theoretical reflections on the working of perfect markets. In neoclassical economic theory, the market is the focal point. Through an economic theoretical perspective involving a descriptive rather than analytical approach to the introduction of the marketisation concept, the following section of this chapter will attempt to answer the question: What is the higher education market in practice?

A variety of marketisation practices exist. A primary issue concerns the intricate relationship between institutional autonomy (especially financial autonomy) and market orientation. It is suggested that institutional autonomy comes down to 'market orientation and flexibility' (Kaiser *et al.* 1992: 25). In this respect, universities traditionally have been 'largely self-governing centers of instruction and research in Europe and the United States …', without being market-oriented in a modern sense (Dill & Sporn 1995: 1). Therefore, it is relevant to draw a distinction between academic autonomy according to the classical Von Humboldt tradition and contemporary 'modern' institutional autonomy involving production processes and organisational issues. It is this latter, so-called procedural autonomy which is associated with market orientation. Procedural autonomy is a *conditio-sine-qua-non* for an effective market orientation. This autonomy gives the institution the 'discretionary space' to react to market signals.

Another manifestation of market orientation in higher education concerns the transition in its funding, especially the funding received from government. This transition is linked with the autonomy theme. The shift from 'budgets itemised by function' towards 'budgets itemised by performance targets' marks the road to market orientation and procedural autonomy (Williams 1995: 184–5). Accordingly, this funding reorientation results in managerialism, as another market-like feature in higher education. Procedural autonomy and managerialism are related to budgeting as follows: output based budgets and performance targets seriously weaken hierarchical relationships between the funding principal and the executive agent, and emphasise managerial responsibilities of the agents. The agents, being professionals, can survey all production procedures and processes. The idea is that the professionals would need flexibility and room to decide on the use of resources, without restrictions due to bureaucratic control. Hierarchy is then replaced by product accountability (Harrold 1998: 8). In this respect, Neave and Van Vught (1991: 252) distinguish between process control and product control. They perceive marketisation as a 'withdrawal from (government) process control', and not necessarily a reduction of (governmental) product control. Still another example of market orientation concerns the demand side of higher education. The market orientation in higher education also manifests itself through a shift from directly subsidising the providers of higher education to a system of demand side financing. Increasingly, students are asked to pay tuition fees, thus covering part of their training costs.

On the demand side, marketisation contributes to consumer sovereignty. Consumer sovereignty implies that the student is a customer, deliberating price/quality ratios, making decisions about the purchase of educational services. As a consequence, consumer decisions determine the revenues of the providers. This demand dependence will induce providers to pay attention to product quality, as well as cost control practices through cost accounting and the use of production and performance ratios. In this respect, it is a prerequisite that the supply-side has a competitive structure. Clearly, consumer sovereignty is lower when providers possess substantial market power.

Finally, marketisation in the public domain may be seen as the formation of quasi-markets, replacing 'monopolistic state providers with competitive independent ones' (Bartlett & Le Grand 1993: 10). Bartlett and Le Grand formulate three conditions which have to be met in order to create competitive quasi-markets. Kaiser and Van der Meer (1999: 4) apply these conditions to traditionally publicly funded higher education systems.

1. *An open market structure.* The market should be open to new providers.

2. *Sufficient individual incentives.* Both consumers and producers are sufficiently stimulated in financial terms and therefore will reveal their preferences (students and other clients) and efficiently produce research and teaching (institutions of higher education).

3. *Information about the quality of teaching and research.* Customers and institutions of higher education must have cheap access to accurate and reliable information about the quality of all teaching and research provided.

These conditions correspond to the aforementioned descriptions of marketisation. At the same time, Bartlett and Le Grand (1993) emphasise the public origin of sectors such as higher education to which marketisation applies (see also Niklasson 1996). It will be shown in the following sections of this chapter that this concerns a highly relevant issue. The public origin of higher education institutions results in a quasi-market and hybrid organisations. The remaining public involvement may constrain and frustrate the intended marketisation processes by legal restrictions, regulation and, last but not least, the government acting as backstop, or as 'lender of the last resort'.

3.   THE ANALYTICAL BACKGROUND OF MARKETISATION IN HIGHER EDUCATION

While the market is an economic concept, an economic approach of course does not exclude other analytical approaches. For instance, marketisation may be perceived as a political issue and a theme in the political analysis of state control versus private initiative. However, in this section we will employ an economic approach to marketisation.

One may argue that marketisation policies derive directly from mainstream economic theory, that is, neoclassical economics. In neoclassical theory the market indeed results in elegant solutions for allocation and coordination questions. The market is Adam Smith's invisible hand, buttressing efficient allocation and wealth, procuring social efficiency.[1] The market is the central concept in neoclassical theory. Therefore, the introduction of marketisation in publicly provided services such as higher education seems to stem directly from neoclassical theory. However, this conclusion is invalid, and the theoretical background of marketisation policies looks somewhat more complicated.

Neoclassical theory indeed proclaims the market as an efficient mechanism for coordination. At the same time, this theory identifies situations in which the market is unable to establish efficient solutions, for instance, whenever external effects occur. In such situations of a failing market, neoclassical theory argues for government intervention. In neoclassical theory, market failures constitute the reasons for non-market coordination. Thus, external effects associated with higher education form the justification of public provision and government intervention in the higher education sector. The

---

[1]   Social efficiency exists whenever it is impossible to make one consumer better off without making others worse off. This welfare position is the so-called Pareto optimality (see Bohm 1973: 1).

neoclassical motto might be formulated as follows: 'Market coordination, unless ...'.

Neoclassical analysis has formulated three situations in which the market fails, that is, public goods, externality, and increasing returns to scale. In case one of these phenomena arises, a call for non-market coordination mechanisms results, that is, government intervention and provision. In contrast to market failures, Wolf (1979) formulates non-market failures. Wolf shows that government intervention in the case of market failures cannot always guarantee efficiency and equity. Due to the principal-agent problem, for instance, the governmental bureaucracy may provide latitude to the pursuit of private goals such as on-the-job consumption, and will cause rising production costs. Wolf's analysis points to the fact that market failures 'provide only a necessary, not a sufficient justification for public policy interventions' (1979: 138). The policy to remedy market failures will cause new failures, that is, non-market failures. This inference does not originate from Wolf,[2] but is part of a broad development in economic theory that incorporates institutional settings and informational problems. The institutional setting concerns aspects such as property rights, incentive and organisational structures, internal regulations and external legislation. These aspects have their impact on economic behaviour and performance. For example, it is the institutional setting of the bureaucratic organisation that provides scope for the attainment of private goals. In a bureaucracy there is no for-profit incentive that will encourage workers' performance. This institutional theme is well-elaborated in new institutional economics.

Ronald H. Coase can be seen as the founding father of new institutional economics. New institutional economics criticises a basic feature of neoclassical economics. In neoclassical economics, the analysis is focused on optimal market decisions, taken by producers and consumers, given price and cost data. At the same time, it is assumed that the market presents these data without cost. In a perfect-competition setting every market partner is equipped with the relevant information to take optimal decisions. However, this setting is highly unrealistic. Therefore, Demsetz (1991: 43) calls neoclassical theory the 'Nirvana approach'. In his article, 'The nature of the firm', Coase (1937)[3] points out that the economic behaviour in the market place is highly complicated by the lack of relevant information. As a

---

[2] Wolf bases his analysis predominantly on public choice theories of government deficiencies, as formulated by Buchanan, Weingast and Niskanen.

[3] The 1991 Nobel Prize, which Ronald Coase received, was first of all based on a paper he wrote in his twenties. 'And it is a strange experience to be praised in my eighties for work I did in my twenties' (Coase 1994: 8).

consequence, Coase introduces the transaction costs of the use of the market mechanism, for example, the cost of negotiating, contracting and enforcement. This introduction marks a fundamental change in economic analysis. It brings about a shift in attention from final decisions on production and consumption to a focus on procedures and institutional settings determining these decisions. The information problems which economic actors have to cope with bring the organisational and institutional theme within the sphere of economics.

An example from higher education may elucidate this neoclassical approach. Positive external effects seem to be part and parcel of higher education production; its social benefits tend to exceed its private benefits, without this being reflected in market prices. According to the neoclassical approach, this is a market failure that should be remedied through governmental intervention, for example, public provision. On the other hand, new institutional economics points to informational problems and the accompanying costs of the various options for 'organising' production or consumption. In this respect, it is useful to look at the effects of external effect remedies that use a market-oriented approach, such as subsidised vouchers, and confront them with solutions involving a more dominant role for the government. Such an application of the new institutional perspective leads to a 'look-and-see' approach. Given the externalities of the higher education sector, a mixture of market and non-market elements may lead to a solution for the allocative problem at hand. 'Whether it (compensation for external effects) is desirable or not depends on the particular circumstances' (Coase 1960: 34). The, as yet unstable, notions of informational problems and subsistent cost mould these particular circumstances and it is impossible to articulate these 'particular circumstances' in a straightforward normative way. For instance, given utility maximising behaviour, a higher education institution will be induced to pay more attention to the price/quality ratio if input funding is replaced by a voucher system. And it is claimed that this redirected attention will promote efficiency. Therefore, marketisation must be judged from the new institutional perspective, and calls for the consideration of a variety of 'social arrangements', each with its ensuing effects on efficiency.

From this discussion, a few conclusions may be inferred. Firstly, the difference between neoclassical and new institutional economics may demonstrate that the marketisation in traditionally publicly provided services such as higher education has its theoretical basis in new institutional economics, and certainly not in neoclassical analysis. Secondly, new institutional economics emphasises the importance of interrelated concepts such as information cost, incentive structures, institutional setting (at a system level), and organisational design. As a consequence, these interrelated concepts result in a pragmatic approach to economic problems; straightforward normative solutions hardly exist. Finally, the prominent position of the informational problem in the new institutional economics justifies the next section's focus on accounting principles and management information in relation to marketisation processes.

4. INSTITUTIONS OF HIGHER EDUCATION AS HYBRID ORGANISATIONS

Marketisation in higher education results in higher education institutions becoming more and more 'hybrid' organisations: 'that is, bodies which operate in both the public and the private domains, both fulfilling public duties and developing commercial market activities' (Van Twist & In 't Veld 1999: 3). They become a mixture of both a governmental institution and a commercial enterprise. Hybrids are often regarded as a phenomenon that can contribute to a more customer-oriented, efficient and innovative organisation (see e.g. In 't Veld 1995). On the other hand, hybrids also are seen as an undesirable development which should be denied the right to exist (see e.g. Garette & Quelin 1994). Following the lead of Van Twist and In 't Veld (1999: 8–12), a more detailed examination of the strengths and weaknesses of hybrid organisations is presented below.

Strong points of hybrid organisations
Strong points of hybrid organisations include that they:

1. are stimulated to perform better because they have to compete with others;
2. are interested in new developments and innovations because of their need for distinction;
3. have significant synergetic effects, for example, the organisation becomes more customer-oriented, more efficient and more effective;
4. adapt a more enterprising attitude also in their relation to principals and that the entire organisation, more than before, searches for ways to improve the efficiency of its production process and quality of its products;

5. fulfil public duties at less cost because of the generation of additional income via their commercial activities (hybridity can contribute to savings of public funds and the mitigation of financial needs);
6. fulfil unmet demands in the market by developing commercial sidelines;
7. have a positive impact on staff motivation and remuneration.

Weak points of hybrid organisations
Hybrid organisations cause problems due to:

1. the risk of unfair competition. This is the case when public funds are partly used for commercial activities which therefore can be carried out (far) below the market price. The competition is also unfair when the commercial activities profit from fiscal benefits (e.g. hybrids are not subjected to VAT and do not have to pay corporation tax);
2. subverting public duties. Market activities can bring large benefits to staff directly involved, leading to the disregard of public higher education goals. Autonomy and professional integrity may also be harmed when academic staff offer themselves as consultants to the highest bidder;
3. wealthy customers being favoured over those who have less ways and means of having their demands satisfied by the hybrid;
4. the undesirability of the government taking entrepreneurial risks, causing the taxpayer to become an unsolicited shareholder in commercial activities and having to pay for the losses;
5. the uncertainty in the lines of responsibility arising from the organisation no longer being primarily oriented to its principal, but developing a multitude of client relations.

The practical issue for the government is how to deal with the challenges and risks of hybrid higher education institutions. Two options are available:

1. Prohibition of hybrid organisations.
2. Regulation of hybrid organisations.

Van Twist and In 't Veld (1999: 15–16) argue that the second option should be preferred. In their words:

> *In our view, it is of the essence to make good use of those strong points and to bring the risks arising from the weak points under control ... It is necessary to come to acceptable details of composite forms that are oriented on government as well as on market. Acceptable are those composite forms that can reduce the contradictions in the impulses*

> *connected to hybridity to allowable proportions. Thereto specific*
> *arrangements have to be designed.*

Points of departure for such regulatory arrangements are given by Van Twist
and In 't Veld (1999) for the hybrid university:

A.   Conditions from the public domain of universities:

- the public duty (teaching and research) may not be endangered;
- the students should not become victims of entrepreneurial activities;
- the prestige of the university as a public institution may not be harmed;
- there should be some interconnection between commercial activities and
  the core business of the university.

B.   Conditions from the private domain:

- there may not be unfair competition with private enterprises;
- there should be distinct agreements on the nature and proportions of the
  commercial activities;
- entrepreneurial risks should not be shifted onto the taxpayer.

C.   Accountability of universities:

- accountable for public duties;
- accountable for commercial activities;
- monitoring and supervision of the hybridity in the relation between
  public duties and commercial activities.

Universities, increasingly becoming hybrid organisations, should be
accountable regarding their public tasks (through monitoring) as well as
regarding their commercial activities (through warranty of quality).
Accountability is, of course, impossible without accounting. In the next
sections it will be shown that the marketisation of higher education requires
important changes in the accounting systems used by these institutions.

5.   INSTITUTIONAL SETTING AND ACCOUNTING SYSTEM

As was stated in section 3, new institutional economics focuses on the role of information in production processes. In section 4 it was shown that marketisation has changed universities and colleges into hybrid organisations. This section underscores the basic institutional economic notion that organisational type (non-profit organisations, hybrid organisations or business enterprises) and informational issues are highly interconnected. On the one hand, institutional economic theory tries to prove that marketisation may increase efficiency by the introduction of incentives to perform better and to respond to consumer preferences. On the other hand, these incentives shape new management information requirements which will be reflected in the accounting system.

Sound management of non-profit organisations such as churches and charities requires accounting principles just as much as for-profit enterprises do. Regarding the non-profit organisation, an essential element of sound management is 'an accounting system that will insure strict adherence ... to restrictions and other requirements imposed by law, by other institutions, or by individual donors' (Niswonger & Fess 1977: 13). At the same time, it may be noted that the scope of a non-profit accounting system will be relatively limited. It is predominantly oriented to external information requirements. In contrast to the business enterprise, the non-profit institution is not familiar with earning net income or dependence on investment. Monetary indicators such as profit and owner's liability value do not dictate the performance of the non-profit organisation. Non-profit organisations are in the 'business' of creating value. However, this creation cannot be fully reflected in monetary terms. For example, higher education institutions are assumed to produce substantial positive externalities, which by definition are not expressed in monetary terms. Therefore, the non-profit organisations' existence depends to a large extent on budgets, and not on market revenues. This budget dependence affects its accounting system. The system is supposed to provide financial data for internal management purposes, as well as to external parties. For reasons of budget restrictions, non-profit organisations often employ *fund accounts* to ensure that expenditures are made only for authorised purposes.[4] A key topic in accounting for the non-profit organisation is budgeting and appropriation control. 'The budget is

---

[4]   A fund account registers expenditures that must be accounted for by earmarked resources. 'Nonprofit organizations typically establish multiple self-balancing funds, which group resources that are similarly restricted in terms of specified objectives. This procedure is known as *fund accounting* ...' (Wasch 1993: 11).

prepared by management and subsequently reviewed, revised, and approved by the governing body ... The specified amounts are then recorded in the appropriation accounts and can be spent only as designated in the budget' (Niswonger & Fees 1977: 789).

The commercial accounting system focuses on value creation by market exchange. Hendriksen and Van Breda (1991: 162) claim that 'in the West accounting occurs in the framework of private capitalist economies permitting the use of exchange prices as measures of economic values'. 'Accounting information is composed principally of financial data about business transactions, expressed in terms of money' (Niswonger & Fess 1977: 11). For the business enterprise the accounting system constitutes a tool of management to govern the organisation which is subjected to (uncertain) market forces mainly expressed in figures about costs, revenues, turnovers, investment, assets, liabilities and debts.[5] Revenue data play a particularly crucial role. For the market firm these data reflect its commercial performance. At the same time, revenue data must be compared to cost data in several respects and at a variety of aggregation levels. Such comparisons constitute the basis for the value creating nature of the commercial firm. It is this value creating nature of the business enterprise that brings about a variety of commercial accounting fields.[6] For example, financial accounting employs accounting principles 'in preparing annual reports on profitability and financial status for ... stockholders and the investing public'; cost accounting is 'concerned with the costs of manufacturing processes and of manufactured products', and management accounting is 'preparing future financing or developing data for use by the sales manager in determining the selling price' (Niswonger & Fess 1977: 11–12). Ultimately, the business enterprise depends on its profitability and its attractiveness as an investment option. This dependence implies an accrual basis accounting system.

---

[5] *Assets*: any physical thing (tangible) or right (intangible) that has a money value is an asset. Assets are customarily divided into distinctive groups for presentation on the balance sheet. The two groups occurring most frequently are (1) current assets; and (2) plant assets or fixed assets.

Liabilities: debts owed to outsiders (creditors). They are frequently described on the balance sheet by titles that include the word 'payable'. The two categories occurring most frequently are (1) current liabilities; and long-term liabilities.

[6] This value creating nature may explain the name 'accrual basis accounting' for the accounting system of the commercial enterprise. On the other hand, the so-called 'cash basis accounting' applies to organisations purely funded by budgets. In the budget-funded organisation, the accounting focuses on an appropriate spending of the budgets. In this respect, a fund account is typical for cash basis accounting.

In non-profit organisations such as universities, the organisational goals differ strongly from those of the business firm. University goals aim at standards in research and education. In this respect, it is important to observe that the attainment of these goals cannot be reflected in financial data. In contrast to the management information in the business firm, the management information in the higher education institution will have a predominantly non-financial status.

It is the quantitative nature of the business figures expressed in money which offers clear-cut information by summary representations of complex phenomena. The summary nature of the figures is forcefully validated by their market lineage. Market prices may express a range of relevant circumstances, which is not by definition valid in a bureaucratic environment. The profit figure represents the ups and downs of the organisation in the single notion of the profit figure. Formulated in the context of new institutional economics, it is the bottom line of negative net income that constitutes the basic incentive to manage the business enterprise efficiently towards positive profit results. At the same time, profitability is decisive for capital market access. These circumstances demand adequate information, which is supplied by the accompanying accounting system. The non-profit organisation lacks this strong incentive basis. In the non-profit institutional setting, it is hierarchy and regulation that shape the accounting principles, underscoring external accountability. This difference emphasises the interrelation between the nature of the institution and its informational requirements, which is the main theme of new institutional economics.

6.   THE LIMITS OF COMMERCIAL ACCOUNTING IN INSTITUTIONS OF HIGHER EDUCATION

Firstly, this section will address the consequences of marketisation for the accounting practices of the higher education institution. Secondly, it will be demonstrated that the marketisation of the higher education institutions raises serious problems in terms of accounting principles. These accounting issues mark the problems surrounding higher education institutions that can be characterised as hybrid organisations.

Accounting consequences
A prominent item in marketisation trends is the transition from input funding to funding based on output and prices. The focus shifts from financing providers towards financial dependence on the sale of services, and

attractiveness to shareholders. In a competitive environment, this transition bends management towards client satisfaction. It also leads to a need for a different type and role of management information. The information required shifts from bureaucratic information for allocating budgets and the way budgets are spent, towards information on the different market revenues and costs of provision.

It is beyond the scope of this chapter to fully address the accounting consequences of marketisation for higher education institutions. Only a few examples will be provided, along the lines of the main accounting documents of the business enterprise, that is, the balance sheet account and the revenue and expense account (profit and loss account). Concerning the balance account, the hybrid nature of the higher education institution will profoundly alter the nature and significance of the capital concept. Capital is strictly defined as the difference between assets and liabilities. The profitability of the enterprise determines the state of this difference, expressing its final performance. Another balance sheet issue regards the economic property of the assets. The nature of the capital and profit concept, as used in accrual basis accounting, requires that the assets allocated in the production processes be owned by the enterprise. In this respect, it may be noted that governmental transfer of the real estate assets to the higher education institutions (e.g. in the Netherlands in 1994) is fully in line with these accrual basis accounting principles. At the same time, this transfer shows that in a hybrid organisation capital is not ultimately dependent on profitability, but on governmental policy.

Consequently, marketisation induces substantial changes in the nature and the significance of the revenue and expense account balance of higher education institutions. Firstly, there is the dominance of the profit issue. Secondly, the revenue side will immediately reveal marketisation activities. For instance, tuition fees may grow in significance. Simultaneously, the revenues generated from contracts (for research and education) will increase. On the expense side, marketisation necessitates the application of cost accounting principles to maintain a sound and commercially successful pricing policy. The cost accounting principles will induce the introduction of depreciation entries for durable assets. Another consequence is that the accounting principles prescribe the application of the 'matching principle'; revenues and cost must be accounted for in the period concerned. This principle is the basis for a sound depreciation policy. For commercial activities such as contract research and courses, it is essential to apply cost accounting principles. In this respect, *project budgeting* may be appropriate.

Firstly, project budgeting may induce sound cost recovery practices. Secondly, such budgeting may preclude cross-subsidisation.

Finally, the marketisation processes will induce higher education institutions to employ adequate treasury management practices such as cash flow management, banking arrangements, short- and long-term investments, and capital financing (HEFCE 1996: 1). In this respect, it is common, as in the profit sector, to use ratios for solvency, liquidity and profitability.[7] It is meaningless to apply these ratios without the application of the corporate accounting principles.

Inconsistent accounting
Marketisation in governmentally funded higher education institutions implies the adaptation of revised accounting practices. This also works the other way around: the success from market activities depends on the merits of the accounting system. The appropriateness of the accounting system constitutes a necessary condition for successful institutional change driven by marketisation.[8] It may be questioned whether in higher education institutions the accounting system fulfils this condition. The basic reason for this doubt lies in the hybrid nature of the higher education institutions, as part government agency and part commercial enterprise. After a marketisation process, the higher education institution turns out to be a hybrid, unable to straightforwardly fully apply the accrual basis accounting principles. At the same time, this claim implies that the marketisation process will not produce its expected efficiency contribution. A variety of issues may support this claim. However, it is beyond the scope of this chapter to deal with this theme in detail. Two questions corresponding to two basic functions of the accrual basis accounting system will be addressed. On the one hand, this accounting system plays an internal role in directing the operations of the enterprise. On the other, this system provides information on profitability and financial status for shareholders and the investing public. Broadly seen, there is an internal and an external function (see Wasch 1993: 10–13).

---

[7]   *Profitability (rate of profit)*: the ability of a business to earn a reasonable amount of income.
     Liquidity: the relative ability to convert assets into cash, sometimes referred to as the nearness of assets to cash. It also refers to the relationship between a firm's short-term liabilities and its cash and near-cash items.
     Solvency: a broader term than liquidity referring to the ability of a firm to obtain cash, or have cash available, for whatever purpose the business requires. More specifically, solvency is the ability of a firm to pay its debts when they become due.
[8]   The appropriateness of the accounting system is certainly not a sufficient condition for marketisation success, as it does not guarantee sound management practices.

Internal function

Central to the internal function of the commercial accounting system is the value creating process. The nature and scope of this function will depend on the size of the enterprise and the complexity of the production processes. However, basically, the end products of accounting must facilitate comparisons between revenues and costs to evaluate the production processes in the value creation perspective. Focusing on the revenue side of such comparisons, it is important to note that for higher education institutions the 'revenues' are predominantly determined by non-market decisions, that is, by government budgets. Consequently, this entails that revenue cost comparisons become highly artificial and without meaning. This problem might be addressed by fund accounting. For example, market activities such as contract research may be accounted for separately. However, a new question will emerge, concerning cost accounting. Higher education activities are characterised by highly complex production processes which are labour-intensive and may show substantial economies of scope.[9] This fact complicates the determination and control of costs. In particular, in accepting market orders, cross-subsidisation lies in wait (Winston 1999: 15).[10] Cross-subsidisation practices conflict with the basic matching principles of cost accounting. According to these principles, sound value creation evaluation is reached by balancing revenues with the costs concerned. This implies that the costs and revenues must be imputed to an identical period. In particular this may raise serious problems for costs. For example, fixed assets by definition must be related to various periods, and require a depreciation policy choice. Subsequently, it will be very complicated to choose a rational depreciation method for fixed assets which are funded partly by a government budget and, moreover, which are partly used for commercial objectives such as contract research. In this respect, another question emerges: the economic lifetime of fixed assets. For example, it is very difficult to calculate the economic lifetime of laboratory equipment. At the same time, this calculation is indispensable for determining the depreciation period and cost. On the other hand, the matching principle requires proper imputation of the costs to the transactions that produce the market revenues. This will also be a complex matter due to

[9] Economies of scope concern a reduction in average cost brought about by the joint production of two or more goods (or services) by a single university, rather than by several universities. The similarities of the production technology permit the use of the same factor inputs for the different products, for example, teaching and research.

[10] Winston (1999) claims that the market metaphor is inadequate for both public and private universities. We have focused on the marketisation policy concerning public universities. However, our main conclusions may still be valid for private higher education institutions.

the combination of the multi-product nature of the higher education activities and the variation in funding methods of the production factors. For instance, there will be production factors or facilities allocated on a non-market, policy basis to pursue a specific political goal. However, such a facility may be partly used for a commercial activity. In such a case, the institution must use artificially calculated opportunity costs.

External function
Concerning the external function of the accrual basis accounting system, it can be argued that its application to the market-oriented higher education institution is artificial. Profit and financial status play a central role in the accrual basis accounting system. Financial ratios inform the external stakeholders of the business enterprise and the general public and concern profitability, liquidity and solvency.[11] In different respects, these ratios and underlying figures are of a doubtful nature. Firstly, the factors that determine the profit figure do not exclusively depend on market processes. To a large extent, the profit result will be determined by governmental funding decisions. Therefore, the profit figure of the higher education institution may vary widely from year to year, and neither reflects market performance nor institutional potential in this respect. Secondly, it does not make much sense to express the profitability in a ratio based on liabilities or capital. The governmental budgets periodically defray the costs of the production processes which might be expressed on the revenue side of the revenue and expense account balance. The balance sheet account mirrors the debts and assets situation at a certain moment for which budgets flow is irrelevant, as budgets do not concern the financial position at a certain moment. Basically, the budget-funded institution may operate without debts (liabilities or capital) or without juridical ownership of assets. Therefore, the balance sheet account of the hybrid is predominantly an artificial affair, from which debt figures cannot be used meaningfully in ratio calculations. Moreover, there do not exist shareholders who have an interest in the 'financial status' of the market-oriented higher education institution (Winston 1997: 34). In line with this inference, it must be claimed that the significance of the solvency ratio or liquidity ratio for hybrids is very questionable. Firstly, once more these ratios are based on artificial balance sheet data. Secondly, these ratios would have to warn against impending bankruptcy. However, the government backup makes bankruptcy rather hypothetical, in spite of proclaimed financial autonomy. This deficient information of the accrual basis accounting system in the hybrid setting leads to the more general conclusion that will be formulated below.

[11] Recently, Koelman has calculated financial status ratios concerning the Dutch higher education institutions (Koelman 1998).

The marketisation trend shifts the emphasis in the management of an institution from hierarchy and regulation towards incentives and managerial discretion. The higher education institution is increasingly encouraged or forced by the government to carry out contract research and contract education and to handle output based budgets. Financial autonomy and responsibility for real estate assets fit in this marketisation trend. It concerns institutional changes in higher education that require a different type of information, that is, managerial information based on financial data and shadow prices. We have argued that the balance sheet account and the revenue and expense account balance cannot produce reliable information on costs and profits which is required for the market-like situations promoted by the marketisation policies. For example, the matching principle appears to be inapplicable. A more basic conclusion is that the inconsistent application of the commercial accounting principles disrupts the incentives that marketisation aims to promote. It may be claimed that the limited 'bottom line environment' (no real threat of bankruptcy) of the market-oriented higher education institution provides latitude for ignoring the market incentives; for example, the governmental budgets may remove the threat of serious market signals. Therefore, the inconsistent application of the accrual basis accounting system and the limited working of incentives may strengthen each other.

Finally, the accounting problems identified ask for solutions. For instance, hybrids may require an explicit planning mechanism, in the same manner as non-profit organisations do. Such a mechanism will set priorities, determine resource allocation patterns and decide what programme services will be provided (see Wasch 1993: 6). At the same time, it must be stressed that non-profit characteristics such as external reporting requirements, diffuse objectives and accompanying measurement difficulties apply to hybrids as well, and will frustrate the planning mechanism. Nevertheless, the hybrids may apply 'business tools' such as variable costing and flexible budgeting, standard cost, and work measurement techniques, to reduce inefficiency (see Wasch 1993: 2).

7.   CONCLUSIONS

Marketisation of higher education, constituting one of the major institutional changes in European higher education over the last fifteen years, was the central issue in this chapter and was defined as the introduction of market-type mechanisms. Market-type mechanisms are arrangements characterised by the presence of at least one significant feature of markets (competition, choice, pricing, dispersed decision-making, monetary incentives, and so on). Contract research and contract teaching (providing programmes for specific customers) are the two types of marketisation that are mentioned most often.

In most Western European countries up to now the introduction of market-type mechanisms has been an incremental process of relatively small steps. Government regulation has been and will remain a major coordinating mechanism in higher education. For that reason, markets in initial higher education can never be more than *quasi-markets*.

In section 3 it was pointed out that the theoretical underpinning of marketisation processes does not lie in neoclassical economic theory. This point of view may be contrary to popular belief. Although the market is central in neoclassical analysis, it is the modern micro-economic approach of new institutional economics that constitutes the theoretical base for marketisation. In contrast to neoclassical economics, new institutional economic theory proclaims a pragmatic approach to the market failure questions. Higher education, having positive external effects, does not per se require governmental intervention.

The introduction of marketisation has various consequences for the organisation, management and mode of operation of higher education institutions. In general, one can argue that marketisation in higher education causes higher education institutions to become more and more 'hybrid' organisations, that is, bodies which operate in both the public and private domains, both fulfilling public duties and undertaking commercial market activities. As a result they become a mixture of both a governmental institution and a commercial enterprise.

In section 4 it was argued that hybrid institutions of higher education have strong and weak points. Strong points are particularly the generation of additional income and the development of a more enterprising attitude. Important weak points relate to unfair competition with private firms and the exclusion of public duties. Concerning the weak points of hybrid institutions of higher education it was concluded that regulatory arrangements are necessary to bring the risks arising from them under control.

Hybrid institutions of higher education will have to be accountable regarding their public tasks as well as regarding their commercial activities.

Accountability, however, is impossible without accounting. However, what kind of accounting is required? This question was tackled in the remaining sections of this chapter.

Because of their market activities, institutions of higher education have more sources of income than they have ever had before. These new flows of money have to be accounted for in a proper way. It was shown in section 5 that market-oriented activities require accounting principles which basically differ from those applied to traditionally publicly funded institutions which do not, or only to a very small extent, undertake contract activities. Organisation type (non-profit organisation, hybrid organisation or private enterprise) and informational issues are highly interconnected. The move to marketisation necessitates commercial accounting principles (e.g. accrual basis accounting). In a market-like environment the accounting system is an indispensable source of management information.

However, as was explained in section 6, the application of commercial accounting principles in these hybrids is problematic. Non-market financial data such as government budgets distort the comparison between costs and revenues. Therefore, it turns out to be extremely difficult to realise consistently the internal function of the commercial accounting system. At the same time, consistent internal information is indispensable to meet the market signals. The proper realisation of the external function of commercial accounting is not without problems either. It has been pointed out that the information products of external commercial accounting are more or less meaningless in the hybrid setting of market-oriented institutions of higher education. Moreover, hybrid higher education institutions do not have shareholders. This absence attenuates the managerial incentives and may even result in adverse effects.

Finally, it has been argued that incentives and accrual basis accounting principles are highly interactive. Establishing incentives by means of marketisation induces the accrual basis accounting system. On the other hand, inconsistent application may disrupt these incentives. Nevertheless, to promote efficiency, hybrids may use accounting tools such as variable costing, standards for cost, and work measurement techniques.

References

Bartlett, W. and J. Le Grand (1993), The theory of quasi-markets, in: J. Le Grand and W. Bartlett (eds.)., *Quasi-Markets and Social Policy*, London: Macmillan.

Bishop, M., J. Kay and C. Mayer (1994), *Privatisation and Economic Performance*, Oxford: Oxford University Press.

Bohm, P. (1973), *Social Efficiency: a concise introduction to welfare economics*, New York: Wiley.

Coase, R.H. (1937), The nature of the firm, *Economica*, vol. 4, pp. 386–405.

Coase, R.H. (1960), The problem of social cost, *Journal of Law and Economics*, vol. 3, pp. 1–44.

Coase, R.H. (1994), *Essays on Economics and Economists*, Chicago: The University of Chicago Press.

Demsetz, H. (1991), The exchange and enforcement of property rights, in: H. Demsetz (ed.), *Ownership, Control and the Firm*, vol. I, Oxford: Basil Blackwell, pp. 31–46.

Dill, D. and B. Sporn (1995), The implications of a postindustrial environment for the university: an introduction, in: D. Dill and B. Sporn (eds), *Emerging Patterns of Social Demand and University Reform: through a glass darkly*, Tarrytown, NY: Elsevier Science/IAU Press, pp. 1–19.

Garette, B. and B. Quelin (1994), An empirical study of hybrid forms of governance structure: the case of the telecommunications equipment industry, *Research Policy*, pp. 359-412.

Harrold, R. (1998), Resource allocation, in: B.R. Clark and G. Neave (eds), *The Encyclopedia of Higher Education*, Oxford: Pergamon Press, pp. 1464–76.

Hendriksen, E.S. and M.F. van Breda (1991), *Accounting Theory*, 5th edn, Homewood: Irwin.

Higher Education Funding Councils (1996), *Treasury Management Value for Money: national report*, May.

Kaiser, F., R.J. Florax, J.B. Koelman and F.A. van Vught (1992), *Public Expenditure on Higher Education*, London: Jessica Kingsley Publishers.

Kaiser, F. and P.H. van der Meer (1999), *Market-type mechanisms in higher education. An exploration into conditions for competitive markets in five Western higher education systems*, paper presented at the Politicologenetmaal, Doorn.

Koelman, J.B.J. (1998), De financiële positie van hogescholen. Kengetallen, normen en een empirische toepassing, *Tijdschrift voor Hoger Onderwijs*, vol. 16, pp. 275–97.

Neave, G. and F.A. van Vught (1991), Conclusion, in: G. Neave and F.A. van Vught, (eds), *Prometheus Bound*, Oxford: Pergamon Press.

Niklasson, L. (1996), Quasi-markets in higher education. A comparative analysis, *Journal of Higher Education Policy and Management*, vol. 18, pp. 7–22.

Niswonger C.R. and P. Fess (1977), *Accounting Principles*, 12th edn, Cincinnati: South-Western Publishing Co.

OECD (1997), *Ministerial Symposium on the Future of Public Services*, http://www.oecd.org//puma/gvrnance/minister/glossary.htm

Twist, M.J.W. van and R.J. van In 't Veld (1999), Public organizations in the market place. Risks, profit opportunities and conditions for existence, *NIG Working Papers*, no. 99–5, Enschede.

Veld, R.J. In 't (1995), *Spelen met vuur. Over hybride organisaties*, Den Haag: Vuga.

Wasch, R.S. (1993), Budgeting in nonprofit organizations, in: R. Rachlin and H.W.A. Sweeny (eds), *Handbook of Budgeting*, 3rd edn, New York: Wiley & Sons, Inc., chapter 31, pp. 1-39.

Williams, G.L. (1995), The 'marketization' of higher education: reforms and potential reforms in higher education finance, in: D. Dill and B. Sporn (eds), *Emerging Patterns of Social Demand and University Reform: through a glass darkly*, Tarrytown, NY: Elsevier Science/IAU Press, pp. 170–93.

Winston, G.C. (1997), Why can't a college be more like a firm?, *Change*, vol. 29, pp. 33–8.

Winston, G.C. (1999), Subsidies, hierarchy and peers: the awkward economics of higher education, *Journal of Economic Perspectives,* vol. 13, pp. 13–36.

Wolf, C. jr. (1979), A theory of non-market failure: framework for implementation analysis, *Journal of Law and Economics,* vol. 22, pp. 109–39.

Chapter 9

Hey, big spender!
Institutional responsiveness to student demand

HANS J.J. VOSSENSTEYN AND IAN R. DOBSON

Key words: institutional responsiveness; marketing; marketisation

1.   INTRODUCTION

In many countries, market-like mechanisms have been introduced into the traditionally public domain of higher education. The main drive for this has come from the government's realisation that it has only limited steering capacity through planning and control mechanisms (Van Vught 1997). Many governments aim at enlarging the adaptive capacity, flexibility, efficiency and quality of higher education. In short, governments took a step back and, by implementing market-like policy instruments, they hoped to make higher education institutions more accountable and responsive to the needs of society. These new steering strategies have led to developments such as deregulation (by providing more autonomy to institutions); competition (between public and private institutions for student places and research funds); the implementation of quality assessment; and the introduction of or raising of customer (tuition) fees (Dill 1997).

Responsiveness to the needs of society implies that higher education institutions are affected by demands from stakeholders such as the government, business, the academic community (peers, disciplines and other institutions) and students. In this chapter, the key focus is responsiveness towards the student population. The student perspective is of particular interest because, as a result of the 'massification' of higher education, there appears to be a growing diversity within the student population. The expanded variety of available study modes, and the diversity of the students themselves (as reflected in income level, social background, age, nationality and occupational status) imply that one can no longer speak of the 'standard' student. This increased diversity of the student body increases the pressure on the institutions to respond to the demands of the student clientele.

Not just the demands as such are important, but also the fact that the institutional resources are dependent on the number of students enrolled and on the students' achievements. The allocation mechanisms used by governments distribute public subsidies between institutions and put an increasing emphasis not just on the number of students, but also on their performance. As Vossensteyn *et al.* (1998) show, students have indirect allocative power because they can vote with their feet.

What is more, many governments are requesting that students should contribute more to the costs of their training. Students have started to become 'big spenders' in terms of educational expenses. The 'massification' of higher education not only led to an enormous growth in the funds needed for higher education, it also created a growing potential source of revenue. In some countries, such as the Netherlands, Poland, Russia, the United Kingdom and the United States, tuition fees are becoming an increasingly important source of income for higher education institutions. In countries like Australia, tuition fees have gradually been reintroduced. In other countries such as Austria, Germany, Portugal and a number of Central European and African countries, the introduction or increase in tuition fees in public higher education is under discussion (Eurydice 1999).

As a result of all this, higher education institutions are increasingly forced to realise that students are important customers who behave in many ways like the consumers of other goods and services, demanding a rightful say in service quality and delivery. Institutions, therefore, may be expected to become more responsive to student demand. Thus the central question we would like to address is whether higher education institutions indeed are becoming more customer-oriented as their revenue becomes more dependent on students.

After a brief reflection on the 'marketisation' of higher education and the supplier-customer relationship in higher education, institutional responses towards a stronger customer position of students are explored. We will do this using insights from the marketing literature, focusing on pricing, product, provision and promotion strategies. Our arguments will be illustrated by giving evidence from two countries, Australia and the

Netherlands, where students increasingly have been asked to contribute to the costs of their study. The chapter concludes with the notion that higher education institutions tend to increase their efforts in the field of communication and counselling towards their (potential) students, encouraged as they are both by government demand for accountability and by the demand for transparency and quality on the part of students.

2.   MARKETS IN HIGHER EDUCATION

In studying the reactions of higher education institutions to increased student demand, we are particularly interested in the phenomenon of higher education markets. In general, the concept of the 'market' is subject to varying interpretations and definitions. Following Leslie and Johnson (1974) we define a market as 'an area over which buyers and sellers negotiate the exchange of a well-defined commodity'. As such, the basic characteristics of markets are prices, competition (i.e. the market structure) and freedom of choice. The price mechanism provides information on the comparative value of goods and services and as such provides direction to the demand and supply of goods (Van der Aa 1998; Walsh 1995). In this sense, market mechanisms can be regarded as incentives to make well-informed decisions. In examining a dynamic sector such as higher education, it is important to recognise that there is not a single market, but rather multiple and interrelated markets, such as for teaching programmes, research and a labour market for academic professionals (Dill 1997).

The 'marketisation' of higher education is a trend that is taking place in the broader context of the general shift towards decentralisation, the increase of competition and the introduction of 'managerial approaches in the public sector'. The so-called 'new public management' literature, which received a lot of attention during the 1980s and 1990s, also discussed market-like approaches which aim to create a more direct link between the suppliers and users (customers) of public services in order to make suppliers more accountable and responsive to the needs of society (Hood 1991; Osborne & Gaebler 1992). Examples of this development can be found in the United States and the United Kingdom where the traditional role of government as both the provider and purchaser of health care and social security services was altered by the creation of quasi-markets where the government buys services through contracts from more or less independent service providers (Le Grand & Bartlett 1993). Other ways of introducing market mechanisms into public services are through charging user fees for public services, or outright privatisation (Walsh 1995).

Higher education is one of the public services which also has been increasingly exposed to market forces (Goedegebuure *et al*. 1994; Williams 1995). The transition of an elite system of higher education to a 'mass' system has been accompanied by the desire to allocate public funds more efficiently and to make higher education institutions more accountable for their use of public funds. Many governments for instance have moved from input-based budgeting, whereby the state supplies educational services, towards output- and performance-based budgeting, in which suppliers receive resources to the extent to which they provide services that satisfy the consumers (Williams 1995).

The marketisation of higher education is also reflected through the increase of students' contributions to the costs of their training. The number of countries where tuition fees are charged or their introduction is considered is increasing. Indirectly, students also are contributing more to the costs of their training because in many student support systems grants are gradually being replaced by loans (Vossensteyn *et al*. 1998).

The rationale for student contributions lies in the 'human capital' perspective, which means that graduates, on average, have better labour market prospects and higher future earnings compared to non-graduates. However, the private benefits argument will have to be balanced with the external effects, or public good character of higher education. Higher education has an effect on the nation's competitive position and its economic growth (Bowen 1977; OECD 1998). In addition, universities have some general societal responsibilities: to truth, to professional integrity and to long-term cultural traditions (Williams 1995).

An analysis of the provision of a commodity such as higher education through structures that incorporate — to some extent — elements of market-type mechanisms, will have to pay attention to criteria such as (Le Grand & Bartlett 1993):

- *efficiency*, which refers to the conception that public services have to offer 'value for money';
- *choice*, which concerns the extent to which customers can choose with respect to the quantity and quality of services and providers;
- *responsiveness*, which is the idea that higher education institutions take into account the demands of their stakeholders (students, business, government); and

– *equity*, which states that services should be delivered on the basis of need, irrespective of factors such as income, socio-economic status and gender.

The central issue of this chapter, which is the responsiveness of higher education institutions to their student clientele, is covered particularly by the second and third criteria. Higher education institutions can only be responsive to the demands of students, and students are only able to make well-founded educational choices if the market is transparent and all stakeholders are financially motivated (Dill 1997). Thus, both providers and purchasers need to have access to accurate and reliable information about the quality of the educational services provided. In addition, providers and purchasers ought to be motivated to react to market signals such as the financial consequences of their choices. For instance, students will only reveal their real preferences if they feel the monetary consequences of their behaviour. Likewise, higher education institutions will only charge 'reasonable' prices if competition (or regulation) forces them to look closely at their costs.

2.1 The student perspective

Traditional economic theory assumes that people try to maximise their 'utility' given their preferences. In terms of educational choice, this implies that, from the full range of alternatives, (potential) students will try to choose an educational career which will bring them an optimal ratio of costs and benefits (Johnes 1993). Costs refer mainly to contributions students and their families have to make towards training costs, living costs and earnings foregone. Benefits relate to the monetary benefits of future job positions.

However, research on educational choice has shown that student choice is not only driven by financial motives, but also by a range of other factors, such as the student's social background, academic ability, aspirations, etc. (Hossler *et al.* 1989). Tuition fees and financial subsidies seem to have a limited effect on overall enrolment rates (in the United States), but may have a different impact on students from different socio-economic backgrounds and in different educational sectors (Leslie & Brinkman 1987; Heller 1997). Furthermore, the variety among students also seems to translate into the different importance attached to different motivations for college choice.

Students seem to behave according to different decision styles (Teunis 1996). Some students make use of a *rational style* in which they try to choose an institution and programme that will bring the highest expected utility. Others use a more *intuitive style* in which emotions dominate the educational choice process. The final category is the *dependency style* in which students make individual choices based on the opinion of 'important others', such as parents and friends. This approach suggests that (potential) students make only limited use of information on educational opportunities.

Nevertheless, it seems obvious to expect that students as consumers will wish to acquire the knowledge and skills that will raise the value of their own future labour and possibly bring other benefits as well (Williams 1995). In addition, one may expect monetary motives to be stronger in cases where the students' financial contributions to the costs of their training are higher.

2.2   The institutional perspective

If higher education institutions, in terms of resources, become more dependent on students, either by students' direct contributions or by their intermediary role in the funding formulae used for allocating public budgets, we would expect that institutions also will become more sensitive to student demand. Therefore, we would expect institutions to develop strategies to successfully recruit students and provide them with a quality education. Following this line of argument, providing information on the quality of a study programme (in other words: its value added compared to other programmes) to (potential) students is an important element in the university's strategy (Dill 1997). Information on the quality of higher education is also important for governments as they are the principal funding agents in most countries. Governments will want to hold higher education institutions accountable for the use of 'taxpayers money'. However, in many higher education systems, information on the price, costs and quality of study programmes is unavailable or limited. As such, students would have to rely upon academic (research) reputations and the status of institutions and accreditation or government licensing of programmes. Only in a limited number of countries have initiatives been taken to overcome these 'informational market failures'. For instance, 'league tables' or rankings based on student surveys, institutional data, graduation rates, duration of courses, quality of services, job placement rates of graduates, etc., are published in popular journals and magazines in Germany, the Netherlands and the UK. In addition, many governments impose quality assurance systems in order to stimulate the improvement in the quality of teaching, learning and research. Both developments have in common the assumption that if more knowledge about alternatives, programmes and the quality of teaching and learning is made public, the market would function better and higher education institutions would be more responsive to student demand, because students will actually use such information in their enrolment decisions (Dill 1997).

With respect to the issue of prices acting as a signalling device, it must be remembered that even in the market-oriented system in the United States, history has demonstrated that tuition fees do not always seem to be a sufficient incentive to make higher education institutions provide satisfactory market information about their programmes (Dill 1997). Nevertheless, one can expect that in the situation of a growing dependency on income generated from student contributions, higher education institutions will be inclined to respond to student demand and will increase their efforts to convince (potential) students to choose their particular institution ahead of others.

2.3   Marketing in higher education

The literature on the marketing of higher education may provide some useful insights in our analysis of institutional responsiveness to student demand in Australia and the Netherlands. Marketing policies and instruments are particularly important in highly competitive higher education markets. For example, they have a long tradition in the United States (see e.g. Simerly 1989) and appear to be of growing interest in European countries (Clark 1998). Marketing is an organisational orientation which puts the customer at the centre of the decision-making process, and can bring about a shift in culture in higher education (Smith *et al.* 1995). The logic of marketing is very simple: 'It identifies consumer needs, then develops, produces, promotes, and delivers a product to fill those needs' (Topor 1983). For non-profit organisations, such as higher education institutions, this is an oversimplified perception of the marketing concept, because higher education institutions have to be accountable to a variety of customers and stakeholders. Even if one focuses only on the student–institution relationship (leaving aside the relationships between higher education institutions and governments, employers, business, alumni, parents, donors, etc.), institutions must be aware that students enter higher education for a range of reasons, including career development, delayed career choices, intellectual curiosity and self-development, and moderated by the variety of income levels, social backgrounds, age, nationality and occupational status of students (Conway & Yorke 1991). Given this variety within the student clientele, higher education institutions have to deal with a complex range of smaller markets (niches) each of which needs a different information stream if institutions are to be genuinely more responsive to their customers.

From the marketing literature, one can find four major instruments — the four Ps — which higher education institutions might use in their marketing strategies towards students (Smith *et al.* 1995):

1. *Price*: Higher education institutions might influence the attractiveness of their products through pricing strategies, which concern charging tuition fees or providing student support. However, in many countries, tuition and student support policies are fully regulated by government.
2. *Product*: Institutions might try to address the needs of a particular group of students or a wide range of students through offering a particular mix of programmes. One can think of programme diversity in the sense of offering programmes at different levels, in different disciplines, or at different locations. In addition, institutions might want to attract students through providing other facilities, for example, concerning sports and culture as well as welfare and housing services.
3. *Provision*: Institutions might influence their attractiveness by the mode of delivery, that is, the way in which they offer their programmes. This could be, for example, through classroom-based teaching, problem-based or computer-based learning, part-time education, distance education or dual learning structures in which working and learning are combined.
4. *Promotion*: Institutions might develop strategies for promoting their products. In doing so, first, they will have to identify their target group. Then they will have to communicate with the potential students to create awareness and promote their services. Finally, institutions might seek to improve the satisfaction of students through surveys, counselling, alumni policies and graduate monitoring.

3.   MARKETISATION IN HIGHER EDUCATION: AUSTRALIA AND THE NETHERLANDS

The increased acceptance of the extent to which market mechanisms are permitted to influence the provision of formerly bureaucratically organised public services has also become manifest in Australia and the Netherlands. These two countries are outstanding examples of places where national economic pressures accompanied by a huge expansion in the demand for higher education can be viewed as the driving forces behind a gradual increase in competition, contract activities in the fields of teaching and research and increased private contributions. In order to facilitate the introduction of these market-like mechanisms, existing regulations have been relaxed through providing institutions with more autonomy in areas such as funding, staffing and curriculum organisation (Williams 1995).

3.1 Australia

To a large extent, one can equate the recent 'marketisation' in Australian higher education with the payment of fees.

For Australian students, there had been a system of (at least) partial fees for higher education, which was removed (from 1974) following the election of the Whitlam government in November 1972. By 1974, therefore, Australian higher education was funded virtually exclusively from government sources. Between 1974 and 1985, Australian higher education was free of tuition fees except for some contributions demanded from students to fund student facilities including catering facilities, sports centres, counselling services, housing and job finding services, and cultural and political student associations.

In 1985, higher education fees began to appear again. Initially, the government established a 'Higher Education Administration Charge' (A$250 per student) followed by fees for certain Australian postgraduate students in 1986. In particular, these postgraduate fees had an impact on the concept of 'the market' for universities. Universities were quickly able to work out which courses had a 'market value', and which courses did not. As a result, there has been an explosion in the number of students enrolling in coursework MBAs (Masters of Business Administration), and in the number of universities offering the degree. Also, many masters by coursework programmes in health sprang up to meet an apparent demand in the student market.

The most common fee in Australian higher education is HECS — the Higher Education Contribution Scheme — which was introduced in 1989 (Chapman 1997). In its first years of operation, all undergraduate students paid HECS at the rate of about 23% of the average costs of study. HECS is an ingenious scheme, in that students have the choice of either paying their tuition fees 'up front' and receiving a 25% discount or repaying their HECS debt through a contingent liability scheme after graduation. In the latter case, graduates are permitted to repay it via the taxation system once their annual salary reaches about the average Australian earning income (around

A\$20,000 in the early 1990s). This system was seen by most students and parents as being 'fair'.

In 1997, the uniform tuition fee aspect was removed from the scheme; HECS was increased and differentiated into three cost bands based on a combination of the relative cost of course delivery and the relative 'profitability', that is, the rate of return of certain programmes. For instance, law, which is relatively inexpensive to deliver, was placed in the top HECS band (along with medicine, dental science and veterinary science) on the grounds that graduates could anticipate higher future incomes.

1998 saw a new set of changes, in that universities were permitted (within constraints) to charge full fees for local undergraduates who were admitted on top of the agreed number of funded undergraduates by the Commonwealth government. These students were not allowed to make use of the HECS payments. However, universities were limited in the numbers they were permitted to accept on a full fee-paying basis but, nonetheless, a few universities took full fee-paying local undergraduates in the first year of the scheme.

When overseas students were first admitted to Australian higher education institutions, they were funded as a part of foreign aid programmes. Later, there were also 'private' overseas students (paying the same fees as Australian students) but, from 1974, overseas fees were fully subsidised by the government. From 1980, 'private' overseas students were required to pay an 'overseas student charge' (which was well below the average course cost) to the government. Further policy changes saw the establishment of a scheme from 1986 whereby private overseas students paid full fees direct to universities. By 1990, this was the situation for all overseas students but those with scholarships were allowed to pay a reduced rate.

The Dawkins reforms in the 1980s also created new universities out of former Colleges of Advanced Education and, although there is still clearly a pecking order among universities, the quest for students became much more competitive. Massification itself provided access to many more students. The Dawkins reforms also forced all universities to be more accountable for their use of public funds, and a set of documents referred to collectively as 'educational profiles' has become an annual requirement since 1988. The educational profile is an agreement between an institution and the Commonwealth on the range of activities covering teaching and research. The agreed profiles constitute the basis on which Commonwealth funding is provided.

Other factors relevant to the expansion of 'the market' in higher education include the formal 'quality' processes in which Australian universities participated in 1994, 1995 and 1996 (helped, no doubt, by the considerable rewards offered to universities adjudged to have demonstrated their 'quality'), and the various informal 'quality' processes, such as the wider use and publication of the results of the Course Experience Questionnaire, the Graduate Destination Survey, and the annual University of the Year 'competition'.

3.2   The Netherlands

With the publication of the policy document 'HOAK' (*Hoger Onderwijs: Autonomie en Kwaliteit*; *Higher Education: Autonomy and Quality* 1985), the Dutch government indicated that it wanted to revise its traditional 'controlling' strategy and increase institutional autonomy in order to enhance the adaptability and flexibility of the higher education system in response to the growing variety in demand (Van Vught 1997). This increased autonomy was expressed for instance through lump sum funding, which enhanced institutional autonomy in financing, staffing, management, administration and facilities.

Parallel to this, public funding per student declined and the accountability of institutions was stressed. In addition, a funding mechanism that included the performance of institutions in terms of graduate numbers and research output was introduced in the early 1990s.

A system of quality control was instituted by the higher education sector in reaction to the idea that the Minister might establish an inspectorate which would closely monitor the quality of higher education study programmes (Van Vught 1997). The government established an inspectorate which was given the task of 'meta-evaluation'. The quality assessment system is based on separate peer review of teaching and research programmes. It produces reports, written by the visiting committees of external peers, partly based on institutional self-evaluations, which are made public. The media increasingly makes use of the reports on teaching to inform the public about the quality of study programmes and to rank higher education institutions per disciplinary area.

The most important way in which market mechanisms have manifested themselves has been the gradual increase in private contributions that students have to make to the costs of their training. Although tuition fees have a long tradition in Dutch higher education — starting in 1876 — they started to increase gradually from 1980 onwards. On average, the level has been increased annually by NLG 100 up to a level of NLG 2.250 in 1994. Then the government proposed an increase of an additional NLG 1.000 in order to cover a budget deficit. Due to student agitation, parliament accepted a compromise that tuition fees would be increased by NLG 500 over a three-year period (1996–98) on two conditions: one, students from lower-income families would be compensated through the student support scheme by means of supplementary grants; and two, higher education institutions should ensure that students could complete their degrees within the nominal duration of study (*studeerbaarheid*), thereby reducing total outlays on student support. The Minister established a so-called incentive fund (*Studeerbaarheidsfonds*) to encourage educational innovations and to stimulate institutions in guaranteeing that study programmes could be completed within a reasonable time frame. Higher education institutions could draw money from this fund if their 'quality management plans' were accepted. These quality management plans were assessed by an independent committee in three annual rounds, starting in 1996.

The increased attention paid to quality has led also to the publication of the government sponsored *Hoger Onderwijs Keuzegids* (Higher Education Consumer Guide), through which the Ministry of Education has supplied information to potential students about the range of study programmes offered as well as about aspects of organisations, facilities, support, etc. It was first published in 1992. In addition, a monitoring system providing information on the labour market position for graduates was set up in 1995.

Over time, students have been asked to contribute more to their study costs through the revisions in the system of student support. Grants have gradually been reduced and replaced by loans. Furthermore, study progress requirements, which made students' grant support dependent on academic achievement, were imposed in 1993.

4.   INSTITUTIONAL RESPONSIVENESS TO STUDENTS

The introduction of market-type elements and quality assurance systems in Australia and the Netherlands was partly carried out in the belief that this would improve educational quality and provide better information to clients and the general public. One therefore might expect institutions to become more responsive to the demands of students. Looking at the various marketing instruments, we will now explore whether higher education institutions in Australia and the Netherlands have in fact taken initiatives to become more sensitive to the demands of students. We will explore and discuss the use of pricing, product, provision and promotion strategies of the institutions.

4.1   Australia

Pricing
There are limits to the extent 'price' can be varied by institutions. For instance, HECS levels are set by the government, and institutions have little if any capacity to vary the levels. The situation is further complicated by the fact that HECS is charged not according to the study programmes students are enrolled in, but on the subjects (courses) which are the components of their programmes. In other words, a BA student enrolled in humanities subjects will pay less HECS than another BA student enrolled in psychology, economics or mathematics subjects which carry a higher HECS charge.

It is with overseas students that the concept of marketisation became very clear in Australia. Education has become one of Australia's principal exports. A rapid increase in the enrolment of overseas students, to the point that they comprised 11% of the total number of students in 1998, has made Australia one of the leading countries in education export. Competition between universities has become fierce, and most universities now have substantial 'International Student Offices' to promote themselves, and to provide student support when overseas students are in Australia. The countries from which most students come are Malaysia, Singapore and Hong Kong. The sensitivity of the overseas student market to the current economic situation of these Asian countries seems to be limited, which was shown during the Asian currency crisis of 1996–97 (Dobson, Hawthorne & Birrell 1998). However, there remains disquiet at the declining pattern of applications for student visas from some Asian countries.

Full fees for overseas students are required to cover both costs of tuition and a capital component. Despite this, there is some room for price adjustment through practices ranging from 'woolly' accounting to providing students with 'scholarships' which grant discounts of 25% or 50% off the prescribed course fee. Other forms of competition between institutions come through fees payment plans, discounts for siblings or alumni, variable entry standards and recognition of prior study for credit, as well as course content.

Despite the fact that universities are now permitted to charge full fees to Australian undergraduates on a limited basis, few universities have taken up this opportunity. (There were only 449 equivalent full-time undergraduates out of a population of over 275,000 in the first semester of 1998.) Much of the demand for full fee-paying places by Australian students is in law. Medicine would also have no trouble attracting local students willing to pay for a fee-paying place (even at A\$25,000 p.a.), but medicine was specifically precluded by the government as an option. In some cases, the 'fee-paying' component of this new scheme has been illusory, because the institutions provide 'scholarships' equal to the size of the fee to some of the students. In addition, some students may have entered these fee-paying undergraduate courses in the expectation of winning a subsidised (HECS) place in their second year. Some universities also have attempted to attract students from institutions with a lesser reputation into later years of fee-paying courses through claiming that they offer a degree from a 'prestige' university.

Product
Universities endeavour to differentiate their programmes from those offered by other universities, but perhaps more important than this is the way universities seek to differentiate themselves as institutions from other universities. An important influencing factor in all this is the fact that there is a fairly clear institutional pecking order among Australian universities in any given state. The universities at the top of the pecking order also tend to be the older universities, and have medical schools. These are the universities which attract final year school students with the highest entry scores, and they are also the institutions least likely to talk about 'value adding' for their students. Universities also seek the hallmark of external organisations to indicate the professional standing of their courses, and institutions are more likely to repackage existing subjects into new 'courses' for which there is demand, that is, shaping products to meet the needs of niche markets.

In an earlier study, Dobson, Sharma and Haydon (1998) explored a situation in which the academic success of students might become very important for the funding of institutions. They particularly focused on the quality of students, whereas the universities also may have a major influence through improving educational processes. Because the distances in Australia are considerable, only few students move interstate for undergraduate studies, unless they are seeking a place in courses not offered in their own state. Therefore, some universities have sought to 'poach' high scoring 'year 12' students from other states. For instance, the University of Adelaide has found it necessary to offer scholarships to South Australian students as a counter-attack to the University of Melbourne which has aggressively sought to attract some of the country's best students from other states, including South Australia.

Provision

The apparent expansion in the diversity of modes of delivery of courses is also very relevant. The preferred mode of delivery as far as most students are concerned remains full-time, on-campus attendance. However, in light of the needs of many other students, for whom full-time attendance is not possible, there has been an expansion in part-time and distance education modes. Part-time delivery has been particularly important in the expansion of enrolments in business courses, the largest field of study in Australian higher education. Part-time and distance education are also important in the postgraduate market. Some universities have also increased the availability of laboratory-based subjects by offering classes at weekends or by block teaching laboratory sessions in such a way that personal disruption to students is minimised.

Universities have become aware of the need to provide 'quality' in their service. For instance, one can read sometimes in the higher education press of one or other group of overseas students' dissatisfaction with some aspect of their lot. Recently, there was a Deakin University fee-paying postgraduate who actually sued his university on the grounds of 'poor service'. Universities which might have taken 'quality' for granted in the past are now much more diligent in using quality assurance processes at all levels. This is not to say that 'quality' did not exist before students became 'customers', but it is now the case that many universities have incorporated formal quality assurance processes into their activities.

Promotion

Certainly all universities are now more publicity conscious than they perhaps were ten years ago. For most universities, their Strategic Plan heads the suite of publications which seeks to 'place' the university in the market. 'Gloss' is particularly important for the better established fee-paying markets: the overseas student and Australian postgraduate markets.

Some promotion is generated externally, through various student satisfaction and graduate outcomes surveys, and by magazine surveys, such as the one conducted annually by *Asia Week*, which is particularly important for universities in their efforts to compete for Asian-based fee-paying students.

4.2   The Netherlands

Pricing
As far as pricing for educational services is concerned, it should be stressed that tuition fees for regular full-time degree programmes are basically set by the government. From 1996, institutions have been allowed (within certain boundaries) to set their own fees for part-time students and for full-time students who have exceeded the student support eligibility period of six years. This concerns around 18% of the total student population. However, recent research at CHEPS (Jongbloed & Koelman 1999) has shown that institutions make little use of the opportunity to vary their tuition rates for specific groups of students. In determining these 'sanctioned' tuition rates, institutions are concerned with guaranteeing access rather than generating additional income or marketing aspirations.

Institutions are not very active in providing scholarships to students, since student support is mainly organised at the national level. The universities of technology, in particular, have experimented with providing scholarships to high scoring secondary school leavers to persuade them to enrol in an engineering course. In addition, institutions have limited 'hardship' funds for regular full-time students who are no longer eligible for student support. However, they do not use these as a marketing instrument to distinguish themselves from other institutions (as is often the case in the US).

Concerning other teaching activities, such as contract teaching and MBA programmes, these are marketed at cost recovery or competitive prices by the institutions.

Product
Changes in the 'product' mix have definitely occurred in the Netherlands. Huisman (1995) showed that in the period 1974 to 1993 institutions expanded the number of programmes and specialisations to satisfy student demand, partly because institutions became more dependent on student numbers for their state revenues. Since the mid-1990s, programme differentiation in higher education has levelled off because the government tightened the regulations for setting up new programmes and changed the incentives in the funding system from an intake- to an output-orientation. Furthermore, the government (pressed by employers' organisations) has asked institutions to voluntary reassess the nomenclature of their courses and programmes to render them more transparent. (This issue is elaborated further in the chapter by Jenniskens and Morphew.)

In addition, there has been a huge expansion in the market for post-initial training and lifelong learning since the early 1990s. As such, many institutions expanded the range of courses offered at competitive or cost recovery rates. Many MBA programmes have been set up not just by private higher education institutions. These developments have been triggered partly by the growing demand for post-initial training and in reaction to decreases in public funding. The marketing of post-initial courses is also a response to the growing competition from private higher education institutions.

Provision
Many new teaching and learning approaches have been developed and employed as a result of studies on how students learn (see e.g. Terenzini 1998). For instance, when it became clear that the Maastricht University had relatively higher graduation rates as a result of educational innovations (e.g. project-based and problem-oriented teaching), many other institutions started to integrate such methods into their programmes. This was partly in reaction to recommendations made by peers in quality assessments of teaching.

Distance education is one of the areas which is developing relatively fast (Collis & Van der Wende 1999). Recently, this development received a substantial impetus through the facilities offered by new information and communication technologies (ICT). A number of private institutions, such as the *Leidse Onderwijsinstellingen* (LOI), offering business-oriented programmes and official degree programmes are active in this field. They compete with the Open University, which was established in 1984, offering publicly subsidised opportunities for retraining and obtaining a recognised university degree. Furthermore, the use of ICT in traditional higher education institutions through (computer aided) teaching was stimulated by the money allocated through the *Studeerbaarheidsfond*. This was established in 1996 to encourage institutions to strengthen the quality of study programmes and to make it feasible for students to complete the programmes within a limited period of time (Wijnen 1999).

Promotion
The communication and information strategies of Dutch higher education institutions towards their (potential) student population have taken place in three stages as was argued by Jansen (1996). Until the mid-1980s, the information presented to future students was sober, unprejudiced, independent and focused purely on the contents of study programmes. However, in a period of high unemployment in the late 1970s a number of institutions stressed the relatively good labour market prospects of some of their study programmes. This period, in which universities recruited their

students in a 'collegial way', was followed by a decade of commercial competition. In this second stage, from 1985 to 1994, the inflow of new entrants levelled off. This tendency, accompanied by governmental cutbacks to the education budget, reduced the amount of public funds for the institutions. The higher education sector gradually turned into a market where institutions had to compete for students. This became particularly visible through the appointment of professional marketeers and public relations officers and through hiring professional advertising bureaux. The communication to, and recruitment of, future students became highly professional. Institutions tried to distinguish themselves from one another. In the third stage, since 1994–95, a slight decrease in student numbers, accompanied by developments towards performance-based funding, resulted in institutional policies directed at limiting the actual duration of study. In this period, when tuition fees increased, grants were replaced by loans and study progress requirements were introduced. More and more, students demanded value for money, particularly during the somewhat heated debates on the proposals to increase tuition fees in 1995 (Jansen 1996).

Probably the most important changes have taken place in institutions' communication strategies towards their (potential) clients. Since the mid-1980s, institutions have set up large advertising campaigns in newspapers and magazines. In addition, many information services were developed for secondary school pupils. More recently, under pressure from the increased amount of information available on the quality and performance of institutions, the communication strategies towards potential target groups were focused more on programme content, quality and student performance. The scores in national surveys on student satisfaction, the outcomes of quality assessments, the position of graduates in the labour market, the ICT facilities offered by the institutions, as well as the ranking of cities in terms of attractiveness to students, are all used in promotional campaigns. Finally, institutions appear to try to build a corporate image, that is, they present themselves as entrepreneurial or innovative.

Concerning the feedback institutions seek from students, we detect an increased interest in student assessment of the educational experience, course content, examinations, teachers and facilities. In addition, many institutions are seeking ways of improving student counselling and trying to better guarantee students' rights (to get information, to have a say and to complain) and obligations of the Student Charters (Jongbloed en Weusthof 1998). Furthermore, some universities have started requesting their teaching staff to develop and enhance their teaching skills. Finally, Dutch institutions have also started to take an interest in their alumni. Although alumni are not yet playing an important role (compared to the United States), universities in particular are developing alumni policies. For instance, alumni are increasingly involved in PR activities, in communication with future students and in management tasks (Van Vonderen 1995; Voorwinden 1999). Institutions also are strengthening their relationship with graduates through offering post-initial training opportunities.

5.   CONCLUSIONS

In many western higher education systems, the introduction of market-like mechanisms has contributed to the strengthening of the supplier–customer relationship between higher education institutions and their students. The increase in the diversity of the student body due to the massification in higher education and the fact that institutional income is becoming more dependent on the number of enrolled students, either directly through tuition charges or indirectly through the allocation of public funds, have furthered this relationship. Therefore, it can be expected that students will become more demanding concerning the quality of the educational services offered to them, and that institutions will become more responsive to student demand. In this chapter this relationship has been explored for the Australian and Netherlands cases.

It was observed that in both countries institutions have developed initiatives in areas such as quality improvement and performance orientation and in generating additional sources of revenue, for example, through contract activities. These initiatives were partly a reaction to cutbacks and governmental policy incentives to ensure that institutions paid more attention to their performances as well as to the quality of their services. The initiatives also resulted in increased responses to the needs of students and other stakeholders. Higher education institutions therefore employed marketing strategies in order to fine tune their services to the wishes and needs of their potential students. In analysing these strategies, four marketing instruments were used: pricing, product, provision and promotion.

As far as price setting is concerned, tuition charges for regular full-time undergraduate students have remained under strict government regulation in both countries. However, Australian institutions are increasingly exploiting the opportunity to attract full fee-paying students from overseas and from Australia in addition to the student numbers subjected to the HECS fees agreed to by the Commonwealth government. Up to now, Dutch higher education institutions do not extensively make use of the freedom they have to charge their own tuition rates to particular groups of students (part-time students and students who have 'used up' their student support entitlements).

Product differentiation is also strongly regulated by the government in both countries. Notwithstanding this, institutions try to offer new programmes and courses that address needs and trends in student demand. In Australia, as well as in the Netherlands, we observed a large degree of activity in the field of contract teaching and so-called post-initial training courses (e.g. MBA) for students who already had completed a first degree. In the Netherlands, the growth in programmes and specialisations has been halted by the government for the sake of transparency in programme supply.

The way in which higher education programmes are provided has undergone significant changes during the last decade. New approaches to teaching and learning have been introduced aimed especially at creating more individual responsibility and initiative on the part of students. Again, these developments are a reaction by institutions to the demands of students, as well as to the increased call for accountability and quality from government. Although growing diversity in the modes of delivery aims to serve the needs of students, it is also a way for institutions to look for new student markets and to make use of new technologies.

Concerning the promotion instrument, we have observed that, in Australia, institutions have actively 'explored and exploited' markets for overseas students, for example, through setting up International Student Offices. Furthermore, universities have increased their willingness to be flexible in ways to make the 'product' suit the 'customer'. In the Netherlands, institutions have become very active recently in their communication with and recruitment of potential students. Professional advertising campaigns that focus more on the content and quality of study programmes have become important.

It can be concluded that many developments indicate that higher education institutions in Australia and the Netherlands have become more responsive to the demands and needs of students. However, it is not clear yet to what extent institutional responses are new initiatives or a re-packaging of existing material and whether this increased institutional responsiveness can be attributed to the demand of the student clientele or to pressures of other stakeholders (governments, business). What is clear is that the market-like relationship between students and institutions offers some interesting opportunities for further study, particularly as students' private contributions to the costs of their training start to receive much more attention in many countries.

References

Aa, R. van der (1998), *Consumentenkeuze in het hoger onderwijs, Een internationaal vergelijkend onderzoek*, Rotterdam: Nederlands Economisch Instituut.

Bowen, H.R. (1977*), Investment in Learning: the individual and social value of American higher education*, San Francisco: Jossey-Bass.

Chapman, B.J. (1997), Conceptual issues and the Australian experience with income contingent charges for higher education, *Economic Journal*, vol. 107, May, pp. 738–51.

Clark, B.R. (1998), Creating Entrepreneurial Universities: organizational pathways of transformation, Oxford: Pergamon.

Collis, B. and M. van der Wende (eds.) (1999), *The Use of Information and Communication Technology in Higher Education: an international orientation on trends and issues*, Enschede: CHEPS and Faculty of Educational Science and Technology, University of Twente.

Conway, A. and D.A. Yorke (1991), Can the marketing concept be applied to the polytechnic and college sector of higher education?, *International Journal of Public Sector Management*, vol. 4, no. 2, pp. 23–35.

Dill, D.D. (1997), Higher education markets and public policy, *Higher Education Policy*, vol. 10, no. 3/4, pp. 167–85.

Dobson, I.R., L. Hawthorne and B. Birrell (1998), The impact of the 'Hanson' effect and the Asian currency crisis on education exports, *People & Place*, vol. 6, no. 1, pp. 44–51.

Dobson, I.R., R. Sharma and A. Haydon (1998), Undergraduate intakes in Australia — before and after, *Higher Education Management*, vol. 10, no. 1, pp. 43–54.

Eurydice (1999), *Key Topics in Education, Volume I, financial support for students in higher education in Europe: trends and debates*, Brussels: European Commission, Education Training and Youth.

Goedegebuure, L., F. Kaiser, P. Maassen, L. Meek, F. van Vught and E. de Weert (1994), *Higher Education Policy: An international comparative perspective*, Oxford: Pergamon Press.

Heller, D.E. (1997), Student price response in higher education, An update to Leslie and Brinkman, *Journal of Higher Education*, Vol. 68, No. 6, pp. 624-659.

Hood, C. (1991), A public management for all seasons?, Public Administration, vol. 69, no. 1.

Hossler, D., J.M. Braxton and G. Coopersmith (1989), Understanding student college choice, in: J.C. Smart (ed.), *Higher education: Handbook of theory and research*, Volume V, New York: Agathon Press.

Huisman, J. (1995), *Differentiation, Diversity and Dependency in Higher Education*, Utrecht: Lemma.

Jansen, C. (1996), Van onafhankelijke studievoorlichting naar verantwoorde werving, Integratie van instroom-, doorstroom- en uitstroombeleid, in: *Tijdschrift voor Hoger Onderwijs en Management*, vol. 4, pp. 30–34.

Johnes, G. (1993), *The economics of education*, London: The MacMillan Press LTD.

Jongbloed, B.W.A. and P.J.M. Weusthof (1998), *Student en Kwaliteit, Een internationaal inventariserend onderzoek naar de positie van de deelnemer aan het hoger onderwijs*, Enschede: CHEPS, University of Twente.

Jongbloed, B.W.A. and J.B.J. Koelman (1999), *Het retributiebeleid van instellingen voor hoger onderwijs, Een empirisch onderzoek naar effecten, motieven en vormgeving*, Den Haag: Sdu.

Le Grand, J. and W. Bartlett (eds.) (1993), *Quasi-Markets and Social Policy*, London: MacMillan Press Ltd.

Leslie, L.L. and P.T. Brinkman (1987), Student price response in higher education, *Journal of Higher Education*, vol. 58, pp. 181-204.

Leslie, L.L. and G.P. Johnson (1974), The market model and higher education, *Journal of Higher Education*, vol. XLV, no. 1, pp. 1-20.

OECD (1998), *Human Capital Investment: an international comparison*, Paris: Centre for Educational Research and Innovation, OECD.

Osborne, D. and T. Gaebler (1992), *Reinventing Government: how the entrepreneurial spirit is transforming the public sector*, Reading MA: Addison-Wesley.

Put, T. van der (1996), *Werken aan kwaliteit en studeerbaarheid*, Landelijke Studenten Vakbond, Den Haag: Vuga.

Simerly, R.G. (ed., 1989), *Handbook of marketing for continuing education*, San Francisco: Jossey-Bass.

Smith, D., P. Scott and J. Lynch (1995), *The role of marketing in the university and college sector*, Leeds: Centre for Policy Studies in Education, University of Leeds.

Stuurgroep Kwaliteit en Studeerbaarhcid (1995), *Rapportage Stuurgroep Kwaliteit en Studeerbaarheid*, Zoetermeer: Ministerie van Onderwijs, Cultuur en Wetenschappen.

Terenzini, P.T. (1998), *Research and Practice in Undergraduate Education: and never the twain shall meet?*, Paper presented at the 1998 CHER Conference in Kassel, Center for the Study of Higher Education, The Pennsylvania State University, Pennsylvania.

Teunis, U. (1996), *Studie- en Beroepskeuzevoorlichting: het effect van arbeidsmarktinformatie*, Maastricht: ROA.

Topor, R. (1983), *Marketing Higher Education: a practical guide*, Washington DC: Council for Advancement and Support of Education.

Vonderen, J. van (1995), Alumni: stand van zaken alumnibeleid Nederland, in: *Tijdschrift voor Hoger Onderwijs en Management*, nr. 5, pp. 6-7.

Voorwinden, R. (1999), Azen op alumni, *Intermediair*, 18 maart.

Vossensteyn, J.J., B.W.A. Jongbloed and J.B.J. Koelman (1998), *University Funding Mechanisms: a comparative analysis of the funding of universities in eight Western European countries*, Enschede: CHEPS, University of Twente.

Van Vught, F.A. (1997), Combining planning and the market: an analysis of the Government strategy towards higher education in the Netherlands; *Higher Education Policy*, vol. 10, no. 3/4, pp. 211–24.

Walsh, K. (1995), *Public Services and Market Mechanisms: competition, contracting and the new public management*, London: MacMillan Press.

Wijnen, W.H.F.W. (1999), *3000 x beter: Slotrapport Studeerbaarheidsfonds*, Adviescommissie 'Beoordeling Projectvoorstellen Studeerbaarheidsfonds, Zoetermeer: Ministerie van Onderwijs, Cultuur en Wetenschappen.

Williams, G.L. (1995), The "marketization" of higher education: reforms and potential reforms in higher education finance, in: D.D. Dill and B. Sporn (eds.), *Emerging patterns of social demand and university reform: through a glass darkly*, New York: IAU Press.

Chapter 10

Analysis of institutions of university governance

A classification scheme applied to postwar changes in Dutch higher education

HARRY DE BOER AND BAS DENTERS

Key words: democracy; public management; university governance

> *One sort of constitution may be intrinsically preferable, but there is nothing to prevent another sort from being more suitable in the given case; and indeed this may often happen.*
>
> Aristotle, *Politica*, 1296[b]

1.   INTRODUCTION

Governance within higher education is a most complicated issue. Managing a university, variously described as 'monadic chaos' or 'organised anarchy', is a redoubtable challenge. Of all issues currently under discussion in the world of higher education, few are more controversial than those pertaining to the institutions of governance (Neave 1988).[1] Who should govern a university, how, and to what ends, have been recurring questions in the history of universities (De Groof *et al.* 1998). Constitutional issues such as these have been raised passionately, again and again, though obviously there have been quiet times too (Bargh *et al.* 1996). Matters of institutional design

---

[1]   Here we use the term institutions of university governance to refer to the rules and formal procedures pertaining to the making of decisions on policies and their implementation within universities. We occasionally also refer to these institutions of governance as 'constitutions', 'constitutional designs' or 'institutional arrangements'.

211

are deemed of particular importance because, right or wrong, they are considered as essential for realising people's visions of the ideal university (Moodie & Eustace 1974: 23). As such, these issues easily touch upon values like effectiveness, efficiency, the quality of primary processes, democracy, institutional autonomy, academic freedom, or the university's role towards society. Therefore, discussions of institutional design derive their importance and their fervour in part from the fact that they inspire the 'affirmation of legitimate values and institutions' (March & Olsen 1983: 292).

Because the university is one expression of a nation's historic memory, and no country's history is the same as its neighbours', it should be no surprise that structure, practice and procedures within universities show a wide diversity across national systems of higher education (Neave & Van Vught 1991: x–xi). Each country has specific institutional arrangements, though sometimes drawing on the inspiration, success or symbolic importance of practices from abroad. From the moment the first medieval 'universities' evolved, there has been a substantial variety in the institutions universities employed for the management of their affairs. Take for instance the organisational structures of the first archetypal universities in medieval times. The University of Bologna had a structure in which sovereign power was vested in the student community (the 'student dominion'), while the university in Paris was a magisterial university (the master's guild). And Oxford, while borrowing heavily from the Parisian model, adopted its own particular set of institutional arrangements.

The constitutional design of universities has been under discussion ever since. Cobban (1975: 35) states that 'whatever the difference in scale and technology, there is a hard core of perennial problems which have taxed the minds and ingenuity of university legislators from the thirteenth century to the present day'. On the threshold of the third millennium, winds of change have greatly affected the institutional landscapes of university governance in a variety of European nations. Many apologies of reforms in the Western public sector in the 1990s, including higher education, were larded with the 'reinvention' rhetoric that is fashionable in today's literature on public management. In Osborne and Gaebler's best seller *Reinventing Government* (1992) the focus is on 'community-owned' and 'decentralised government', alongside pleas for 'results-oriented', 'enterprising' and 'market-oriented' government. This reinvention rhetoric implies a preoccupation with the dual aims of democracy and effectiveness in public management. By and large this is what is at stake in several Western higher education systems, especially the ones that have, or used to have, a 'state-control model of university governance' (see, amongst others, Maassen & Van Vught 1994).[2]

---

[2]   We should emphasise that this does not imply that the demands for change underlying national government legislation to change institutions of university governance were

It remains to be seen whether the impact of these changes has been merely rhetorical. To what extent have ideas of democracy, decentralisation, efficiency and effectiveness been effectively embodied in traditional and modern institutional designs? In order to provide a systematic answer to such questions we will employ a set of dimensions to classify some main characteristics of the constitutional designs for university governance. This classification scheme will provide us with a basis for a systematic description of institutions of university governance that might be used for two types of descriptive analysis:

1. Synchronic or cross-sectional analysis: comparison of different systems at one moment in time, for example, what are the similarities and differences between the national laws determining the contemporary institutions of university governance in OECD countries? Or, alternatively, what are the similarities and differences between university charters (or similar documents) determining institutions of university governance in a single country?
2. Diachronic or longitudinal analysis: comparison of changes within one system over time, for example, what is the nature of the changes in institutions of university governance in a particular country since 1945?

The results of both synchronic and diachronic analyses will invite at least two new sets of questions for future research. On the one hand, how do we explain variations in institutional arrangements in these different settings? Do these choices reflect different normative theories of constitutional design or are they reflections of radically different local conditions? On the other hand, one might ask whether universities with radically different institutional designs also differ in their performance? In fact, this pertains to the often 'taken-for-granted' assumption that 'governance makes a difference'. But does it? And in what way? Our current aims, however, are more modest, and relate to the use of our tool for descriptive purposes. In this chapter we will employ our classification scheme for a diachronic analysis. We will apply it in a description of changes in the Dutch system of higher education in the period since 1945.

With respect to our classification scheme we readily acknowledge that it only refers to the formal structure of university governance. We recognise

---

primarily motivated by any desire to change internal relations within universities. Often these changes were primarily motivated by a desire to strike a different balance between the state and the universities. Changes in intra-university arrangements were merely the by-products of these new forms of state-university relations (De Groof *et al.* 1998: 13; Neave 1997).

that formal, constitutional rules are not, necessarily, exact guides to the actual conduct of governance (see, for instance, Moodie & Eustace 1974). Although a university's constitutional rules do not provide a complete description of the university's system of governance, it is worthwhile to have a closer look at these constitutions because without understanding these rules we cannot properly understand what is happening within a university (Moodie & Eustace 1974: 17). Institutions of governance — setting the goals of universities and their most important governmental bodies — provide the boundary framework within which the members of the academic community are supposed to act (Neave & Rhoades 1987: 214).

In the next two sections we will introduce two basic dimensions of institutional design that will provide the cornerstones of our classification scheme. These dimensions are: (i) the choice between democracy (government by all members of a community) and guardianship (government by the most qualified members of a community); and (ii) the choice between concentrated or divided powers.

2.   DEMOCRACY AND GUARDIANSHIP

A key concept in the description of the institutions of governance of social organisations is democracy. Universally, this notion has concerned political philosophers interested in the topics of power, authority, order, discipline, steering and freedom. Even though these thinkers have written about democracy, the notion of democracy means different things to different people. In part, this is due to the specific historical conditions in which these concepts were employed. The concept of democracy as used in the works of Plato and Aristotle is completely different from the one employed by a political scientist like Robert Dahl.

The concept of democracy, however, is used by virtually everyone to refer to a system that in one way or another is characterised as 'rule by the people'. But then: who are the people? Who are the 'Demos' or, in other words, who are the 'citizens' who are entitled to rule? A common answer to this question is based on the principle of affected interests (Dahl 1989). This principle states that every adult who is affected by a collective decision should have a say (participate) in making that decision. If we apply this deceptively simple criterion to the context of universities, it is immediately evident that it is not at all clear whose interests are at stake in academic decision-making. For some, the 'academic community' may be considered too narrow, because it would imply that non-academics working at universities were to be excluded. A more inclusive definition, for example, 'those who are on the university payroll constitute the "Demos"', would still exclude students. But even if we agreed that the university 'Demos' comprises academics, non-academics and students, the issue need not be resolved completely. In Portugal, for instance, ex-students form another constituency, represented in university governance. Should they be regarded as members of the university's 'Demos'? And, in the Netherlands, lay members are included in university councils, because it was argued that society at large also had a stake in university decisions. It is clear therefore that various 'democratic' systems may be based on radically different definitions of the 'Demos'. Rather pragmatically we will consider systems as democratic provided they allow participation in university decision-making by academic staff, non-academic staff and students.

A distinctive feature of the democratic creed is the assumption that every adult is qualified to participate, either directly or indirectly through the choice of representatives in making decisions that affect his/her fate (Dahl 1989). Therefore, nobody from the 'Demos' should be excluded from making major decisions. This principle of inclusion is highly distinctive. It means that we do not consider the 'student guilds' of the medieval universities of Bologna and Padua as democratic, because the academics were not allowed to take part in decision-making. It also implies that the notions of self-governance and collegiality, often used and abused in discussions on institutions of university governance, are not necessarily compatible with the concept of democracy (see, amongst others, Bess 1992; Chapman 1983: 14). Generally speaking, institutional self-governance and collegiality (as it is found, for example, in Oxford or Cambridge) typically refer to joint decision-making and shared authority among professionals, while non-academic staff and students are excluded.

The concept of democracy is not without its critics (e.g. Dahl 1989). Many of its opponents forcefully reject democracy, because they argue that 'ordinary' people are clearly not qualified to govern themselves. Not everyone is equipped with the expertise and knowledge that is required to govern. Therefore political power should be entrusted to a minority of persons who are specially qualified to govern on the basis of their superior knowledge and virtue. These highly qualified rulers are often referred to as the guardians. Advocates of 'rule by guardians' argue for the hierarchical subjection of ordinary citizens to the rule of a few enlightened rulers. A textbook example of a plea for hierarchy and guardianship stems from Plato. He firmly believed that some men are superior in their knowledge and that they should be carefully selected and rigorously trained for political leadership. Essential in guardianship is the assumption that people are incompetent, or are insufficiently competent to govern themselves. Consequently, the fundamental distinction between democracy on the one hand and guardianship on the other concerns the question: who is qualified to govern? Are all community members capable of making community decisions, or should the right to participate in decision-making be reserved for a body of meritorious leaders who possess exceptional knowledge and virtue?

According to Dahl (1989: 52):

> *Both as idea and as a practice, throughout recorded history hierarchy has been the rule, democracy the exception. ... In practice, then, hierarchy is democracy's most formidable rival; and because the claim of guardianship is a standard justification for hierarchical rule, as an idea guardianship is democracy's most formidable rival.*

This is the case in the history of university governance too. In practice, in the Western world, the 1970s are generally regarded as the heydays of academic democracy. In several West European countries, university governance was being 'democratised' in the sense of allowing for (equal) representation of the constituent groups on all university bodies (see, amongst others, Daalder & Shils 1982). But, if we employ our rather exacting definition of democracy, in practice, throughout history, democracy in universities has been rare. In their comprehensive analysis of power and authority in British universities, Moodie and Eustace (1974: 228) argue that:

> *The right to take decisions, generally speaking, has either been vested in or has gravitated to those who are informed or learned in relevant ways, or who are at any rate believed to do so.*

Moreover, academic democracy, as an idea, has been heavily criticised. For various reasons it was argued that democracy would weaken academic control over teaching and research, and would gradually result in a decline in academic standards (e.g. Lijphart 1983). These arguments — true or false — can be reduced to the presumption that not all members of the university community (as defined above) are equally enlightened and therefore not every person is equally qualified to rule.

In the organisational context of a university, however, there are at least two bases for legitimate claims to enlightenment. On the one hand one might refer to being a scholar or an expert in a particular academic field (professional authority). On the other hand one might refer to a set of skills related to the 'art of governing' (managerial authority). In fact, the entire notion of academic self-governance has rested upon the claim that scholarship is the primary source of authority within universities, if only because no other source is as firmly rooted in the very essence of universities. For ages, academic communities have argued over the legitimacy of these competing sources of authority. A combination of these rival principles is embodied in the notion of the university as a 'professional bureaucracy' (Mintzberg 1979). The distinction between these two sources of authority is important for our understanding of university governance. Academics and administrators, or managers, play different roles. They operate in partly different environments. This leads academics and managers to construct different — though equally valid — perceptions of reality. These different roles and perceptions may be reinforced or tempered by the choice of the institutions of university governance (Birnbaum 1989).[3]

The distinction between the concept of democracy and the concept of guardianship refers to the first dimension in our classification of university governance structures. The fundamental difference between these concepts manifests itself in radically different systems of selecting rulers. In contemporary democracies, the citizens typically elect those who are to govern. Except for some short-lived experiments in direct democracy, academic democracy has been synonymous with representative democracy. In an academic *democracy* no one belonging to the university 'Demos' should be excluded from the right to vote in elections of representatives who will participate in making the major decisions.[4] *Guardianship* provides an alternative mode of governance. Under this regime, office holders are appointed on the basis of their competence. This competence may bear reference to (some combination of) professional expertise, and managerial expertise. In the following section, we will introduce a second distinctive feature of organisations: the distribution of powers.

---

[3] We will discuss different systems for the allocation of powers over these two distinct groups of actors later in this chapter.

[4] The issue of elections may be very complicated (see Neave 1988). For one thing, the nature of the electoral system will depend on the definition of the 'Demos'; this determines which constituencies are allowed to vote. Many of these complications are due to the fact that powers of governance may be distributed over a number of public offices.

3.   DISTRIBUTION OF POWERS

The concept of power, from the perspective argued here, refers to the legitimate, formal prerogatives of making decisions that are binding on others. In both democratic systems and guardianships, powers may be more or less concentrated. At one extreme, powers may be concentrated in one locus of power. On the other hand, they may be widely dispersed over subsystems within the organisation. The concentration of authorities — 'all' powers in the hands of one body consisting of one or more persons — is often regarded as undesirable, because subjects are at the mercy of an omnipotent ruler, elected or not.

This is a widespread concern both in political theory and in the specialised literature on university governance. In political theory, Aristotle was an early advocate of a mixed constitution. He argued that a mix of democracy (in performing legislative functions) and oligarchy (in performing executive responsibilities) offers probably the best constitution that can realistically be hoped for (Sabine & Thorson 1973: 115–17). Later, the division of powers was conceived as an institutional safeguard against the risks of power concentration. Political philosophers such as Locke, Montesquieu and Kant argued that the freedom of subjects (as guaranteed by inalienable civil rights) is best protected by means of a separation of powers.[5]

Concerns about the dangers inherent in the concentration of powers are also to be found in the literature on institutions of university governance. Clark (1983: 265) points out that the history of higher education clearly shows that anything approaching a monopoly of power becomes the greatest single danger in the operation of a system of higher education. Take, for instance, the situation in the medieval university of Bologna once again. The concentration of powers in the hands of students — with their elected rector — led to a situation in which the statutory controls imposed by students on the tutors were formally so rigorous that, according to Cobban (1975: 63), it might be termed a quasi-totalitarian regime.[6] And Clark (1983: 265) concludes that:

---

[5]   A pure separation of powers, however, is nowhere realised in practice, because a well-defined, conclusive distinction among powers is hardly possible (Van der Pot & Donner 1983). In fact, the very idea of the separation of powers transformed into a system of checks and balances has essentially the same function: the protection of individual freedom.

[6]   This system did not last long. The student dominion ended by the mid-fourteenth century when students lost their controlling power over the appointment of the teaching staff (Cobban 1975).

Dominating trustees in some early American colleges could and did fire presidents and professors for not knowing the number of angels dancing on the head of the ecclesiastical pin, or, in the twentieth century, for simply smoking cigarettes and drinking martinis.[7]

Another argument in favour of the distribution of powers is based on the presumption that decisions based on joint decision-making are more generally accepted. In such a vision, consultation and participation improve the effectiveness of decision-making. Advocates of this line of argument may readily acknowledge that concentration of power might sometimes be helpful in higher education, protecting scholarship or helping to build distinctive enterprises, or activating an immobilised system. In this respect, concentrated powers can respond more quickly, because cumbersome procedures of joint decision-making are avoided. According to Clark (1983: 265), however, concentration of powers does not work well for long, because it soon freezes an organisation around the views of just a few.

Powers may be distributed in either of two ways. The first option is to distribute powers horizontally, that is, powers are divided between two or more bodies on the same level. The second option is to distribute powers vertically, that is, powers are distributed over different organisational layers. In the remainder of this section we address the 'horizontal' and 'vertical' dimensions of power distribution separately. These two dimensions are relevant for both the concept of democracy and guardianship, that is, dispersion of powers might be used in university constitutions where the main office holders are elected (democracy) or appointed (guardianship). Moreover, as is evident from Aristotle, dispersion of powers may even be used to obtain the 'best of both worlds'.

3.1   The horizontal dimension

An important decision to make in constitutional design is whether there should be some form of separation of powers or not. If not, the constitutional design is monocentric. If it is decided that powers are dispersed, there are in theory two main alternatives for a horizontal distribution of powers. Parliamentary government (based on the idea of *fusion of powers*) is a form of governance in which executive authority emerges from, and is responsible to, legislative authority (Lijphart 1984: 68). Alternatively, presidential

---

[7] To be sure, this does not imply that the power of the university president is without any checks.

government (based on the notion of *separation of powers*) implies a high degree of independence between the executive authority and the legislative office.

This may manifest itself in a number of different ways. First, the distinguishing feature of a parliamentary system is that the executive is elected or appointed by the legislature and not as in presidential systems: elected by the people or selected by another principal. In a university setting, a parliamentary system might imply that a representative university council (democracy) or the classical senate (guardianship)[8] elects or appoints the rector[9] who is accountable to that representative council or senate. In this system, the council or the senate can also dismiss the rector from office. By contrast, in a presidential system, in a university context, the president is able to act 'independently' from the council or senate. In such presidential systems, the authorities of president and council or senate are clearly separated.

Second, in parliamentary systems the chief of the executive or the executive board is responsible to the legislature in the sense that he/she is dependent on the legislature's confidence and may be appointed and dismissed by the legislature. In a presidential system, however, the chief executive is relatively independent from the legislature and, apart from exceptions, cannot be dismissed. The chief executive is in charge for a fixed term.

Third, a final contrast between parliamentary and presidential systems refers to the membership of the governing bodies. In principle, a system of separation of powers implies independence of the executive and legislature and, hence, the rule that the same person cannot simultaneously serve in both. A fusion of powers implies that the same persons may be members of both the executive and the legislature (monism). In several countries, however, parliamentary systems do have an incompatibility rule (dualism). Therefore, it is possible to make a subdivision in the class of parliamentary systems, viz. that between monistic and dualistic systems. According to this subdivision, parliamentary systems may differ in the degree of independence of the executive (relatively high degree of independence: dualism; relatively low degree of independence: monism).

---

[8] In this context all constituencies of the university 'Demos' are represented on the university council and, consequently, it is labelled 'democratic'. In the classical university senates, 'only' full professors hold seats ex officio and, consequently, this type of university is to be considered as a 'guardianship'.

[9] Terms may be very confusing, because in parliamentary systems the head of the university may also be called 'president' or, alternatively, in presidential systems these executives may be referred to as 'rectors'.

In all three respects, the difference between presidentialism and parliamentarism is that between a system based on a clear separation of powers and a system based on a fusion of powers. Presidentialism and parliamentarism are two rather distinct alternatives for a monocentric system with concentrated powers.

The formal distinction between two systems is relatively unambiguous. In practice, it becomes somewhat blurred, however, once we realise that there is no deterministic relation between formal arrangements and the primacy of influence of either the executive or the legislature. In principle, three kinds of relationship between the executive and legislature might emerge under both presidential and parliamentary systems (Lijphart 1984: 78).[10] There may be executive dominance, legislative dominance, or a more or less balanced relationship between the executive and the legislature. In practice, maybe counter-intuitively, there is some evidence suggesting that separation of powers rather than fusion of powers could result in a relatively strong position of the legislature vis-à-vis the executive. Parliamentary systems apparently develop a tendency towards executive dominance.[11]

Both systems have their strengths and weaknesses. There is, for instance, the problem of executive stability in parliamentary systems. When the legislature — in the case of university governance, the university council or senate — uses its right to dismiss the executive (that is, the rector), frequently, the functioning of the rectorate will be seriously undermined, and as a result may damage the university severely, especially when it comes to strategic, long-term issues. On the other hand, presidential systems face the potential problem of deadlock. Should the executive and the legislature be unwilling to compromise, constitutional provisions may be necessary to overcome the deadlock. In the absence of such provisions deadlocks might paralyse the university.

---

[10] The distinction between an executive and legislative power implies that we will leave the judiciary aside.

[11] See Moodie and Eustace (1974), especially chapter X, for such a discussion in the context of British universities. Similarly, the effects of monistic and dualistic arrangements in parliamentary systems are difficult to predict. The choice for the monistic variations is often justified by pointing out its assumed positive effects on legislative influence. In this line of thought it is argued that the executive will not develop into a completely separate body, but will remain at arm's length of the legislature. On the other hand it seems plausible that the executive (e.g. a rector) may derive substantial power from his/her double role, resulting in a position of executive dominance over the legislature (for a discussion in the context of Dutch local government see Elzinga 1998).

The above discussion leaves us with four alternative models for the allocation of powers in universities. In theory all four models are conceivable under both a democratic system and guardianship:

1. *Concentration of powers* (monocentrism). This implies an almighty ruler at the apex of the university. Such a rector, or equivalent, holds both the (main) executive and legislative powers, whether he/she is appointed (guardianship) or elected by the university 'Demos' (democracy).[12]

2. *Monistic fusion of powers.* This implies that the legislature (either senate or council) has the power to select and dismiss the executive (e.g. the rector) and hold this office holder accountable. Moreover, the executive remains a member of the legislature (no incompatibility).

3. *Dualistic fusion of powers.* Here too the legislature (either senate or council) has the power to select/elect and dismiss the executive (e.g. the rector) and hold this office holder accountable. However, in this variant, the rector cannot be a member of the council or senate (legislature) at the same time (incompatibility).

4. *Separation of powers.* This corresponds to a situation where a clear separation of powers exists between the rectorate and the representative council or senate. Again, both the rector and the council may be either elected or selected. Both types of office holders are able to operate more or less independently from one another.

3.2   A horizontal subdivision

The issue of the design of institutions of university governance is further complicated by the distinction between 'monocephalic' and 'bicephalic' structures (Neave 1988: 111). This distinction refers to the locus of executive powers. We have argued that two types of qualifications may be relevant for university leadership: specialised knowledge in an academic discipline or general knowledge of the art of governing. In debates on university governance, it is more or less generally accepted that the former type of qualification provides entitlement to participation in executive matters. In *monocephalic* systems this has resulted in a unified structure in which the head of the university is the head of both the academic and

---

[12] Note that we do not label a system as 'purely democratic' when the rector, or equivalent, is elected by the professors only.

administrative hierarchy. In *bicephalic* systems, however, the role of the administrative hierarchy is more prominent. In these structures the rector, or equivalent, is the head of the academic hierarchy, elected by it. But this academic hierarchy is run parallel to an independent administrative hierarchy. This dual structure is to be found in most 'continental' structures of higher education (e.g. Norway, Sweden,[13] Germany and the Netherlands) and has a long history in university governance (Neave 1988; 1997). An important reason for the existence of a separate administrative chain of command alongside the academic hierarchy is the desire of national governments to ensure a certain degree of continuity and to provide some guarantee that the university is managed in accordance with public laws. The apex of the administrative hierarchy therefore is typically appointed by the state and is variously titled as Kanzler, Curator or Director.

3.3   The vertical dimension

The vertical dimension refers to the relations between centralised and decentralised systems. In a fully centralised system, one or more governing bodies at the central level are empowered to take 'all' the decisions for the whole organisation. Powers, however, can also be allocated to lower levels in the organisation. The autonomy of the decentralised units in using these powers may be more or less strongly restricted by various modes of central supervision and financial arrangements. These arrangements of central control are generally introduced to 'organise the anarchy' resulting from the existence of partly autonomous subsystems.

Most students of university governance will probably recognise the inherent tension between subcentral autonomy and the necessity of some mechanisms for central control. If we compare universities to other kinds of organisations, academic institutions are traditionally characterised by a relatively high level of decentralisation. One of the organisational features of universities is the diffusion of decision-making power throughout the organisation (see, amongst others, Maassen & Van Vught 1994). The rationale for this decentralisation is based on the presumption that if production processes are knowledge-intensive, there is a need to decentralise. When knowledge in such a process is highly dispersed, as in the university, with its highly specialised academics, this rationale implies the need for a radical decentralisation of decision-making powers. Many

---

[13] In Sweden, the 1964 reform created the externally appointed head of the entire administration of a university. This position of the Director was abolished, however, by the 1993 reform.

traditional universities have been organised along such lines. Universities are, in Clark's view (1983: 266–7), 'semi-autonomous departments and schools, chairs and faculties that act like small sovereign states as they pursue distinctive self-interests and stand over against authority of the whole'. The chair-faculty structure that was predominant until the late 1960s in most West European countries and principles like 'departmental autonomy', are the reflection of an essentially highly decentralised system.

Decentralisation does not necessarily go hand in hand with a democratic system. In the case of systems of higher education it is quite the contrary. The traditional chair-faculty structure in Germany, for instance, used to be inherently non-democratic. It was based on a system of patronage in which members of the non-professorial class remained highly dependent on individual chair holders (Neave & Rhoades 1987: 211–12).

Advocates of decentralisation would argue that devolution of powers allowed for greater flexibility, increased capacity to acknowledge and deal with 'local' needs and situations, and relieved the administrative burden at the central level. On the other hand, decentralisation might result in a lack of coordination, a loss of economies of scale or 'tribalism' ('Balkanisation'). As a consequence, one analyst argued that universities must continuously be urged to seek the 'benefits of association' (Clark 1983: 269).

That universities are frequently regarded as highly decentralised organisations does not mean that there are no differences among universities in this respect. Generally, several principles may be used to codify the distribution of responsibilities between central and subcentral levels. First, it is possible to enumerate the powers of the central level, and prescribe that all remaining powers are by definition local. Thus the scope of central powers is restricted to those decisions that are specifically mentioned in the constitutional laws. On first sight this might be considered as an indication of severe limitations on central powers. We should keep in mind, however, that central powers may be defined as rather broad and vague, which would still allow the centre wide opportunities to exercise significant powers. A second possibility is that law determines the powers of both the central and decentralised units. A third possibility implies that powers of the decentralised units can be enumerated, leaving the remaining powers to the central level. Finally, the constitution might allocate overlapping powers to the organisational layers, deliberately introducing elements of competition into the organisation. This is the case in the relations between Dutch central and local governments, where the central level uses broad regulations, leaving it up to the decentralised units to fill in the details when implementing central policies (co-governance or 'medebewind') (Toonen 1987: 82–5).

Once more it is difficult to translate formal arrangements into statements on the actual distribution of influence between organisational layers. First, it is difficult to determine the exact degree of decentralisation. These arrangements are multifaceted, including such items as the nature and number of responsibilities, the opportunities to initiate policies, the nature of supervision, the disposal of means, the way office holders are elected or appointed, and so on. It relates to numerous issues which cannot be discussed here in detail. Second, even when one has overcome this hurdle the same institutional arrangements may have radically different effects on influence relations under different conditions. A highly centralised system of faculty funding may work out very differently in the case where a faculty is able to fund part of its activities through alternative sources of revenue (e.g. revenues through commissioned research) compared to the case in which the faculty is totally dependent on central funding (Bleker & van den Bremen 1983: 18–19).

In this chapter we will not be able to conduct a complete analysis of influence relations between central and decentralised bodies in universities. We will restrict ourselves to a qualitative assessment of these relations.

4.   APPLICATION OF THE CLASSIFICATION SCHEME FOR UNIVERSITY GOVERNANCE STRUCTURES

Our analysis is based on four dimensions. The first dimension refers to the degree to which an organisation may be characterised as either a democracy or a guardianship. The second dimension pertains to the *horizontal* distribution of powers in an organisation, that is, the distribution or concentration of powers between a legislature and an executive authority. Here we distinguish between four main types: power concentration, monistic fusion of powers, dualistic fusion of powers and separation of powers. Our third dimension refers to a possible further refinement of the horizontal distribution of powers. In some countries, the executive power in universities is not concentrated in one office (monocephalic system), but is dispersed over two offices (bicephalic system). Our fourth dimension relates to the *vertical* distribution of powers, or the degree of decentralisation in the organisation (see table 1).

In the following descriptions we will use these four dimensions for an analysis of the changes in the institutions of university governance in the Netherlands since 1945. We will concentrate on developments in national legislation and ignore possible variations at the level of individual universities even though local situations may differ even when national laws are highly prescriptive.

Table 1: Institutions of university governance in the Netherlands, 1945–2000

Period	democracy vs.guardianship	distribution of powers	monocephalic vs. bicephalic	decentralisation
prior to 1970	guardianship	fusion of powers: monistic	bicephalic	very decentralised
1970–97	democracy	fusion of powers: dualistic	bicephalic	decentralised
from 1997	guardianship	monocentric	monocephalic	'centralised'

A striking feature of the governance structure of Dutch universities prior to 1970 was its clear bicephalic structure.[14] Authorities of academic and non-academic affairs were clearly separated. At the apex of the administrative hierarchy the *college van curatoren* ('board of curators') was responsible for upholding laws and regulations, for the administration of the university finances, and for personnel policies. They hired and fired, for instance, junior academics, student counsellors and other employees, whilst they made nominations for positions of full and associate professors after having consulted the faculty and the *college van rector en assessoren* (see below). In this system, the *college van curatoren* consisted of five to seven persons, all appointed for a four-year term by the national government. This body generally acted as a mediator between national government and the university. The *college* was accountable to the Minister under this institutional regime. According to the *Wet op het Wetenschappelijk Onderwijs 1960* (Act on Higher Education 1960), the chair of the *college van curatoren* legally represented the university. A professional administrator, the *secretaris*, who was in charge of the central administration of the university, assisted the *college van curatoren*. The *secretaris*, nominated by the *college van curatoren*, was appointed by the national government. Over the years the position of this *secretaris* became more important.

---

[14] As mentioned earlier, local situations might differ. Regarding the bicephalic structure there were at least two exceptions: the Agricultural University of Wageningen and the relatively young University of Twente had a monocephalic structure in which (some) curators and senate members were united in one executive body.

The other pillar in the bicephalic structure of those days was the senate. This body, originating from 1815 as *Senatus Academicus*, was responsible for all academic matters. It consisted of all full professors of the university and embodied academic self-governance. The chair of the senate was held by the *rector magnificus*, who represented the university in academic affairs. The *rector magnificus* was appointed by the national government after the senate's nomination of at least two candidates (full professors). The *rector magnificus* was assisted by a *secretaris* selected from and appointed by the senate. The executive board of the senate was comprised of the *college van rector en assessoren*, consisting of the rector, the registrar and at least four representatives from the faculties (usually the full professors of the faculty). Although Dutch universities in those days had a clear-cut dual structure, one of the curators (usually the president-curator) and the *rector magnificus* met regularly to discuss daily matters.

Obviously Dutch universities prior to 1970 cannot be labelled as 'democratic' according to our definition in section 2. All the main players were appointed by the national government, even though the senate had the right to nominate candidates for its chair. Junior academics, non-academics and students were not represented in the formal governance structure though they could participate in committees at the central and faculty level. Consequently, stating it in terms we used in section 2, the system should be labelled as a system of 'guardianship'.

With respect to academic affairs, the system was characterised by a fusion of powers, held by the senate and an executive body (*college van rector en assessoren*). In the terminology introduced in section 3.1, we can characterise this system as parliamentary, since the executive body emerged from, and was responsible to, the legislative authority (i.e. the senate). Moreover the system was monistic, because the members of the *college van rector en assessoren* were also members of the legislature. It should be noted, however, that contrary to a complete parliamentary system, the senate did not appoint the rector (though it played a role in nominating the rector).

Another salient feature of the institutions of Dutch university governance prior to 1970 was its chair-faculty structure. The faculty was a compound of chairs of full professors. The predominance of strong collegial rule by chair holders was a strong decentralised element in the institutional structure. Decentralisation, however, was by no means complete. The faculty was obliged to contribute to the university's policies, that is, to contribute to the preparation of strategic plans and budgets and to provide information to curators regarding the use of facilities, personnel, and so on. All in all, we

may characterise the pre-1970 system of Dutch universities as a
guardianship, based on a monistic fusion of legislative and executive power,
and a bicephalic allocation of executive powers, with a high degree of
decentralisation.

The 1960s witnessed a growing concern in the Netherlands, as elsewhere,
about the effectiveness and efficiency of the traditional forms of university
governance in an era of unprecedented expansion of participation in higher
education. In 1967 these concerns resulted in proposals by an important
academic advisory committee (Maris Committee) to centralise the structure
of university governance. This committee proposed, amongst other things, to
allocate the major decision-making powers to a presidium of three persons
that would be accountable to the Minister. The proposal, however, was not
implemented. The publication of the Maris report more or less coincided
with a radical change in public opinion. Political and social democratisation
was high on the public and political agenda. The previous worries about the
effectiveness and efficiency of universities were overshadowed by demands
for democratic participation of junior academics, staff and students in
university decision-making. The spirit of this democratic movement left
deep scars on a new Act of university governance, which parliament passed
in 1970.

The most striking feature of the new Act — the *Wet op de Universitaire
Bestuurshervorming* (WUB) — was its emphasis on democratisation. Both
the senate and the *college van curatoren* were abolished. The WUB created a
system of functional representation in university and faculty councils.
Academics (professors and other academic staff), non-academics and
students were given the right to elect representatives to these legislative
bodies. Members served for at least a two-year period, except for students
who served for only one year. The meetings of the councils were public. The
chair of the university council was a council member elected by other
council members. The university council had a final say in budgetary
matters, institutional plans, annual reports, general academic procedures, and
the university's internal regulations and rules. The *college van bestuur*
carried out the executive function. This chief executive board consisted of
three to five members; one of them was the *rector magnificus*. All members,
including the rector, were appointed by the national government. The board
of deans and the university council had the right to submit nominations to
the Minister. The tasks of the previous *college van curatoren* were then
performed by the executive board. This body became responsible for the
'administrative hierarchy' within the university.

This system of university governance closely resembled the concept of democracy as previously defined. All constituencies of the university 'Demos' were represented and could participate in major decision-making through their elected representatives. The WUB system was not fully democratic, however, because some of the main players, that is, the *college van bestuur* were appointed. In this respect the model was more like Aristotle's model of mixed governance (see section 3). In terms of the distribution of powers, these arrangements may well be considered as an example of dualistic fusion of powers, since an incompatibility rule was applied (i.e. members of the chief executive board, including the rector, were not members of the university council). Moreover, the structure, as before, was bicephalic, because executive powers regarding academic and non-academic affairs were separated.

Within the universities the WUB Act introduced a new organisational layer, the *vakgroep* ('department'). The *vakgroepen* were small clusters of professors and their assistants working in the same sub-disciplinary area. They had substantial powers regarding the design and implementation of teaching and research programmes, although they were accountable to the faculty council, the equivalent of the university council at the faculty level. In a sense, one might say that these groups replaced the powers of individual chair holders in the pre-1970 system. Still, the collectivised powers in academic affairs of the smallest units in the university organisation implied a highly decentralised system of governance.

The participatory governance structure of the WUB existed for some twenty-five years. Over the years, however, the balance of power between the executive and the legislature in universities shifted. The initial dominance of the legislature (university council) gradually gave way to a more or less balanced relationship between these two bodies. Subsequently the balance was tilted even further, eventually resulting in executive dominance. This gradual shift towards executive leadership corroborates the hypothesis that parliamentary systems apparently develop a tendency towards executive dominance (see section 3.1).[15] Put succinctly, in the midst of the 1990s, Dutch university governance was characterised by (1) a substantial degree of democracy; (2) a dualistic fusion of powers; (3) a bicephalic structure of the executive; and (4) a decentralised system. The earlier dominance of the democratic legislature, however, was largely replaced by the primacy of the guardians, that is, the *college van bestuur*.

---

[15] See also De Boer *et al.* (1998) for empirical support for this shift in the balance of power between the executive and the legislature in Dutch university governance in the period 1970–97.

In 1997, the Dutch parliament, once again, accepted a new bill on university governance. The introduction of the Act *Modernisering Universitaire Bestuursorganisatie* (MUB) implied a substantial change, at least in theory.[16] The MUB Act abolished the system of co-determination by board and council. At the central level nearly all powers regarding both academic and non-academic affairs were attributed to the *college van bestuur* which consisted of three appointed members (including the *rector magnificus*). The *college van bestuur* was accountable to a 'new' supervisory body, the *raad van toezicht* (a lay member body of five persons appointed by and accountable to the Minister).[17] At the faculty level, the dean became the 'omnipotent ruler'. At both the university and faculty levels, representative councils were retained but they lost most of their earlier powers (e.g. the right to reject the budget proposal).

So, for the first time in the history of Dutch higher education, universities now have a monocephalic structure, that is, the integration of authorities regarding academic and non-academic affairs in one body (the *college van bestuur* and the dean at the central and faculty level respectively). We would also argue that the new institutions are to be considered as a system of guardianship in which executive and legislative powers are concentrated, even though the academic community has its representatives in relatively powerless councils. All the members of the crucial governing bodies — *raad van toezicht, college van bestuur* and *decaan* — are appointed.

The issue of centralisation is one of the most delicate topics. With respect to academic affairs, however, it seems fair to say that, according to the MUB Act, the governance system in itself is more centralised than it used to be. The MUB abolished *vakgroepen*. The dean, appointed by the *college van bestuur*, is now responsible for the design and implementation of the teaching and research programmes. One might argue that in this respect the 'managerial' legitimacy replaces pure academic legitimacy. Because the dean has become one of the key players in university governance in the Netherlands, we would argue that the system as such is not fully centralised, but it is less decentralised than before. All in all we would characterise the contemporary institutions of university governance as a guardianship having a monocentric, monocephalic and 'centralised' constitution.

---

[16] One might differ in opinion on how dramatic the changes were in practice. One could argue that in some respects the MUB was more or less a codification of an already existing practice (De Boer *et al.* 1998).

[17] One might hold the opinion that this new body resembles the old *college van curatoren* to a large extent.

5.   FINAL REMARKS

There has been a substantial variety in the institutions of university governance ever since the first universities were established. In this chapter, we characterised different institutional designs of university governance using a classification scheme based on four dimensions. Most available descriptions of institutions of university governance either fail to develop the analytical tool used in the analysis or are based on only one or two dimensions. In this chapter, we have tried to provide an explicit and multidimensional classification scheme which is firmly based in normative theories of institutional design. This multidimensional scheme allows for a differentiated comparison of institutional arrangements. It may be applied to compare institutions of university governance at one point in time (synchronic analysis) or to characterise institutional change over time (diachronic analysis). Moreover, the scheme can be used at different levels of analysis. National laws on university governance from different countries may be compared, but the four dimensions may also be used at the level of individual universities.

In this chapter, we have used the scheme to characterise changes in the institutions of Dutch university governance since 1945. Our analysis has shown that on all four dimensions, institutions of university governance have changed radically: the current institutional arrangements (guardianship, monocentric, monocephalic and centralised) are little less than the perfect antithesis of the system adopted in the early 1970s (democracy, fusion of powers, bicephalic and decentralised). Our analysis also clearly illustrates that the new institutional arrangements for university governance are by no means a return to the 'ancien regime' in use prior to 1970. Even though the contemporary institutions, like the pre-1970 period, might be characterised as a system of guardianship, the nature of guardianship has changed considerably over the years: from a system essentially based on academic professional skills to a system based predominantly on administrative and managerial skills. Moreover, the wide dispersion of powers (in three dimensions) that was characteristic for the situation prior to 1970 has been replaced by arrangements that imply a high degree of concentration of powers (monocentric, monocephalic and 'centralised').

After having characterised institutions of university governance in terms of the scheme's four dimensions, one wonders if such institutional changes lead to variations in performance. After all, most reorganisations are inspired (or rationalised) by arguments relating to the prospective beneficial effects of institutional change. Over the years, reforms in institutions of university governance in the Netherlands have been advocated on the basis of presumptions about potential effects on effectiveness and efficiency. Whether these promises have actually been fulfilled is essentially an unanswered question. This poses a major challenge for future research.

References

Bargh, C., P. Scott and D. Smith (1996), *Governing Universities: changing the culture?*, Buckingham: Open University Press.

Bess, J.L. (1992), Collegiality: toward a clarification of meaning and function, in: J.C. Smart (ed.), *Higher Education: handbook of theory and research*, vol. VIII, Bronx, NY: Agathon Press, pp. 1–36.

Birnbaum, R. (1989), Leadership and followership: the cybernetics of university governance, in: J. Schuster, L.H. Miller and Ass. (eds), *Governing Tomorrow's Campus: perspectives and agendas*, New York: MacMillan, pp. 27-41.

Bleker, H. and W.M. van den Bremen (1983), *Macht in het binnelands bestuur: een theoretische en empirische verkenning van macht- en invloedsverhoudingen tussen bestuurslagen*, Deventer: Kluwer.

Boer, H. de, B. Denters and L. Goedegebuure (1998), On boards and councils; shaky balances considered: the governance of Dutch universities, *Higher Education Policy*, vol. 11, no. 2–3, pp. 153–64.

Chapman, J.W. (ed.) (1983), *The Western University on Trial*, Berkeley: University of California Press.

Clark, B.R. (1983), *The Higher Education System: academic organization in cross-national perspective*, Berkeley: University of California Press.

Cobban, A.B. (1975), *The Medieval Universities: their development and organization*, Chatham: Methuen & Co.

Daalder, H. and E. Shils (eds) (1982), *Universities, Politicians and Bureaucrats: Europe and the United States*, Cambridge: Cambridge University Press.

Dahl, R.A. (1989), *Democracy and its Critics*, New Haven, CT: Yale University Press.

Elzinga, D.J. (1998), Monisme en dualisme: een sterke raad, een sterk college, een sterk apparaat, in: A.F.A. Kortsen and P.W. Tops (eds), *Lokaal bestuur in Nederland: inleiding in de gemeentekunde*, Alphen aan den Rijn: Samsom.

Groof, J. de, G. Neave, and J. Svec (1998), *Democracy and Governance in Higher Education*, The Hague: Kluwer Law International.

Lijphart, A. (1983), University 'democracy' in the Netherlands, in: J.W. Chapman (ed.), *The Western University on Trial*, Berkeley: University of California Press, pp. 212–30.

Lijphart, A. (1984), *Democracies: patterns of majoritarian and consensus government in twenty-one countries*, New Haven, CT: Yale University Press.

Maassen, P. and F. van Vught (1994), Alternative models of governmental steering in higher education: an analysis of steering models and policy-instruments in five countries, in: L. Goedegebuure, and F. van Vught (eds), *Comparative Policy Studies in Higher Education*, Utrecht: Lemma, pp. 35-63.

March, J.G. and J.P. Olsen (1983), Organizing political life: what administrative reorganization tells us about government, *American Political Science Review*, vol. 77, pp. 281–96.

Mintzberg, H. (1979), *The Structuring of Organizations: a synthesis of the research*, Englewood Cliffs, NJ: Prentice-Hall.

Moodie, G.C. and R. Eustace (1974), *Power and Authority in British Universities*, London: George Allen & Unwin.

Neave, G. (1988), The making of the executive head: the process of defining institutional leaders in certain European countries, *International Journal of Institutional Management in Higher Education*, vol. 12, no. 1, pp. 104–14.

Neave, G. (1997), *The European dimension in higher education: an historical analysis, background document to the Conference: The Relationship between Higher Education and the Nation-State*, Enschede, The Netherlands.

Neave, G. and G. Rhoades (1987), The academic estate in Western Europe, in: B.R. Clark (ed.), *The Academic Profession: national, disciplinary and institutional settings*, Berkeley: University of California Press, pp. 211–70.

Neave, G. and F. van Vught (eds) (1991), *Prometheus Bound: the changing relationship between government and higher education in Western Europe*, Oxford: Pergamon Press.

Osborne, D. and T. Gaebler (1992), *Reinventing Government: how the entrepreneurial spirit is transforming the public sector*, New York: Plume.

Pot, C.W. van der and A.M. Donner (1983), *Handboek van het Nederlandse staatsrecht*, Zwolle: Tjeenk Willink.

Sabine, G.H. and T.L. Thorson (1973), *A History of Political Theory*, Hinsdale, Il: Dryden Press.

Toonen, T.A.J. (1987), *Denken over binnenlands bestuur: theorieën van de gedecentraliseerde eenheidsstaat bestuurskundig beschouwd*, 's-Gravenhage: Vuga.

Chapter 11

Institutional change in doctoral education
The graduate school

JEROEN BARTELSE AND LEO GOEDEGEBUURE

Key words: doctoral education; graduate school; innovation

1.   INTRODUCTION

Since the first doctorate was conferred more than eight centuries ago, this apex of university education has proved crucial to the continued existence of academic work by preparing new generations of scholars. Over the last decades, concerns have been expressed regarding the function and organisation of doctoral education. A number of European countries have faced important reforms in this area. One of these reforms regards an institutional change: the rise of the graduate schools.

In Finland, France, Germany and the Netherlands, for example, policies have been implemented to stimulate the development of these schools. Yet the nature and pace of change differ across countries and fields of study. Graduate schools sometimes prosper, whereas in other cases they only develop sparsely or not at all: design and reality do not always coincide. In this chapter these policies and their outcomes are discussed.

Policies on graduate schools commonly take the form of stimulation programmes. These programmes outline the concept of the graduate school in a number of criteria or characteristics. Initiatives to establish graduate schools should meet these criteria in order to obtain funding or recognition. Hence, a policy refers to a more or less coherent government programme that formulates a certain idea of the graduate school and launches a number of measures for the realisation of this idea. The process in which this policy becomes — or fails to become — a stable and meaningful practice for the actors is coined *the institutionalisation process*. This is a process in which institutional change actually takes place. We consider this the 'final' stage of the policy or innovation process (Rogers 1983).

Both in Germany and the Netherlands, the two countries that will receive specific attention in this chapter, the development of graduate schools has had a high profile. But along the process of institutionalisation much has happened to the original policy idea: the graduate schools have been established in some fields of study, but in other cases they have never evolved, have disappeared, or sometimes were transformed into alternative organisational forms of doctoral training. Over the last years, we have been engaged in a study concerning the development of graduate schools across countries, with the following principal research question: *How do policies regarding new organisational formats such as the graduate school institutionalise in different systems of doctoral education, and what factors can explain the outcomes of this institutional process?*

The objectives of our study are both theoretical and practical. First, we aim to advance our understanding of processes of institutional change in higher education in relation to government policies. Second, we are interested in the practical implications of our model. If reality does not always coincide with (policy) design, what then happens during the process in which graduate schools are being adopted, or not adopted, in the field? An explanation of the discrepancies that occur between policy and reality may contribute to a more appropriate design of policies in the area of doctoral education. In this chapter, we focus particularly on the theoretical approach and conclusions of the research project.[1]

The structure of this chapter is as follows. In section 2, we sketch the background of the rise of graduate schools in European higher education. Next, in section 3, we develop a theoretical perspective based on a model of institutionalisation and derive four hypotheses regarding the institutionalisation of graduate schools in different systems of doctoral education. In section 4, we summarise various ways of conceptualising the institutionalisation process of graduate schools. On the basis of a comparative analysis, in section 5 we assess the viability of the theoretical model. Section 6 draws some tentative conclusions.

---

[1]   For a reflection on the practical implications of this research project, see Bartelse 1999; and Bartelse *et al* 1999.

2. THE RISE OF THE GRADUATE SCHOOLS IN EUROPEAN HIGHER EDUCATION

Doctoral education is the subject of critical discussion. Questions have been raised on the appropriateness of doctoral education both inside academia and by governments, business communities and the public. These issues are not new, but are connected to larger societal and academic developments.

In the 1950s, 1960s and 1970s, following rapid economic growth and in the context of the overall geo-political situation (such as the cold war and the space race), large sums of money were injected into research and development. This was the period of the 'grant-swinging' game in the United States: 'there were few conceivable questions that someone did not try to put to some empirical test in some grant application' (Hesseling 1986: 35). During the last two decades, however, the investment in research and development as a percentage of the gross national product (GNP) of most Western countries has not increased, and in some cases even dropped (OECD 1995). Other needs and priorities are competing for resources. This reappraisal of the role of academic research and research training is not only reflected in funding cutbacks; in modern society, academic research and research training face a more *critical and demanding public*: in terms of its aims and functions, its place in and relevance for society, and its effective and efficient performance (see Lapidus 1994).

Another important development is the *mass enrolment* that higher education has faced. 'The second half of this century will go down in history as the period of the greatest expansion in higher education, world-wide' (Van Vught & Westerheijden 1993: 102). Access to higher education was boosted for a variety of reasons mainly relating to economic and societal pressures, deliberate policy programmes to enhance participation, and demographic trends. Doctoral education is losing its elitist character as well, which is curious enough given the cutback on expenditure on research mentioned earlier. In the United States, less than 600 doctorates were conferred by only 14 universities until 1920. Doctoral education in this part of the world has since become paramount (Bowen & Rudenstine 1992: 19). In Europe, the participation rate in doctoral work gradually increased in the 1950s and 1960s, but only since the last decade has the growth figure been profound (figure 1). Several governments are deliberately stimulating enrolment in doctoral education (such as France and the Netherlands). In contrast to the United States, Europe has not developed structures to cater for large-scale postgraduate training for students with an increasing variety of backgrounds.

Figure 1: Doctorates awarded in Germany, France, the Netherlands and UK

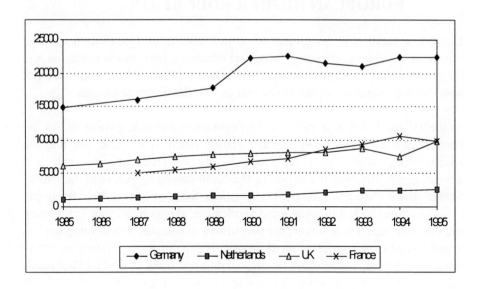

Source: OECD 1995

A third development which encourages a reappraisal of doctoral education is the *expansion of knowledge* (see Clark 1993). Two implications for doctoral education can be seen in this regard. First, a 'knowledge intensive' society calls for highly trained professionals and thus longer training periods. Doctoral education can play a role in answering this call. However, the spread of high occupational expertise not only requires doctors trained for scholarly work, but also doctors trained for occupations outside academia. A second component of the growth of knowledge relates to the location of research and research training. Clark (1993: 361) concludes that:

> *The expansion of knowledge at the hands of research creates research settings that leave teaching and study behind. Within and beyond the grounds of universities, research finds homes where little or no teaching goes on and where few if any students are found.*

Regarding research training, Blume (1995: 14) remarks that universities are not the exclusive home of research training:

> *A good deal of training is provided informally, on the job, and in the growing numbers of industrial training centres. ... In a number of Western European countries also, much of the best scientific work takes*

place in institutes which are not formally part of the higher education system.

Rethinking the role of, and relations between, universities, research institutions, centres of excellence and the like, implies reconsidering the location and organisation of research training.

These issues have not gone unnoticed by national governments, and several reforms have been initiated. Inspired by the American example, several European governments have stimulated the development of graduate schools. In other countries, higher education institutions themselves chose to establish variations of the graduate school. The following examples illustrate these developments.

In 1986, the German *Wissenschaftsrat* proposed the creation of *Graduiertenkollegs.* In 1989, the federal government and the *Länder* agreed to jointly support such a system. By 1997, around 280 of these schools had been founded. In Britain, the call to improve postgraduate training

> *tended to require an increased level of 'centralised' monitoring and support of individual programmes and students, and all institutions have had to establish policies and procedures for such activity* (CGE 1995: 9).

This, together with the identified trends and issues in this study, stimulated institutions to establish graduate schools. In 1990, the French Ministry of Education created the opportunity for universities to establish *écoles doctorales* (De Wied 1991: 21). In the Netherlands, the Minister of Education and Science established a system of graduate schools in 1991.

Although the idea of the graduate school is employed and developed quite disparately within and between countries, we suggest that the concept of concentration best captures its basic feature. Concentration signifies the process in which various aspects and capacities of doctoral education are brought together. Doctoral education in Europe was scattered across universities and research institutions; now collaboration, and at times the incorporation of previously independent faculty entities and individuals into graduate schools takes place. Doctoral students are brought together to conduct their research and receive their training. Clearly, concentration takes various forms, ranging from frail constructions of collaboration between institutions to the establishment of special institutes for research training located between 'four walls'. Yet, its prominence in the doctoral education policy landscape is unmistakable.

The design of graduate schools seems to be contingent on circumstances related to existing practices and tradition. For the policy-maker, it is questionable whether these institutions can be designed nationally at all. Nevertheless, graduate schools have been planned in the Netherlands and Germany, and policies were implemented in the early nineties. Since then, their establishment in the two countries is considered a prominent development — although the pace and nature of development differ across the two countries and in different fields of study. In the report of an international committee that studied new organisational forms of graduate research training, it was observed that:

> *new policies towards postgraduate research training need to take account of specific national circumstances and traditions. The various national debates, as well as experience, show that complex issues arise here, to which we can do no more than allude* (De Wied 1991: 22).

As to disciplinary traditions of doctoral education, diverging trends can be observed as well. In the natural sciences, graduate schools are relatively easily adopted, whereas in the various social sciences there is a mixed record of success. This variety formed the starting point of our study and we have developed an explanation for the different outcomes of institutional change that can be observed.

3.   THEORETICAL PERSPECTIVE

There is a line of scholarly thought that specifically addresses the role of institutions in social life: institutional analysis. Since the 1980s, this perspective has faced a revival under the heading 'new-institutionalism'. New-institutional analysis emerges in various disciplines, and is conducted quite disparately across them. The common factor seems to be that institutions matter, but controversies exist on exactly what institutions are, how they work, and what their explanatory role and use can be (Norgaard 1996: 34; De Boer *et al.* 1998). Many overviews of these 'new-institutional schools' can be found in the literature[2]. Here, we suffice to note that there is not one institutional perspective. From various approaches, theorists stress different roles and conceptualisations of institutions. Keman (1997: 19) asserts that:

> *there is not a systematic or generally accepted theory of institutions available to overcome the almost inevitable eclecticism by which the various approaches are characterized.*

Given this range of perspectives, it becomes imperative to define one's conception of an institution and to clarify the particular new-institutional approach this study will follow. If a broad or unclear institutional approach is chosen, the action situation becomes obscured: 'anything goes' for an institution and explanatory variables can be mixed up with the variables to be explained.

We define an institution as a social establishment with a stable character which provides a common frame of reference for the actors in a field. The institutions of interest in this study concern doctoral education and are located at the disciplinary and national level. We note that systems of doctoral education vary between countries and disciplines rather than between, for example, universities or departments. These national and disciplinary influences make up distinct constellations of institutional factors. This specific set of institutions is referred to in this study as 'the institutional context of doctoral education'.[3]

Although institutions, being social facts, may be perceived differently (individual social constructions), the ordering of day-to-day life implies a certain sense of common knowledge. Particular institutional contexts, such as an organisation, a football team or a doctoral system, provide specific shared

---

[2] For a more detailed description of disciplinary orientations in new-institutional thought, see DiMaggio and Powell 1991: 1-38; Hendriks 1996: 92-101; Keman 1997: 11-23; Norgaard 1996.

[3] At this point, we find no reason to locate the institutional factors solely on one of these levels: the disciplinary or the national. A discipline in one country may develop different institutions of doctoral education compared to the same discipline in another country, although related disciplines often share particular institutions of doctoral education irrespective of the national context (see also Braxton & Hargens 1996). The delineation of this set of institutions deflects from a traditional focus — in studies on higher education — on either the discipline *or* the national context. Rather, we try to capture institutions that matter for those who operate within the institutional context of doctoral education, such as doctoral candidates, professors and university administrators. These institutions are nationally *and* disciplinary bound.

meanings for its 'members' which are not shared by people outside these structures. Institutions reduce complexity and give meaning to social reality — they provide a 'repertoire' through which actors define and appraise the world around them. In this sense, institutions are a resource for human action.

However, institutions do not dictate social action. They can also be considered to provide an opportunity set for social interaction. If, under political, economic or normative pressures, the institutional context does not provide adequate 'standard procedures', it is eventually the actor who makes the decision and acts. Sometimes institutional conditions may be conflicting, sometimes external circumstances or events may bring the actor to act in alternative ways. The human factor can play a decisive role. Yet, if it is ultimately the actor who makes the decision, then institutions can also be considered to restrict the number of alternatives and allow or forbid particular actions. In this sense, institutions are conceived as constraints on human activity.

Hence, the influence of institutions on social life can be considered both constraining and resourceful: two sides of the institutional coin. This refers to a dilemma which lies at the heart of new-institutional thought and relates to a classic dispute in the social sciences: the role of agency and structure. Can social life be explained by the behaviour of actors (the behaviourist or reductionist perspective) or are social structures or institutions the pivotal factors (the classic institutional perspective)?

In the many new-institutional approaches, these two perspectives on social life can also be recognised. We appreciate both perspectives for their explanatory value. Human creativity may lead to institutional change; yet, in accomplishing this, it is subject to existing institutions. As Giddens (1977: 121) puts it: 'social structures are both constituted by human agency, and yet at the same time are the very medium of this constitution'. Therefore, we propose a model that accommodates these two traditions, in a *complementary* rather than a competitive approach.

The two theoretical perspectives suggest different explanations of the institutionalisation process of policy innovations such as the graduate school. Rational choice theorists seek explanations of institutional change in the behaviour of self-interested individuals. Their key assumption is that human activity is goal-oriented and instrumental, and that actors try to maximise their goal achievement or utility (Eggertsson 1990; Tsebelis 1990: 6; Green & Shapiro 1994: 13). The degree of utility or *profitability* of the policy innovation will provide actors with the determining reason for their decision to establish or accept graduate schools or not. The notion of profitability refers to the degree to which the policy innovation satisfies the needs of the actors involved. In sociological approaches, institutional change is considered to depend on 'supra-individual units of analysis', such as norms, values, social structures or taken-for-granted scripts, rules and classifications. A policy innovation that is compatible with these existing institutions will be more easily adopted than policy innovations that are in conflict with them. This notion of compatibility refers to the degree to which the policy innovation matches the existing institutional context, or makes up an institutional logic.

The concepts of compatibility and profitability play an important role in studies on the diffusion of innovations in organisations. In his book *Why Innovation Fails* (1980), Levine offers an interesting modelling of both the process and the outcomes of institutionalisation on the basis of the notions of compatibility and profitability. We have used his work to develop a model of institutionalisation of graduate schools in different contexts of doctoral education.

We define *compatibility* as the degree of fit between the policy innovation and the existing institutional context. Conflicting rules, norms or organisational structures may generate confusion and threats. If a graduate school is inconsistent with the existing institutional context, it may be rejected or denied. Incompatibility in this study thus relates to a mismatch between the innovation — the graduate school — and those institutions that are shared by the 'members' of the doctoral system. Compatibility, as such, refers to preservation rather than to change, and can be seen as a measure of dissatisfaction: the greater the degree of compatibility, the lesser the degree of dissatisfaction.

Profitability is defined as the degree to which the innovation satisfies the needs of the actors. Within a certain institutional context, actors assess the graduate school on its merits and may assign a certain degree of profitability to it. The concept of profitability can be considered a degree of satisfaction: the greater the degree of profitability, the greater the degree of satisfaction. Unlike compatibility, profitability refers to the agency-side of social life. It is about the 'practical' advantages that actors conceive.

Positive or negative degrees of compatibility and profitability set in motion two mechanisms which describe what happens during the institutionalisation process. The first mechanism is institutional contraction. If a policy innovation is perceived as incompatible or unprofitable, it will be rejected by the institutional context. The second mechanism is institutional expansion. If a policy innovation is perceived as compatible and profitable, it will be accommodated within the institutional context. These processes, in turn, lead to four possible states of institutionalisation:

- *Diffusion*, which occurs if the policy innovation is adopted throughout the entire doctoral system according to the original policy idea.
- *Termination*, which takes place if the policy innovation is not established or if newly established institutional structures are abolished.
- *Resocialisation*, which occurs if the policy innovation diffuses throughout the system but changes in the institutionalisation process. The outcome is a different institutional form than envisaged in the policy idea.
- *Fragmentation*, which happens if in some instances the policy innovation is adopted according to the original policy idea, while it is rejected at other locations.

In order to gain insight into the combined impact of the variables on the states of institutionalisation, four extreme combinations can be depicted. The policy innovation can be:

1. compatible and profitable
2. incompatible and unprofitable
3. incompatible and profitable
4. compatible and unprofitable.

We infer an hypothesis for each combination below.

Combination 1 refers to a strong degree of compatibility and a strong degree of profitability. Both variables induce the same mechanism, that of institutional expansion. As the policy innovation is compatible with existing institutions, it will be incorporated easily into the institutional context. As the policy innovation is perceived to be prevalently profitable in the institutional context, a stimulus in favour of pursuing the policy innovation will prevail. The institutional context is expected to expand which leads straightforwardly to diffusion of the policy innovation.

Hypothesis 1: If the policy innovation is characterised by a high degree of compatibility and a high degree of profitability, diffusion of the policy innovation occurs.

Combination 2 couples a strong degree of incompatibility to a strong degree of unprofitability. Again, both variables bring about the same mechanism, which is institutional contraction. As the policy innovation is in clear conflict with the existing institutional context, the policy innovation will be excluded. In addition, the policy innovation is not perceived to be a satisfying new-institutional structure; actors will reject the policy innovation for being disadvantageous. The contraction of the institutional context leads to the termination of the policy innovation.

> *Hypothesis 2*: If the policy innovation is characterised by a high degree of incompatibility and a high degree of unprofitability, termination of the policy innovation occurs.

Combinations three and four involve a more ambiguous process and outcome. Yet, these two instances are of great interest: does successful institutionalisation actually occur and how does it happen; what counts most if the two variables push and pull in contradictory directions? A clarification of this relationship may generate a more complete institutionalisation model and also yield interesting clues for policy recommendations. Not much theorising has focused on this relationship. In sociological and anthropological studies, compatibility receives more emphasis, whereas in economic studies, profitability seems to be the principal variable to explain the outcome of institutionalisation (see also Levine 1980). As pointed out earlier, our study stresses the idea that both variables play an indispensable role in the explanation of specific institutionalisation outcomes.

In a situation characterised by combination 3, two contradictory mechanisms are set in motion. Institutional expansion is expected because of the perceived merits of the new-institutional construct. However, due to disagreement with the existing institutional context of doctoral education, forces seeking to exclude the innovation will be present, which will act in the direction of institutional contraction. If this situation persists, the expected outcome of the institutionalisation process will be resocialisation. The policy innovation is attractive enough to diffuse throughout the system of doctoral education, but due to an institutional mismatch it will be aligned with existing institutions. The outcome of the institutionalisation process will be a modified institutional structure, which differs from the policy innovation that was originally implemented.

Hypothesis 3: If the policy innovation is characterised by a high degree of incompatibility and a high degree of profitability, the policy innovation will resocialise.

In a situation characterised by combination 4, institutional contraction and expansion are expected as well. This time, contraction occurs as a result of the unprofitability of the policy innovation: actors do not perceive the graduate school as meeting their needs. However, expansion is expected given an institutional match: the graduate school fits the existing institutional context easily. The match of institutional characteristics itself does not seem a sufficient condition to bring about institutionalisation. As mentioned earlier, compatibility can be considered a degree of dissatisfaction. Hence, if incompatibility occurs, a degree of dissatisfaction is implied, but if compatibility occurs, only dissatisfaction is absent. At face value, this seems a weak reason to expect institutionalisation, specifically when it combines with a high degree of unprofitability. This suggests that the outcome will be termination. Institutional expansion without reference to a direct profit can be explained by the presence of institutional mimicking and rule-following behaviour. In this situation, actors comply to the institutional expectations of their context as there is no explicit institutional mismatch. An additional consideration in this specific combination of compatibility and unprofitability is the aggregated nature of the variable profitability. The variable does not reflect local considerations with respect to the adoption of a graduate school — but the overall picture of a certain institutional context. We expect the establishment of graduate schools in accordance with the policy idea at a few locations as a result of their specific circumstances. These considerations yield the expectation that the outcome in situation 4 will be fragmentation: the policy innovation will diffuse sparsely throughout the adopting system.

Hypothesis 4: If the policy innovation is characterised by a high degree of compatibility and a high degree of unprofitability, the policy innovation is likely to fragment.

The relationships between compatibility and profitability on the one hand and the states of institutionalisation on the other are presented in figure 2.

Figure 2: The hypothesised institutionalisation model

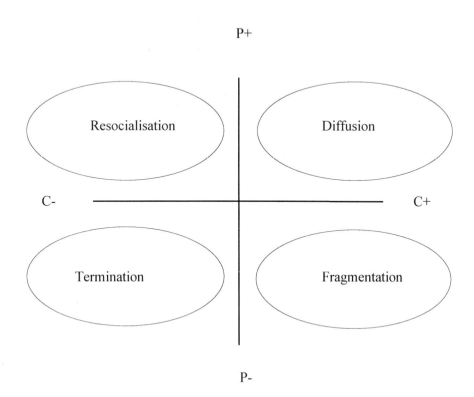

P+

Resocialisation

Diffusion

C-   C+

Termination

Fragmentation

P-

4.   CONCEPTUALISATIONS

4.1   Compatibility

In our daily life, we often refer to compatibility. A nut may fit a bolt, pieces of a puzzle match each other, a lid fits the pot. Here the criterion of compatibility is quite obvious. But in other situations this is not the case. Clothes may fit a person, yet particular combinations of clothes, or colours, are considered to be a complete mismatch. Here the criterion of a match is less obvious. It refers to taste, or involves a complex set of aspects. In order to make any statements on a possible match between institutions, a criterion should be specified that allows comparison. Generally, studies on compatibility specify a number of dimensions upon which the variable is measured. If two objects of study show similarity on relevant aspects then compatibility is concluded, if there is no congruence then incompatibility is concluded. However, the ultimate test of compatibility is how actors perceive themselves. A degree of correspondence may strongly suggest the presence of compatibility, but the actor's perception of fit is the ultimate test. For an empirical investigation at a system level, the criterion of correspondence is a valuable conceptualisation that may well serve in addition to subjective information collected at the level of the individual actor. In the next section, a number of institutional dimensions is suggested. Institutional compatibility can then be determined by comparing the graduate schools to the existing institutional context of doctoral education in terms of each of these categories.

We pursue Clark's (1983) distinction of what he calls the 'basic elements of higher education systems': work, beliefs and authority. For each category, the indicators allow an assessment of the degree to which the policy innovation is compatible with the institutional context into which it is introduced.

Work pertains to the delegation and definition of tasks. Clark (1983: 28), following Durkheim, argues that:

> *... if we reduce a knowledge-bearing system to its primordial elements we find first a division of labour, a structure of organized effort within which many people individually and collectively take different actions.*

With regard to work in a system of doctoral education, two aspects stand out. First, there is the *division of labour*, or the organisation and delegation of work in doctoral education. Second, there is the *content of the work*, which refers to the tasks carried out. The establishment of graduate schools may have an impact on both aspects. It usually involves the concentration of doctoral candidates, staff and resources, which implies a reallocation of tasks among the actors in a doctoral system.

Beliefs regard the symbolic side of social entities. They 'help define for participants who they are, what they are doing, why they are doing it, and whether they have been blessed or cursed' (Clark 1983: 72). Clark demarcates four beliefs that are 'noteworthy and variable' across countries and that reflect and affect the character of a system. These beliefs are very recognisable in systems of doctoral education, and help to characterise their national orientation and distinguish between disciplinary orientations: the *access belief*, which refers to assumptions about the breadth of access to doctoral systems;

the *specialisation belief*, which refers to the range of fields and subjects that should be incorporated into a doctoral programme; the *employment belief*, which refers to the labour market orientation of doctoral education; and finally the *research belief*, which refers in the context of this study to the disciplinary or interdisciplinary orientation of the doctoral programme.

Clark's third basic element is *authority*. This concerns the location and nature of competencies in the institutional context. The indicators that we distinguish are: the *level of authority*, which refers to the level where decision-making power regarding the organisation and content of doctoral work lies; and the *forms of authority*. The introduction of the graduate school may challenge the dominant authority at a particular location, and hence may be conceived as incompatible.

In our empirical investigation, the policy idea of the graduate school is compared to the institutional context of doctoral education on each of the above categories. Compatibility is concluded if we can establish a clear-cut correspondence — or perceived compatibility — on the suggested indicators.

4.2   Profitability

Profitability is the degree to which a policy innovation satisfies the needs of actors who operate within an institutional context of doctoral education. Unlike compatibility, profitability relates to the practical needs of actors, and to the utility and impact of policy innovations on the satisfaction of these needs. Profitability is not an easily measurable, invariant variable. It depends on the dynamic and complex positions of actors who operate within a particular institutional context of doctoral education. When it comes to concepts such as profitability or utility, social scientists often borrow from rational choice theories. For a specification of profitability we have done the same.

Rational choice models do provide useful concepts to frame profitability. They suggest the elements that are relevant for determining the degree of utility, or — in the context of this study — profitability. The following concepts are usually included in an expression of utility: actors, alternatives, preferences and strategies.

Actors
In the institutional context of doctoral education, the following actors can be discerned. (1) Doctoral candidates, those individuals who pursue a doctorate

within programmes of doctoral education. (2) Supervisors, those individuals who are directly engaged in the supervision of doctoral candidates. (3) University administrators, those individuals who are involved in the administrative and regulative procedures of doctoral work. (4) Governmental agencies, those organisations, including research councils, that create or implement policies in the area of doctoral education. (5) The wider public, those actors who have a varying stake in doctoral education, such as future employers of doctors, or industries that make use of the scientific output of doctoral work.

The university is the principal location where the decision is made to establish a research school or not. If a degree of profitability is to be measured, this is the place to measure it. Therefore, as indicated earlier, the principal level where we collected the empirical data is the organisational, or university level. For each case study relevant actors were identified, bearing in mind the different parties.

Alternatives
It is important to bear in mind that the unit of analysis is at a different level than the unit of research. The outcomes of the institutionalisation process are defined at a macroscopic level. These are the outcomes of a complex social process and cannot be considered as clear-cut alternatives for actors to choose. At the level where evidence is collected (i.e. the university), (groups of) individuals have a number of alternatives if the graduate school is the subject of discussion. From the perspective of practical advantage, the obvious alternatives are either adoption or rejection of the graduate school. Between these two options, there are of course more 'moderate' alternatives. For example, conditional adoption might be a viable option if it is possible to adapt the graduate school to an actor's interest.

Preferences
Profits can be derived from various sources.

- *Financial and material resources*: the degree to which an actor can acquire resources through the graduate school. These can be either financial resources or other utilities.
- *Autonomy*: the degree to which the actors acquire freedom to make decisions concerning their own work, and are able to manipulate their environment accordingly, due to the establishment or membership of a graduate school.

– *Quality*: the degree to which actors perceive the quality of their work or working environment to improve as a result of the establishment or their membership of a graduate school.
– *Prestige*: the degree to which actors derive status or reputation from the establishment or their membership of a graduate school, for example as a result of quality improvement or expansion.

We employ these four categories to measure systematically the content of preferences.

Strategies
If the preferences of the identified actors in a system of doctoral education are established, the degree of profitability of a policy innovation in a system is not yet obvious. Strategic behaviour and relative influence in terms of power have an impact on the total degree of profitability in the institutional context. In terms of Clark's metaphor, actors are not in fixed positions on the seesaw. They can move up and down, pick up some extra weight or make coalitions with a (heavy) counterpart or competitor. Power is unequally divided, for example, doctoral candidates are known to have scant potential to influence the direction of graduate schools.

As mentioned earlier, the scope of the empirical study does not go as far as a systematic analysis of strategies and power positions. Hence, these were not included when degrees of profitability were measured. Respondents were asked to indicate to what extent in their perception the graduate school was conceived as profitable in the institutional context under scrutiny for each of the distinguished categories of preferences. In addition, their perception on the profitability of the graduate school at the specific locations of inquiry was assessed. This was conducted in two ways. First, the context of the process of institutionalisation was assessed for each university under examination. This was to grasp the local circumstances into which the research school was introduced. Second, the decision-making process with regard to the establishment of a graduate school was reconstructed. In this respect, attention was paid to those actors who were actually involved in the decision-making process and to the extent of their influence on the decisions. On the basis of an assessment of the information given by the respondents, we tried to make a convincing argument for the *aggregated* degree of profitability for the institutional system under examination.

4.3   States of institutionalisation

Four states of institutionalisation were distinguished: diffusion, termination, resocialisation and fragmentation. The definition of a state of institutionalisation captures two dimensions: a quantitative dimension that refers to the degree of adoption of the graduate school throughout a system of doctoral education, and a qualitative dimension that refers to the institutional form of the graduate school as compared to the original policy idea. As to the *quantitative dimension*, it is necessary to employ a precise demarcating criterion in order to distinguish the states of institutionalisation from each other. In the case studies, the government usually expected a number of graduate schools to emerge in a particular field of study, or a number of PhD candidates to participate in the schools. A state of institutionalisation can be determined on the basis of the degree of adoption of graduate schools as compared to the policy objective. With regard to the *qualitative dimension*, it is not as straightforward to set an indicator. It is easier to identify the deviation of graduate schools from the original policy idea in those systems where graduate schools receive some sort of recognition, or qualify for funding if the policy idea is realised.

The four states of institutionalisation can be identified as follows. *Diffusion* occurs if more than 75% of the planned graduate schools have been established throughout the doctoral system. These graduate schools function in agreement with the original policy statements. *Termination* happens if less than 25% of the planned graduate schools have been established. Major and system-wide malfunctioning of the system of graduate schools may also indicate this state of institutionalisation. *Resocialisation* takes place if research schools have been established that deflect from the originally implemented policy idea. Formal policy documents generally form the primary benchmark for determining resocialisation. At least 25% of the planned graduate schools should have been established for this state of institutionalisation to apply. *Fragmentation* is demonstrated by a situation in which between 25% and 75% of the planned graduate schools have been established in accordance with the original policy idea. In this state of institutionalisation, graduate schools prosper in some locations, but decline in others.

5. EMPIRICAL ANALYSIS

We developed a research design on the basis of John Stuart Mill's book on experimental inquiry (Mill 1843), taking the 'indirect method of difference' as a basis for the empirical investigation and analysis (see Bartelse 1999; Goedegebuure & Van Vught 1996).

Four case studies were selected, representing the four different states of institutionalisation of the graduate school that were distinguished in section 3. Chemistry in the Netherlands was selected as an instance of diffusion; business administration in Germany was taken as an example of termination; law in the Netherlands served as an illustration of resocialisation; and the earth sciences in Germany constituted the case of fragmentation. For each case study, we measured the degrees of compatibility and profitability throughout the institutionalisation process. Two strategies were pursued to collect data and to measure the explanatory variables. The first approach focused on the situation in a particular country and discipline as a whole by way of interviewing specialists in the particular disciplinary field, and through a document study. The second approach comprised site visits to graduate schools (or terminated graduate schools) in each of the four cases, where a number of relevant stakeholders were interviewed. On the basis of the gathered empirical information we constructed degrees of compatibility and profitability at an aggregate level.

A comparative analysis was conducted in three steps following Mill's indirect method of difference. First, for each case, the presence of the dependent variable was assessed against the presence of its hypothesised cause. Second, the so-called negative cases of each hypothesis were assessed: the absence of a certain state of institutionalisation was assessed against the absence of its hypothesised causes. Third, the case studies were compared in order to identify alternative explanations, and to explore the hypothesised relationships further. We summarise the outcomes of this analysis below.

> *Hypothesis 1*: If the policy innovation is characterised by a high degree of compatibility and a high degree of profitability, diffusion of the policy innovation occurs.

In the Netherlands, the opportunity to establish graduate schools was created in 1991. Chemistry was selected as a case of diffusion. In chemistry, the graduate schools became an accepted phenomenon relatively quickly and, by the mid-1990s, the schools covered virtually the whole field and were recognised formally.

The idea of the graduate school was assessed to be compatible with most institutional characteristics of the doctoral system in chemistry. With regard to profitability, the lack of immediate advantages at several locations held back a full-blown diffusion throughout the discipline in the early 1990s. However, in the years that followed, the potential benefits of graduate schools became apparent. Hence, the hypothesised high degrees of compatibility and profitability were found. With regard to the negative case, we did not find evidence in the case studies that high degrees of compatibility and profitability could be associated with other states of institutionalisation. Hypothesis 1 was not rejected.

> *Hypothesis 2*: If the policy innovation is characterised by a high degree of incompatibility and a high degree of unprofitability, termination of the policy innovation occurs.

In 1990, Germany formally established a programme for the stimulation of graduate schools (*Graduiertenkollegs*). In this country we could select the field of business administration as a case of termination. In this area, graduate schools never gained ground. Only one school operates with funding from the *Deutsche Forschungsgemeinschaft* (DFG) and just a few graduate schools accommodate components of business administration. Throughout the research period, degrees of compatibility and profitability were found to be persistently negative. This supports the hypothesis on termination. As to the negative case, we did not find a situation where similar scores on the two explanatory variables corresponded with another state of institutionalisation. Hypothesis 2 could not be rejected.

> *Hypothesis 3*: If the policy innovation is characterised by a high degree of incompatibility and a high degree of profitability, the policy innovation will resocialise.

The field of law in the Netherlands was selected as a case of resocialisation, although the state of institutionalisation changed over the research period. While the situation in the early 1990s can best be described as one of termination, gradually, a number of initiatives were started to concentrate research training in schools or institutes. Many of these initiatives however did not comply with the original policy idea of the graduate school.[4] Only in the

---

[4]   The original policy idea was reconstructed on the basis of the criteria that the Royal Netherlands Academy of Science (KNAW) uses for the formal recognition procedures of graduate schools.

late 1990s did several faculties consider participating in the system of recognised graduate schools.

The measured degrees of compatibility and profitability also fluctuated, but in a pattern that does not oppose the hypothesis on resocialisation. At the time of the introduction of the graduate schools, compatibility and (to a lesser extent) profitability were both perceived to be low — which coincided with a state of termination. Gradually, however, the degree of profitability increased whereas compatibility remained low. During this situation, the state of resocialisation developed. The absence of resocialisation, being the negative case, did not correspond with a combination of incompatibility and profitability in any of the other three case studies. Hypothesis 3 was not rejected.

> *Hypothesis 4*: If the policy innovation is characterised by a high degree of compatibility and a high degree of unprofitability, the policy innovation is likely to fragment.

The discipline of the earth sciences in Germany currently exhibits a state of fragmentation. However, the discipline faces scientific developments that may possibly lead to a changing state of institutionalisation.

The findings in this case study indicate a strong ambiguity with regard to both compatibility and profitability. The idea of the graduate school could be characterised neither as clearly compatible nor as clearly incompatible. Generally, the heterogeneity of the discipline balances out the differences among actors. As to profitability, perceptions of the advantages also varied among actors in the different sub-disciplines and at different locations. In addition, most respondents saw strong disadvantages as well as advantages in the establishment of graduate schools. Hence, we concluded the degree of profitability to be medium. The negative case did not yield further evidence. Consequently, the hypothesised relationship between compatibility and unprofitability on the one hand and fragmentation on the other was not found. Hypothesis 4 was rejected.

6.   CONCLUSIONS

The comparative analysis did not lead to the falsification of hypotheses 1, 2 and 3. Hypothesis 4, however, was rejected. The theoretical framework seems to be largely supported, but needs critical consideration in several respects.

At the systemic level of analysis we have not found relevant alternative explanations for the institutionalisation of graduate schools. The concepts of compatibility and profitability are broad explanatory notions that are rooted in cultural and economic explanations of social life — they incorporate many potentially alternative explanations. Hence, the flip-side of adding parsimony to existing explanations of institutionalisation processes is the restricted empirical content of the theory (Van Vught 1997: 386). In order to prevent compatibility and profitability from being 'container' notions, we went to considerable length conceptualising and operationalising these variables. The distinguished operational categories of the two variables worked well in the empirical study of graduate schools. However, further empirical research is needed to assess whether the conceptualisations are generalisable to other situations, and to find out if other abstractions better grasp the forces at work.

The mechanisms of institutional contraction and expansion were not addressed in detail in the framework of this chapter. However, the notions do provide an account of the process of institutionalisation. They are the answer to the 'how' part of the central research question. The mechanisms of institutional contraction and expansion bridge cause and effect and thereby provide a more complete explanation of institutionalisation. Although the concepts of institutional expansion and contraction, and their indicators, were helpful in describing the process of institutionalisation in the case studies, they appeared to be somewhat crude. We feel the need for a further refinement of the response strategies of actors in connection with compatibility and profitability. Oliver (1991) suggests a typology of strategic responses of organisations to institutional pressures towards conformity. She identifies five types of strategic responses which might also be adopted and adapted as institutional responses to policy innovations: acquiescence, compromise, avoidance, defiance and manipulation (Oliver 1991: 151–9; Gornitzka & Maassen 1998: 4).

A third consideration originates from the falsification of hypothesis 4 on fragmentation. This pertains to the actual institutionalisation model: to what extent does this flaw the institutionalisation model, or should the model be adapted? The quadrant compatibility/ unprofitability (figure 2) is not filled with an empirical observation — the hypothesised relationship on fragmentation was falsified. What happens in cases of medium degrees of compatibility and profitability? The comparative analysis suggests that a state of fragmentation coincides with medium degrees of compatibility and profitability. Theoretically, this makes sense if fragmentation is viewed as situated between termination and diffusion on a quantitative, hence one-dimensional, scale. Profitability works particularly on the quantitative dimension: the degree to which a policy innovation is adopted in an institutional context. The practical advantages motivate actors within a certain institutional context to establish graduate schools; thus profitability works as a degree of satisfaction. Compatibility instead is a degree of dissatisfaction. It may work as a barrier which can stop innovations from institutionalising, or make them turn out differently. Both variables work simultaneously in the institutionalisation process. However, they work differently. Profitability, as a degree of satisfaction, makes things happen. Compatibility, as a measure of dissatisfaction, refers to a 'let-happen' sense of causality.[5] Hence, if profitability is negative, the graduate schools do not institutionalise. If, however, profitability is positive, then the degree of compatibility determines the state of institutionalisation that eventually evolves. Figure 3 reflects the adaptations suggested above.

Figure 3: Adjusted institutionalisation model

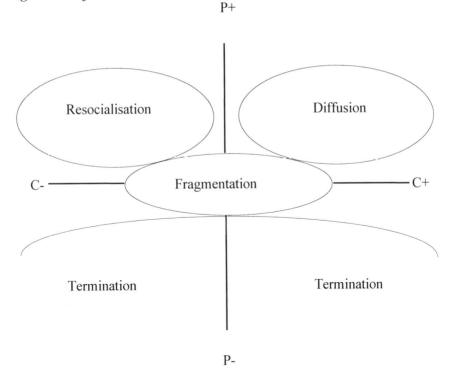

---

[5] Mohr (1996: 22) gives the following illustration of these two types of causality: 'Consider that someone opened the shutter irresponsibly, and a ball broke the window. Both of these factors were causes but in different senses'. Opening the shutter refers to a let-happen sense of causality; a ball breaking the window refers to a make-happen sense of causality.

In this chapter, we outlined what we consider to be a viable theoretical approach with which to study in what way a particular policy innovation — the graduate school — will or will not evolve into an actual institution. Have we realised the theoretical objective of this study, which was *to develop a viable explanation of institutionalisation processes of policy innovations in the area of doctoral education*?

We have not attempted to present a fully fledged theory on institutionalisation. The endeavour has been far more heuristic. We hope to have provided a set of coherent statements to understand the phenomenon of interest. The idea has been to provide an extra dimension to the understanding of the dynamics of (higher education) policy and to develop a workable bridge between as yet rather disparate strands of theorising.

There may be substantive value in going beyond traditional higher education and policy study approaches, which often focus on specific explanations. What we have attempted to argue is that viable empirical research is possible taking two explanatory perspectives together — in a complementary rather than a competitive way. Actors are embedded in what we have termed 'an institutional context' that may affect substantially the way in which they operate. For our object of study — policy innovations in doctoral education, in particular, the graduate school — this is especially appropriate if we are to take the institutional implications of Clark Kerr's (1963) famous expression on the permanence of higher education seriously. Can we say anything about how and why innovations evolve or not in *the* higher education realm par excellence — doctoral education — without explicit reference to higher education as an institution? From the framework sketched above, it follows that our answer to this question is negative. Institutions do provide a logic of their own, and attempts at changing the core elements of these institutions cannot be analysed without reference to this logic. Hence, the attention paid to the constituent elements of work, beliefs and authority in the case studies. In the case of law, for example, deeply rooted convictions and practices have challenged the prosperity of the innovation. Despite a clear-cut incentive to establish graduate schools, the incompatibility of the policy innovation has induced unexpected outcomes.

As suggested, it is also pointless to either abstract or neglect the 'mundane' component of human interaction. Higher education, and universities as a specific form, are not 'above' that which motivates individuals: (strategic) self-interest. Striving and struggling for money, power and prestige is as much part and parcel of higher education as it is of any other social field. This is also reflected in the case studies. Take for example the case of chemistry. After a hesitant start — some faculties lingered over the installation of graduate schools — the prospect of substantive amounts of funds, the quality mark attached to research schools and the accompanying prestige provided the active motivation to establish a graduate school. Therefore, any analysis of change should incorporate this element.

Whether we have captured the balance between compatibility and profitability correctly remains a moot point. There seems to be little doubt regarding the expected outcomes of a policy innovation when both variables are assessed as either positive or negative. But the mixed cases are the interesting ones. Does self-interest overcome the institutional logic and thus result in a new 'institution', or are 'the institutional roots' ultimately stronger? The evidence so far supports the expectation that greater weight should be given to the institutional context than has been the case in previous studies focusing on innovations in higher education. But, basically, the variables work simultaneously, each in their own right: profitability as a degree of satisfaction, compatibility as a degree of dissatisfaction.

We suggest that theoretical efforts should focus particularly on the process of institutionalisation. As mentioned above, the mechanisms of institutional contraction and expansion seem too crude to represent the dynamics of this process. Alternative notions may capture institutional responses to policy innovations more adequately. Furthermore, the conceptualisation and operationalisation of the explanatory variables need additional consideration — not only because they were developed with a particular policy innovation in mind, the graduate school, but also to develop the concepts further as useful theoretical abstractions. The current indicators seem to work relatively well, in particular for the concept of compatibility, which is usually regarded as an awkward concept to grapple with. Profitability was easier to recognise and more straightforward to deal with empirically, but is difficult to judge on an aggregate level. Here, power struggles and strategic self- and collective interest blurred the measurements. A more refined and balanced conceptualisation and operationalisation of this variable seems justifiable.

As to empirical research, we believe that a case study method remains a useful strategy to advance the institutionalisation model presented. Additional cases may flesh out the hypothesised relationships and refine the proposed conceptualisations.

References

Bartelse, J.A. (1999*), Concentrating the Minds: the institutionalisation of the graduate school innovation in Dutch and German higher education*, Utrecht: Lemma.

Bartelse, J.A, H. de Boer, J. Huisman and E. Lugthart (1999), *De Onderzoekschool: een analyse van het functioneren van het beleidsinstrument onderzoekschool*, Enschede: CHEPS.

Blume, S. (1995), Problems and prospects of research training in the 1990s, in: OECD (ed.), *Research Training: Present & Future*, Paris: OECD, pp. 9–40.

Boer H.F. de, A. Gornitzka and P.A.M. Maassen (1998), *Higher education and institutional analysis*, Enschede: CHEPS, University of Twente (draft version).

Bowen, G.B. and N.L. Rudenstine (1992), *In Pursuit of the PhD*, Princeton: Princeton University Press.

Braxton, J.M. and L.L. Hargens (1996), Variation among academic disciplines: analytical frameworks and research, in: J.C. Smart (ed.), *Higher Education: handbook of theory and research*, vol. XI, New York: Agathon, pp. 1–46.

Clark, B.R. (1983), *The Higher Education System*, Berkeley: University of California Press.

Clark, B.R. (ed.) (1993), *The Research Foundations of Graduate Education: Germany, Britain, France, United States, Japan*, Berkeley: University of California Press.

Council of Graduate Education (CGE). *Graduate Schools* (1995), Warwick. (CGE)

Deutsche Forschungsgemeinschaft (1997), *Entwicklung und Stand des Programms 'Graduiertenkollegs'*, Bonn: DFG.

DiMaggio, P.J. and W.W. Powell (1991), *The New Institutionalism in Organisational Analysis*, Chicago: The University of Chicago Press.

Eggertsson, T. (1990), *Economic Behavior and Institutions*, Cambridge: Cambridge University Press.

Giddens, A. (1977), *Studies in Social and Political Theory*, London: Hutchinson.

Goedegebuure, L.C.J. and F.A. van Vught (1996), Comparative higher education studies: the perspective from the policy sciences, *Higher Education, vol. 32*, no.4, pp. 371-94.

Gornitzka, Å. and P.A.M. Maassen (1998), *Governmental policies and organisational change in higher education*, paper prepared for the 11th CHER Conference, Kassel, Germany, 3–5 September.

Green, D.P. and I. Shapiro (1994), *Pathologies of Rational Choice Theory: a critique of applications in political science*, New Haven: Yale University Press.

Hendriks, F. (1996), *Beleid, Cultuur en Institutties: het verhaal van twee steden*, Leiden: DSWO Press.

Hesseling, P. (1986), *Frontiers of Learning: the PhD octopus*, Dordrecht: Floris Publications.

Keman, H. (1997), Approaches to the analysis of institutions, in: B. Steunenberg and F.A. van Vught (eds), *Political Institutions and Public Policy: perspectives on European decision making*, Dordrecht: Kluwer.

Kerr C. (1982) (1963), *The Uses of the University*, Cambridge, Mass: Harvard University Press.

Lapidus, J.B. (1994), *Current issues, influences and trends in doctoral education*, paper presented at the ASHE Conference, Arizona.

Levine, A. (1980), *Why Innovation Fails: the institutionalization and termination of innovation in higher education*, Albany: State University of New York Press.

Mill, J.S. (1967) (1843), *A System of Logic Ratiocinative and Inductive*, Toronto: University of Toronto Press.

Mohr, L.B. (1996), *The Causes of Human Behavior: implications for theory and method in the social sciences*, Ann Arbor: The University of Michigan Press.

Norgaard, A.S. (1996), Rediscovering reasonable rationality in institutional analysis, *European Journal of Political Research*, no. 29, pp. 31–57.

Oliver, C. (1991), Strategic responses to institutional processes, *Academy of Management Review*, vol. 16, no. 1, pp. 145–79.

Organization for Economic Co-operation and Development (1995), *Research Training: present & future*, Paris: OECD.

Rogers, E.M. (1983), *Diffusion of Innovations*, New York: The Free Press.

Tsebelis, G. (1990), *Nested Games: rational choice in comparative politics*, Berkeley: University of California Press.

Van Vught, F.A. (1997), Using policy analysis for strategic choices, in: M.W. Peterson, D.D. Dill, L.A. Mets and Associates (eds), *Planning and Management for a Changing Environment: a handbook for a changing environment*, San Francisco: Jossey-Bass Publishers.

Van Vught, F.A. and D.F. Westerheijden (1993), *Quality Management and Quality Assurance in European Higher Education: methods and mechanisms*, Luxembourg: Office for Official Publications of the EC.

Wied D. de, (1991), *Postgraduate Research Training Today: emerging structures for a changing Europe*, The Hague: Netherlands Ministry of Education and Science.

Chapter 12

Higher education policies and institutional response in Flanders

Instrumental analysis and cultural theory

OSCAR VAN HEFFEN, JEF VERHOEVEN AND KURT DE WIT

Key words: cultural theory; instrumental analysis; policy implementation

1.   INTRODUCTION

After the state reform of 1988, Flanders wanted to act differently and achieve more than Belgium. The Flemish Minister-President Geens declared on 8 November 1988 that: 'We shall have to prove to the current and future generations that what we do ourselves, we do better' and 'The Flemish policy institutions must prove in this new structure that, thanks to the full autonomy in such a vital sector for our community as the education of our youth, in Flanders a different method can be applied' (Vlaamse Raad 1988).

Belgian society and politics traditionally were influenced by three cleavages. In the social and economic field, labour and capital stood against each other. Concerning language, there were tensions between Dutch speaking and French speaking populations. In terms of ideology, Catholics and freethinkers were opponents. These groups were often diametrically opposed to each other and that was a potential threat to the stability of the Belgian state. Many governments fell over linguistic problems.

To overcome the threat of instability, the principle of pacification was introduced. Pacification is based on the idea that one party or group can never take decisions alone or impose them on another party or group. In other words, the majority cannot rule. On the contrary, an agreement or compromise is sought which is more or less acceptable to all parties concerned. It is a process of give and take, often with the government giving to all parties. Establishing a compromise is carried out by an elite, which discretely searches for a solution that is acceptable to all. This often leads to complex results; a complex exchange operation embedded in protective measures. Policy problems are neutralised by being turned into technical exchange questions. The pacification democracy resulted in the so-called politics of the waffle iron (*wafelijzerpolitiek*). Ministerial portfolios of both parts of the country were linked to each other and this led to unnecessary expenses.

Before 1989, as a result of these social, linguistic and ideological cleavages, it was difficult, if not impossible to develop a higher educational policy which would go beyond the previous state of affairs, for example, a policy aimed at the rationalisation of the higher education system. If the Belgian government had developed such a policy, pacification would probably have been in danger. The underlying ideological tendencies would have become manifest again and a crisis would have been hard to avoid. Therefore, it comes as no surprise that the policy documents from this period contain very little explicit statement, minimising the risk of a fundamental debate about policy, something Belgian politics were not ready for.

Furthermore, Belgian educational policies were hampered by the economic recession, as elsewhere, at the end of the 1970s and the beginning of the 1980s. The former Minister of Education, Coens, put it this way (1985: 10): 'Doing educational politics in a time of economic growth must have been a pleasant occupation ... The choices to be made were only: how much "more more" or "less more" was assigned. Today the situation is different'. The Belgian higher educational policy, and in a broader sense the whole government policy, was dominated by financial problems. The increasing public debts and the increasing interest rates made a renewal of the content of higher education policies also unlikely.

The improvement of the economic situation and federalisation in 1989 made it possible for the content of the higher educational policy to come under scrutiny. The new policy-makers responsible for education — the Flemish government and the Minister of Education in particular — focused their attention mainly on the quality of higher education.

Firstly, the Flemish government has attempted to enhance the quality of higher education by increasing the transparency and rationality of course supply, and by refining the system of quality control. Secondly, the Flemish government encourages new educational methods on behalf of the knowledge society, including distance learning, but mainly lifelong learning. Thirdly, the Flemish government promotes the internationalisation of higher education. Among other things, it stimulates participation in European programmes, supports international financial cooperation, introduces adaptations to international systems and subsidises foreign students.

Like in many other European countries, the former Belgian higher education system was a combination of state bureaucracy and faculty guilds (Clark 1983; Van Vught 1995). Flanders is one of the first continental experiences with a state-supervising system. Our knowledge of the success and failure of such major transformations of steering strategies and major policy innovations is limited. We only know that far-reaching policy innovations are difficult to implement (Lindblom 1959, 1979; Korsten 1998). From this perspective the Flemish case is interesting, both from a scientific and an administrative point of view.

In this chapter the effects of changes in steering strategies of Flemish higher education and their impact on universities (in particular, the Catholic University of Leuven and the University of Gent) will be discussed. We analyse the changes in steering strategies, policies and university policy plans from an instrumental perspective and a cultural perspective. Using a power-dependency framework (Van Heffen & Klok 1997) and cultural theory (Thompson *et al.* 1990) we will explain the relationship between governmental policies and institutional performance.

The central research problem is formulated as follows:

What are the effects of changes in steering strategies of the Flemish government and governmental policies with respect to higher education on the policy plans of Flemish universities?

This central problem is elaborated in the following questions:

1. What is the steering strategy of the Flemish government in the field of higher education?
2. What is the content of the Flemish governmental policies on higher education?
3. How are governmental policies and policy plans of Flemish universities related?
4. How can this relationship be explained, taking into account the characteristics of the policy instruments and the institutional culture?

The content of this chapter is as follows. In section 2 the theoretical framework will be presented. Section 3 deals with the changes in the Flemish steering model of higher education. In section 4 governmental policies and university plans on the transparency and rationality of course supply, lifelong learning and internationalisation of higher education will be analysed. Finally, in section 5 some conclusions will be drawn on the basis of the theoretical framework.

2.   THEORETICAL FRAMEWORK: INSTRUMENTAL ANALYSIS, CULTURAL THEORY AND INSTITUTIONAL RESPONSE

2.1   Power-dependencies and instrumental tactics[1]

The outcomes of a policy process are dependent on the activities of policy actors. Generally speaking, human activity is the result of available resources and the motivation to undertake a certain activity (to be able to, and to want to). For an actor to be able to undertake certain activities, the availability of and the access to resources is a necessary condition. Resources can be the personal possession of an individual, but also interpersonal or interactive. Resources are 'interactive' when they can only be used as resources by an actor if at least one other actor recognises them as such. Interactive resources are a part of the reality definitions of actors and are construed and reconstrued in processes of continuing interaction.

Personal or non-interactive resources are, for example:

– Physical goods
– Skills
– Manpower
– Information
– Time.[2]

---

[1] This subsection is derived to a large extent from Van Heffen and Klok (1997).

[2] In human perception, time and activity are inextricably connected to each other. Time can be seen as a scarce good that is necessary for the production of physical and immaterial goods. The amount of time that an actor has available, can be denoted as a time budget

Interactive resources are, for example:

- Money
- Legal rules
- Trust
- Reputation
- Relationships.

For understanding policy processes the 'supply' and the 'flow', the 'function' and the 'spreading' or 'distribution' of resources are important concepts.

Supply refers to the amount of resources that an actor has at his/her disposal. Flow bears reference to the positive or negative variation in this amount. In a multi-actor situation, four types of flows can be distinguished:

1. Obtaining resources from other actors;
2. Relinquish your resources to other actors;
3. Production of resources by the actor;
4. Destruction of resources (use or destruction).

The function of resources is dependent on the activities that an actor wishes to undertake. It is about the special effects and actions that the input of resources accomplishes with regard to certain activities. So, the resource 'metal chisel' is suited for splitting wood, but not for cutting diamonds.

It is well-known that an actor can influence a second actor if the second actor requires resources from the first actor to undertake certain activities. One can see the relation between these actors as a power-dependency relationship, whereby power is defined as the ability to influence the behaviour of another actor in accordance with one's own aims, by changing the availability, characteristics or consequences of behavioural alternatives. Dependency refers to the resources that an actor has control over and that are necessary for another actor to undertake certain activities (Gross & Etzioni 1985). The spreading or the distribution of resources thus influences the available behavioural alternatives.

Instrumental tactics
The activities of an actor can be stimulated, opposed or changed by another actor because the second actor is capable of influencing the motivation and/or the available resources of the first actor (see also French & Raven 1959; Emerson 1962). Thereby the second actor can apply the following

instrumental tactics: facilitate, defacilitate, organise, deorganise, motivate and discourage. These tactics can present themselves in various forms (see figure 1).

Figure 1: Different forms of instrumental tactics

Facilitate - once-only supply of resources - start a flow of resources - functionalise	Defacilitate - depriving of resources - interrupting a flow of resources - defunctionalising
Organise - creation of an actor - reorganisation of an actor	Deorganise - eliminating an actor - reorganisation of an actor
Motivate - provisional facilitation - provisional defacilitation - provisional organisation	Discourage - provisional defacilitation - provisional deorganisation

Facilitation of resources can take place in different ways. An actor can supply resources once-only or he/she can start a permanent flow. It is also possible that he/she can apply changes in an environment, which will make the resources of a second actor relevant for the undertaking of certain activities (function profit). This form of facilitating is denoted as functionalising.

The defacilitation of resources can take place by taking away or destroying the supply of resources, interrupting a permanent flow and the changing of an environment, which will cause resources to partly or completely lose their function (defunctionalisation).

The purpose of organising an actor is that a changed or new actor will develop certain activities. Deorganisation in fact initiates a situation where an actor will no longer be capable of developing 'activities that are not wanted'. By means of organisation and deorganisation, an attempt is made at influencing the deployment of resources by changing the structure of the actor.

The organisation of an actor can refer to the creation of a new actor or the reorganisation of an existing actor. Deorganisation is the elimination or reorganisation of an existing actor.

Motivating an actor is aimed at having this actor display a certain form of behaviour. Motivation can be done by means of provisional facilitation, provisional defacilitation and provisional organisation. Provisional facilitation means that an actor is supplied with resources (once-only or a permanent flow) or that his/her environment is changed, such that his/her (potential) resources become functional, provided that he/she will undertake certain activities. We call threatening to take away, destroy or interrupt a flow and the defunctionalisation of resources of a certain actor if he/she does not undertake certain activities, provisional defacilitation. Provisional organisation means that an actor is confronted with the prospect of the creation of another actor (a competitor) if the first actor refuses to develop certain activities or the first actor can be confronted with the threat of reorganisation.

Discouraging an actor aims to prevent him/her from showing a certain form of behaviour. Discouragement can take place in the form of provisional defacilitation and deorganisation. Provisional defacilitation means that an actor is told that his/her resources will be taken away or destroyed, that a flow of resources will be interrupted or that his/her environment will be changed such that his/her resources will lose their function, if he/she continues to undertake certain activities. One can speak of provisional deorganisation when the threat is expressed that an actor will be reorganised or eliminated if he/she continues to undertake certain (undesired) activities.

The effects of changes in steering strategies and policies
It is possible to deduce from the framework of instrumental tactics that changes in steering strategies and policies cause intended effects if these stimuli influence the motivation, resources or structure of an actor. From this point of view with regard to four imaginary situations the following assumptions regarding the effects of changes in steering strategies of the Flemish government on the policy plans of Flemish universities can be formulated.

Situation 1: Universities are not motivated to implement governmental policies and do not possess (sufficient) resources

1: The continued effect of the Flemish governmental policies on higher education is stronger as these policies contain tactics like 'provisional facilitation of resources' or 'provisional organisation of universities'.

Hypothesis 1 needs a short explanation. If an actor is not motivated to undertake certain activities and he/she does not dispose of sufficient resources, the application of instrumental tactics is dependent on his/her appreciation of the absent resources. In case there is a positive appreciation of these resources, these can be facilitated on condition that the desired activities are undertaken. This tactic is, however, senseless if the actor does not appreciate the resources. Threatening with the creation of a new actor or the reorganisation of the unmotivated actor (provisional organisation) and actually applying these tactics in case threatening does not work seems more obvious.

Situation 2: Universities are not motivated to implement governmental policies and possess (sufficient) resources

2: The continued effect of the Flemish governmental policies on higher education is stronger as these policies contain tactics like '(provisional) defacilitation of resources' or '(provisional) organisation of universities'.

Situation 3: Universities are motivated to implement governmental policies, but do not possess (sufficient) resources

3: The continued effect of the Flemish governmental policies on higher education is stronger as these policies facilitate (sufficient) resources.

Situation 4: Universities are motivated to implement governmental policies and possess (sufficient) resources

4: The Flemish government can refrain from action.

2.2   Cultural theory

Inspired by Durkheim, the British anthropologist Mary Douglas formulated a theoretical framework based upon 'social integration' and 'regulation' of the actions of individuals, which she indicated as group- and grid- dimensions. In this framework not only are individual preferences and individual behaviour classified, but also organisational types and cultural systems (see e.g. Douglas 1970, 1982). Later, Aaron Wildavsky and Michael Thompson elaborated this cultural theory. In cooperation with Ellis, they presented a framework applied in various policy analyses (e.g. Coyle & Ellis 1994; Hoppe & Peterse 1993; Hendriks 1996; Maassen 1996).

The basic assumption of cultural theory is that 'what matters most to people is their relationships with other people and other people's relationships with them' (Wildavsky 1984: 1; see also Thompson *et al.* 1990: 97). Therefore, the social order in which people interact is of utmost importance to them. An important proposition of the theory is that there can be only a limited number of social orders, called cultures or ways of life.

On the basis of the dimensions 'group' and 'grid', four patterns of social relations are distinguished. Group is seen as '... the experience of a bounded social unit' (Douglas 1970: viii). It is thus about the incorporation of an individual in a group or, at least, about the perception that an individual has of it. 'Grid refers to rules that relate one person to others on an egocentered basis' (Douglas 1970: viii) and therefore to the binding nature and the extensiveness of rules or regulations that structure the individual choice processes that precede interactions.

The main points of interest in a group–grid analysis are the different ways of social control.

Individual choice, this mode of analysis contends, may be constricted either through requiring that a person be bound by group decisions or by demanding that individuals follow the rules accompanying their station in life. Social control is a form of power. In the grid-group framework individuals are manipulated and try to manipulate others. It is the form of power — who is or is not entitled to exercise power over others — that differs (Thompson *et al.* 1990: 6).

A combination of the two dimensions leads to four categories of social patterns that are linked to beliefs about man and his/her place in the world: the cultures or ways of life. These cultures are powerless fatalism, hierarchical collectivism, competitive individualism and egalitarian sectarianism.

The fatalistic culture is associated with a low group- and high grid-score. A person with a fatalistic attitude feels subject to many rules and obligations. He/she does not know the security of a group and therefore cannot derive protection or power from a group. The fatalist is a plaything of forces that are difficult to fathom.

The hierarchical culture is closely tied to a high group- and high grid-score. The positions of hierarchically geared people in a certain societal setting can be traced back to the strength of the group of which they are members. In filling the various roles that are linked to these positions, hierarchists are bound by a large number of rules and obligations, but are also subject to the control of the group. For this, the group has various methods of control. The exertion of such power is justified by the idea that different roles for different persons offer people the possibility of living together in more harmony than in other social arrangements (Douglas 1978). The hierarchical culture is riddled with ideas about organisation, technical control and make-ability.

The individualistic culture is characterised by a low group- and low grid-score. The role that an individualist plays is to a considerable extent decided by the person him/herself. An individualist does take part in certain social relations, but does not consider him/herself subordinate to these relations or groups. In the individualistic culture, all roles and (social) boundaries are temporary and (possibly) subject to negotiation. Thompson *et al.* (1990: 7) note that the freedom of control of the individualist does not mean that he/she is not involved in the exertion of power over others.

The egalitarian culture is related to a high group- and low grid-score. The egalitarian is confronted with clear group boundaries ('us against the world') and group decision, but there are few rules and obligations, which does not make it easy to distinguish the different roles in the group. The lack of internal role-differentiation (low grid) causes relations between the members of the group to be unclear. Combined with the fact that authority is lacking, resulting internal conflicts can only be resolved with great difficulty. Individuals only have power over other individuals when they can exert it (temporarily, from case to case) in the name of the group. After all, they do not have a role that permits them to force others to alter their behaviour. The solving of conflicts often takes the form of expelling one or more of the conflicting parties, or threatening to do so. The radical nature of such solutions prevents differences of opinion from being spoken and therefore they continue to boil beneath the surface.

An important assumption in the cultural theory is that beliefs, actions and norms of an individual mesh with 'the organisation of the social relations', the so-called compatibility condition. In this way, the rationality of the individual and his/her choice processes are to a certain extent biased. It is thus a matter of cultural distortion that leads to a certain form of rationality. The cultural theory claims that human decisions are determined by culture but that people also construe their culture in continuing processes of decision-making: '... beliefs are no longer separated from structure or action, but are part of the action itself' (Douglas 1982: 199–200).

Individuals discover their preferences through confirming, adapting or totally changing their way of life. That is to say: preferences are exogenous '... but continuously moulded by the way we organise our lives' (Grendstad & Selle 1995: 10). Cultural theory does not rule out the possibility of people choosing another way of life, but such a dramatic change only takes place if there is a cumulation of disappointments. A disappointment occurs when a reality does not correspond with the expectation of it. Every time someone is disappointed, his/her convictions that are connected to the way of life are affected. If this person is 'sufficiently' disappointed, he/she loses his/her convictions (way of life) and becomes a supporter of another way of life.

Selle (1991: 103) has succinctly described the structure of cultural theory:

> *Value patterns (= shared values) legitimize and reinforce behavioral patterns (= social practices). Together they form 'social orders', 'ways of life' or 'cultures'. It does not make sense to ask which comes first, because the one cannot exist without the other. Together they are supposed to predict political behavior (politics), institutions (polity) and outcomes (policies) ...*

The effects of changes in steering strategies and policies
Cultural theory contains statements about individual and organisational responses to change. We can deduce from cultural theory that (external) changes in steering strategies and policies cause intended effects if:

– the perceived intentions of these (environmental) stimuli are in accordance with the beliefs of the culture in question: Individuals and organisations will not respond positively if their beliefs, interests or goals are at stake. Beliefs, interests and goals are culturally determined;

– the stimuli modify the grid dimension of the culture: Individuals and organisations will change their behaviour if they are not able to resist a reinforcement of rules or regulations that structure the choice processes that precede interactions (grid).

From the point of view of cultural theory, two hypotheses (assumptions 5 and 6) regarding the effects of changes in steering strategies of the Flemish government and governmental policies with respect to higher education on the policy plans of Flemish universities can be formulated:

5: The continued effect of the Flemish governmental policies on higher education is stronger as the assumptions of these policies and the cultural bias of Flemish universities are more alike.

6: The continued effect of the Flemish governmental policies on higher education is stronger as the Flemish government is able to formulate rules or regulations that structure the choice processes of Flemish universities.

After a presentation of the changes in the Flemish steering model (section 3) and governmental policies and institutional policy plans (section 4), the 'instrumental' and 'cultural' assumptions will be tested (section 5).

3.   THE FLEMISH STEERING MODEL OF HIGHER EDUCATION

Generally, government can be considered as the recognised, authoritative leadership of a society. This section pays attention to the steering relationship between government and universities in Flanders. Following Olsen (1988) we distinguish four steering models: the sovereign (or unicentric) state, the institutional state, the segmented (or corporatist) state and the market state.

In a sovereign steering or unicentric model, higher education is seen as an instrument to attain economic or social goals (CHEPS 1998). Tight control over universities and universities being accountable to political authorities are distinctive features of this model. In accordance with ends articulated by the dominating political force, well-trained bureaucrats list the policy alternative strategies and determine the consequences that follow upon each of these strategies. Subsequently one of the alternatives is chosen and implemented. Such a view implicitly presupposes a top-down implementation of a policy. After all, the governing groups in a society have enough power to control the implementation process. 'Policy is taken to be the property of the policymakers at the top' (Hill 1997: 131).

The model of the institutional state emphasises the responsibility of higher education institutions for the protection of academic values and tradition against one-sided interests of political regimes and interest groups.

> *In the field of higher education this model is probably best exemplified through reference to the relationship between the state and the old elitist universities, where there is/was a shared understanding and unwritten conventions of state non interference between state civil service and universities as elite institutions* (CHEPS 1998: 16).

The model of the segmented or corporatist state contains several competing, but legitimate centres of authority and control, inside and outside government. Schmitter (1974: 93–4) defines corporatism as:

> *A system of interest representation in which the constituent units are organised into a limited number of singular, compulsory, non-competitive, hierarchically ordered and functionally differentiated categories, recognised or licensed by the state and granted a deliberate representational monopoly within respective categories in exchange for observing certain controls on their selection of leaders and articulation of demands and supports.*

In the segmented or corporatist state, policy is the result of negotiations in these centres, councils or commissions and reflects the constellation of represented interests.

In the market model the role of the state is minimal. It is supposed that the market is superior to traditional state bureaucracies because market relations are more flexible and therefore lead to socially needed innovations (the innovation argument). Besides, the competition between organisations keeps costs down (the efficiency argument). In this model, policy is the result of bilateral negotiations between governmental actors or between governmental and social actors, for example private-public partnerships.

Olsen's four models will be used to characterise the steering relationships between government and universities in Flanders.

Before 1989 university steering was based on the law of 27 July 1971 on the financing and control of university institutions and the law of 28 April 1953 on the state universities. The actual way universities were treated, differed greatly for free and state universities.

The state universities were directly subjected to the responsibility of the national Minister of Education, who was the organising body of state education. Therefore these universities were influenced directly by the features of the political system of that time: unstable due to linguistic troubles and financially restricted because of the increasing public debt. Moreover strong centralism (everything was decided 'in Brussels') caused strong bureaucratisation. Decisions were executed by the administration, which was politicised. The bureaucratisation was an expression of the hierarchical structure of state education, with the Minister of Education as the centre.

The free universities were relatively autonomous. According to Verhoeven (1982: 131) this can be explained by, on the one hand, the fact that university education has always been seen as necessarily autonomous and organised by private initiative and, on the other hand, because it was entirely clear that interventions could trigger irreconcilable conflict. The government was reluctant to regulate in order to leave the delicate ideological and linguistic equilibrium in the university sector in peace.

This short overview of the governmental steering in the 1970s and 1980s towards state universities and free universities indicates that we cannot describe it homogeneously in terms of one steering model. Policy towards state universities can be described best as a sovereign state model. The model of the institutional state applies to the free universities. But the governmental steering towards both types of universities also had features of the segmented state model, for example, the National Council for State Education (*Nationale Raad voor het Rijksonderwijs*) gave advice on all propositions to change the educational structure, the duration of studies, and the general orientation of education. Among the 21 members of the Council were representatives of the state university education, the state inspectorate and state schools, parents and teachers associations, and trade unions.

The discontent in Flanders about these steering models, especially the way the state higher education was treated, caused a fundamental shift when Flanders received authority over education. With the decree on universities of 1991, the government took an important step towards far-reaching autonomy. The Flemish governmental agreement of 17 June 1995 spoke of a radical enlargement of the autonomy and responsibility for the whole education sector. The decrees only imposed formal requirements (length of the course, division in cycles, possibilities to abridge course duration and so on); the content of education (the course programme) could be decided by the institutions themselves.

The government however did not withdraw entirely: 'The government creates conditions and sets out quality goals' (Van Den Bossche 1995: 9); 'it proposes minimal goals, promotes certain social priorities, secures a number of vital interests and rights, especially for the weaker, and to that aim provides the necessary resources in exchange for clear agreements' (Van Den Bossche 1995: 12). In principle, control was exercised in retrospect. For that purpose a quality control system was established, but the application of the system came under the responsibility of the institutions.

Governmental steering of higher education after 1989 differed greatly from the previous period. An important change is that the steering is now nearly the same for all higher education institutions. With the special decree of 26 June 1991 the former state universities became their own organising body and their autonomy became largely the same as that of free universities.

The new steering model is more like a market model. The government only provides the financial means, and controls in retrospect. The autonomy however is not total, as was indicated above. In other words, the market state model is only partially applicable to the current situation. This also appears from the elements of the segmented state that are still present in the steering model, like advisory councils in the policy network.

4.   GOVERNMENTAL POLICIES AND INSTITUTIONAL POLICY PLANS

In this section we study the effects of the governmental policies on the plans of two major Flemish universities, namely Leuven and Gent. First we will outline governmental policies, then we will discuss the university plans. These policies and plans deal with the transparency and rationality of course supply, new educational methods on behalf of the knowledge society, and internationalisation.

4.1   Transparency and rationality

The transparency and rationality of course supply are dependent on the development of new programmes and the reorientation or adjustment of existing programmes.

Governmental policy
The Flemish government considers it important to increase the rationality of course supply in higher education, because it wants Flemish higher education to be competitive in an international context. This rationalisation and optimisation goal includes the following elements: new programmes and courses; improvement of existing programmes; rejection of inferior courses; 'freezing' (i.e. abolishment but with the possibility of re-establishment) and abolishment of courses; and integration of courses. The instruments to achieve these goals are legislation and information.

Law is used for example to create a system of quality control. The universities' decree of 1991 introduced a threefold quality control system. The institutions themselves are responsible for the internal quality control. Through reviews an external quality control is carried out. A further external control is the meta-evaluation ordered by the government and carried out by an international panel of experts.

The Flemish government tries to influence the development of new programmes by stimulating universities and colleges to be more entrepreneurial and dynamic by indicating in which way higher education should develop (through information in policy statements and so on). The relevant policy documents do not specify clear obligations, but set out the direction to be followed by the higher education institutions. Likewise the government tries to stimulate universities to improve their existing programmes. Furthermore, the former Flemish Minister of Education has stated several times (see e.g. Van Den Bossche 1995, 1998) that the idea of a 'full' university is outdated. The traditional way of thinking, in which each institution tries to complete its supply of courses horizontally or vertically, can no longer be maintained. Instead, universities must strive to become 'valuable'. In other words: they have to become centres of excellence in education and research. As a consequence of this concept of a valuable university, universities should not offer inferior courses. However, no direct policy instrument to achieve this goal is formulated. Here again the Flemish government seems to 'manage by speech', a technique that seems to be used often towards higher education. This technique is based on the idea that when one firmly sets the course, others will follow. Lastly, we have to say that a number of policy measures with regard to the freezing, abolishment and integration of the university course supply will be taken, but only after consultation with the vice-chancellors. This is a good example of the new steering model of the Flemish government (a market-oriented but still segmented state model).

Catholic University of Leuven

In the period under study, there have been two instances of major reorientation of existing programmes at Leuven. The first was an internally motivated Operation Rationalisation that started in 1989. The goal of rationalisation was to enhance the quality of education in the first and second cycle, by limiting the number of courses, reducing the volume of courses, and abandoning the idea of 'encyclopaedic education', which was a burden for both students and teachers. 'Teach the student how to think, not what to think' was proclaimed to be the new motto for the organisation of education in the first and second cycle.

The second major reorientation took place in the two academic years following the universities' decree of 1991, when a number of adaptations made the programmes fit with the new regulations. Inter-university deliberations resulted in a clear distinction between basic courses and advanced courses, including new titles for the programmes. The possibilities for transition from college to university were better defined. The educational regulations (access conditions, content of the programmes, the possibility of half-time study, etc.) were clarified. The 'individually tailored year programme' was introduced and all curricula were based on study points.

More recent initiatives are the involvement of the Catholic University of Leuven in the Consortium for the Innovation of Higher Education; the establishment of the Institute for New Teaching Methods (*LINOV*) (a centre of expertise and study with regard to the use of multimedia and telematics in education); and stimulating educational projects (*onderwijsgerichte onderzoeks-, ontwikkelings- en implementatieprojecten*), that is, projects for the analysis of educational problems, the development of new teaching methods or instruments, and the broad implementation of these initiatives.

University of Gent

The Special Decree of 1991 (which turned the University of Gent from a state university into an autonomous university) brought changes, but mainly at the organisational level. Attention at the central level for educational innovation has only been apparent in recent years. Reorienting or adjusting the content or method of existing programmes is mainly a task at the base level (individual academics, departments and educational committees). Educational innovation takes place both inside and outside the framework of curricular reform. External quality control (the so-called reviews) concerns, among other things, rationalising the structure of the curricula, individualising educational processes and study processes, using active teaching and learning methods, and stressing guidance of learning processes instead of transfer of information.

The University of Gent participates (since 1996) in the Consortium for the Innovation of Higher Education (*Consortium Innovatie Hoger Onderwijs*). This consortium is a cooperative network of Flemish and Dutch universities that aims at promoting innovation in higher education, particularly the systematic use of information and communication technology (ICT). To promote participation in this consortium, the University of Gent has established an internal education fund which supports educational innovation through promoting new educational methods and integrating them into daily practice as quickly as possible.

The University of Gent also participates (as does the Catholic University of Leuven) in the Programme for Innovation of Higher Education (*Stimuleringsprogramma Innovatie Hoger Onderwijs*) of the Flemish community. This programme promotes the design and development (making use of ICT) of innovative learning environments, teaching methods and techniques, and instructional materials.

Summary
The changes in course supply at the universities of Leuven and Gent are mainly internally motivated. The universities make use of governmental funds if the preconditions for obtaining these funds are in line with their policy initiatives. The governmental wishes for transparency and rationality, as expressed in policy statements, do not have a strong impact on the performance of universities. Maybe the system of quality control will have a stronghold on Flemish higher education and will contribute to the attainment of the policy objectives of the government. The assignment of a special government commissioner, Rector of Honour, R. Dillemans, may also have a similar influence. He has to develop a plan for the optimisation of university education. This plan must be finished within five years and in consultation with the vice-chancellors. Whether the quality control system and Dillemans' plan have the desired effects remain to be seen.

4.2   New educational methods on behalf of the knowledge society

Governmental policy
The Flemish government considers lifelong learning or continual training a prerequisite for the good functioning of a modern society.

> *The explosive growth of science (and the subsequent erosion of knowledge) and the rapid evolution towards a knowledge society require not only more elaborate possibilities to update knowledge by retraining, but will make it necessary in a while to think of the initial basic academic training as of the start of a process of lifelong learning. To meet the demands of the buyers adequately, the supply of continuing university training will have to be organised in a very flexible way* (Van Den Bossche 1998: 6).

Although the Flemish government finds lifelong learning very important, it does not take responsibility for the development of it within universities. Rather, it wants to create the conditions in which the higher education institutions can organise such a structure. This implies that higher education institutions cannot rely on a permanent, structural funding. But the former Minister of Education, Van Den Bossche, has promised a stimulation subsidy, that can 'stimulate (universities) in the take-off of this important new component of university activities' (Van Den Bossche 1998: 6).

It seems that for lifelong learning the Flemish government tries to influence higher education by providing information. The former Minister of Education, Van Den Bossche, has stressed the importance of lifelong learning on several occasions. Although the government does not feel directly responsible, it does indicate how a new structure for lifelong learning can be conceived. A good example of this 'management by speech' is the following remark of Van Den Bossche about financing lifelong learning (1998: 6):

> *As far as financing is concerned, there must be striven for an interuniversity mechanism of solidarity, so that towards less prosperous sectors a supply can be developed based on revenues from other programmes that are offered to strong sectors at market prices.*

Catholic University of Leuven
In 1988 the central university level established a Continuing Education Office. It was a limited office whose main task was to support the initiatives of the faculties. When a Council for Continuing Education was formed in 1990, this basic principle of the central role of the faculties in the organisation of continuing education was confirmed. Other principles were that the Continuing Education Office had to be initiating and coordinating; and that the activities had to be self-sustaining, because of the absence of systematic governmental financing.

In 1995 a Continuing Education Think Tank, with internal and external members, concluded that 'the dialogue between demand and supply' had to improve, and that the supply had to be structured in a better way. As a result, a new Council for Academic Continuing Education was established, together with a steering committee for each participating sector (health and welfare; education; government; the socio-cultural sector; enterprises; the professions). Two consultants were recruited to act as intermediaries between the demand and supply side. The Continuing Education Office must become self-sustaining and organise post-academic training for alumni of the Catholic University of Leuven. Nevertheless, the initiatives taken by the faculties remain the most important part of continuing education. Besides, faculties which do not consider lifelong learning an important matter do not have to undertake any initiative and can ignore the wishes of the central university level and the Flemish government.

University of Gent
In the field of new educational methods on behalf of the knowledge society, the University of Gent wants to profile itself mainly in the field of advanced academic courses. The focus on these courses does not mean however that initiatives of continuing education and training receive no attention.

Advanced academic courses are not developed at the central level of Gent University but, as is the case in the first two cycles, at the decentralised level (educational committees). Likewise, there is no central service for post-academic and continuing education. Some post-academic courses (a total of 23 in 1997) are however subject to a formal decision of the Management Committee (including the entrance fee). These do not comprise the many activities that are organised by decentralised bodies and do not lead to a university certificate.

Most post-academic and continuing education is offered by a limited number of faculties, the Department for Teacher Training, the Institute for

Continuing Education of the Faculty of Engineering, the Open University Study Centre, and the Language Centre. There are also faculties which do not undertake such activities because they are not motivated to do so. Besides this, there are diverse training activities (lectures, exhibitions, etc.) for a general public audience. Contract education is not institutionalised. In general, education is supply-driven.

Summary
Lifelong learning is only taken up at universities if individual academics or faculties consider it a matter of major concern. At Leuven and Gent, base level departments which do not care for lifelong learning ignore the plans of the government and the central university administration. Following Clark (1983) and Van Vught (1995), an explanation for this behaviour can be found in the organisational characteristics of higher education institutions.

> *In an organisation where the production processes are knowledge-intensive, there is need to decentralise. When such an organisation is also heavily fragmented, decision making power will be spread over a larger number of units and actors. A higher education institution therefore becomes a federal system; semi-autonomous departments and schools, chairs and faculties act like small sovereign states as they pursue distinctive self-interests and stand over against the whole* (Van Vught 1995: 249).

4.3   Internationalisation

Governmental policy
The internationalisation of higher education is an important issue for the Flemish government. To promote the participation of Flemish institutions and students in European educational programmes and to coordinate national initiatives, the Flemish government has established several agencies (e.g. the Flemish Socrates Agency, the Flemish Lingua Agency, and the Flemish Leonardo da Vinci Agency).

Furthermore, the Flemish government has implemented European directives concerning a general system of recognition of higher education diplomas, the right of students of other EU-countries to subsidies, and a general (European) study-point system which makes it easier to compare the study results of students and to transfer them between institutions.

Finally, the Flemish government provides money for:

- participation in European research programmes;
- international university cooperative projects in the field of education (with Russia, Ukraine, Vietnam, and China as priority partners);
- cooperative projects within the framework of the *'transborder agreement'* (an agreement between the Netherlands, Flanders, Nordrhein-Westfalen, Nieder-Saksen, and Bremen);
- additional study grants in the framework of the ERASMUS programme of the EU.

Catholic University of Leuven
The Catholic University of Leuven has taken several steps to position itself internationally. The European programmes, and especially ERASMUS, have played an important role in this respect. For instance, as a result of the establishment of the Socrates programme, the University of Leuven finalised an institutional contract with the European Commission, drafted a European Policy Statement, and provided extra financing for initiatives taken in the faculties within the framework of Socrates.

The University of Leuven participates in many European programmes (Socrates, Lingua, Tempus, Delta, Med-Campus, Alfa, EU-Canada), but the most successful has been ERASMUS, which is now regarded as 'an evident surplus in our university course offer'. Besides the European programmes, the Catholic University of Leuven also cooperates with foreign universities on a bilateral and multilateral basis. A third element of internationalisation is the development of international course programmes (e.g. Artificial Intelligence; European Master of Public Administration; International Study Program on Statistics; Master of Arts in European Studies).

In general, however, the number of foreign students at the Catholic University of Leuven is relatively smaller than at other Flemish universities. It amounts to 4.2 % in the 1st and 2nd cycle, 26.2 % in the third cycle, and 26 % of the doctorates. The figures for the University of Gent are 2.7 %, 22.2 %, and 27 % respectively.

Although the absolute numbers of foreign students at both Leuven and Gent are amongst the highest in Flanders, the relative numbers are the reason why the Catholic University of Leuven plans to seek cooperation with the Dutch universities for the 1st and 2nd cycle. The university will evaluate, improve, and internationalise the advanced academic courses (3rd cycle) in order to attract more foreign students and doctoral students.

University of Gent

Internationalisation has been a policy issue at the University of Gent since 1987. In that year the European Educational Programmes Department (*Dienst Europese Onderwijsprojecten,* DEO) was established. The direct incentive to do so was the ERASMUS programme of the European Commission, but the department fulfilled tasks with respect to all European educational programmes.

The centralisation policy of the European Commission in the Socrates programme (e.g. the Institutional Contract) was the sign for the University of Gent to partake in further centralisation and overall institutional involvement, and to establish a new internal communication structure: the Faculty Commissions for Internationalisation.

In January 1995, the DEO was transformed into the International Relations Office (*Dienst Internationale Betrekkingen,* DIB). The number of staff was increased and their competence extended. The DIB provides central coordination and support for all international cooperative relations of the University of Gent, including not only the educational programmes of the European Commission, but also the internationalisation projects of the Flemish community, institutional international cooperation, and development cooperation. As far as the European programmes are concerned, with an involvement in about 100 ERASMUS networks, the University of Gent is one of Europe's most active universities. Other European programmes in which the University of Gent is involved, are: Tempus, Leonardo, Jean Monnet, Med-Campus, EC-USA, EC-Canada, Alfa, EU-China, EU-India.

Summary

The governmental policies on internationalisation are aimed at stimulating universities and students to take part in the programmes of the EU and to seek cooperation with universities abroad. Contrary to the policies on traditional course supply and lifelong learning, the policies on internationalisation, namely the provision of extra funds and the establishment of supporting agencies, have a strong effect. The governmental policies in this field (European and national) shape financial and organisational conditions which make it easier for universities and students 'to operate internationally', but the choice to do so is in their own hands.

5.   **CONCLUSION: INSTRUMENTAL AND
          CULTURAL EXPLANATIONS**

The Flemish governmental policies on higher education have only modest effects on the university plans on course supply and new educational methods, at least that is what is concluded from our analysis of governmental and institutional documents and interviews with relevant university and governmental actors. On the other hand, the policies on internationalisation did show some successes. Governmental subsidies and services of special agencies stimulated Flemish researchers and students to participate in international educational and research programmes which paved the way for more structural cooperation between institutions.

In this section we try to explain the effects of governmental policies on the university plans using an instrumental framework and a cultural framework (see sections 2 and 3).

5.1   Instrumental explanations

In general, the governmental policies concerning universities can be considered as facilitating. In 1991 the Flemish government introduced a lump-sum financing system that gave universities much freedom in using allocated funds. One could presume that the call for transparency and rationalisation of course supply, as formulated in the policy statements (Van Den Bossche 1995, 1998), is in terms of the model of instrumental tactics presented in section 2. In our view, this call for transparency and rationalisation is not a precondition for receiving financial means, but a kind of 'moral appeal'. A moral appeal refers to the influencing of norms and values of an actor, which may also cause his/her aims and behaviour to undergo changes. The system of unconditional financing and the policy management by speech (a kind of moral appeal) are in accordance with the fundamental choice for institutional autonomy within a state-supervising model.

From this it follows that implementation and success of governmental policies on rationality and transparency of course supply are fully dependent on the will   (motivation) of universities to make adaptations in their programmes. Compatibility of a policy with the values, beliefs and interests of the dominant coalition of decision-makers at the different university levels is a prerequisite for goal attainment. If a policy is not compatible with these values, the bargaining process between government and universities and institutional internal policy processes becomes lengthy and treacly. The majority of such policy processes disappears into nothingness.

The policies of the Flemish government on new educational methods on behalf of the knowledge society (lifelong learning) can be described as a mixture of provisional facilitation (a once-only take-off subsidy) and management by speech. Some faculties and departments are motivated to develop courses for lifelong learning, others are not. The facilitation of once-only financial resources is no reason for unmotivated university units to change their behaviour. These units do not sufficiently appreciate the take-off subsidy compared to future efforts and costs. Here too the success of the governmental policies is strongly influenced by the compatibility of governmental goals and institutional interests (motivation of universities). Obviously, this conclusion also holds for the management by speech on lifelong learning.

The educational policies on internationalisation are mainly a form of facilitation of financial resources and special services executed by agencies like the Flemish Socrates Agency. These policies link up well with the interests, wishes and intentions of the Flemish universities and therefore could be easily implemented.

Summarising, we may say that:

- the governmental educational policies in question are a mixture of facilitation, provisional facilitation and management by speech;
- the universities are partly motivated and partly not motivated to implement these policies;
- the policies have varying success.

In section 2 we formulated hypotheses with regard to the success of policies seen as instrumental tactics and the motivation of the target group.

In the case of transparency and the rationalisation of course supply, universities possess sufficient resources (lump-sum financing) but are not motivated to behave in line with the governmental policies which were mainly a kind of management by speech. Our hypothesis (2) concerning these circumstances predicted that the effect of a policy is stronger as this policy contains tactics like (provisional) defacilitation of resources or (provisional) organisation of universities. Applied to the Flemish situation this would mean that the government would enforce transparency and rationalisation of course supply by attaching conditions to the financing of universities or by reorganising the decision-making structure of universities. The latter implies empowerment of the central levels of universities, which probably are more willing to follow the governmental line of policy. It goes without saying that instrumental tactics like provisional defacilitation and (provisional) organisation do not fit into the new Flemish steering model, but it is also clear that management by speech is not a policy instrument which will have much effect in the short run. Besides, empowerment of the central levels of universities is ineffective in organisations where production processes need to be decentralised. In such organisations decentralisation is essential because:

- one centre is not capable of processing the necessary information to take all the decisions;
- quick responses to 'local' conditions have to be made;
- creative and intelligent people require room to maneuver (Mintzberg 1983: 96–7).

Otherwise it is difficult to deduce from instrumental analysis which kind of reorganisation of universities is preferable from a governmental point of view.

According to hypothesis 3, the governmental policies on lifelong learning, a mixture of (provisional) facilitation and management by speech, are suitable for stimulating motivated faculties and departments which do not possess sufficient resources for a take-off. But these tactics are unfit in the case of unmotivated university organisations (hypothesis 1) which do not appreciate earmarked financial resources. Here too reorganisation of universities would be an option according to the model of instrumental tactics, but such reorganisation is difficult if not impossible within the chosen steering model.

The governmental policies on internalisation and the institutional intentions in this matter link up well with each other. The permanent flow of financial resources and services stimulates universities to undertake international educational and research activities. The development of these policies and their implementation and effects are in line with hypothesis 3.

5.2   Cultural explanations

In general, academic culture is influenced by the discipline, the higher education institution, the national system as a whole and the academic profession (Clark 1983). Maassen (1996: 53) claims that academic culture is affected through the social institutions in which academics operate: 'Referring to the work of Clark, it is argued that the most relevant social institutional contexts in higher education are the structural systems links, the guildlike professional structures, and the university structures'.

Flemish academic culture is to a large extent egalitarian, which implies the following:

– collective strategies aimed at equal sharing of losses and gains are primary;
– academics control most aspects of their own work and do not have sufficient power to control the work of other academics;
– non-intervention principles between academics, departments and faculties are dominant.

At Gent and Leuven the supervising relation between state and higher education institutions (low grid), the guildlike professional structures (high group), and the decentralised decision-making system (low grid) further this culture.

Cultural theory predicted that the effect of the Flemish governmental policies on higher education is stronger as:

– the assumptions of these policies and the cultural bias of Flemish universities are more alike;
– the Flemish government is able to formulate rules or regulations that structure the choice processes of Flemish universities.

The analysis of policy and implementation processes on rationalisation of course supply, lifelong learning and internationalisation confirms the first hypothesis, but does not allow a pronouncement upon the second hypothesis. Furthermore, the cultural analysis sheds light on the obstacles for implementation of the governmental policies within the institutions.

Universities only pay serious attention to governmental policies, if these policies are compatible with the values, beliefs and interests of the dominant coalitions of decision-makers at the different university levels. Especially decentralised levels at Flemish universities (faculties and departments) are powerful. Their behaviour is decisive for the success or failure of the continued effects of a policy. For example, regarding continuing education at the Catholic University of Leuven or internationalisation at the University of Gent, the central level of each university claims to be ahead of the governmental policies. But the implementation of these plans takes place at the base level. The central decision-makers, the Academic Council (*Academische Raad*), do not have the power to force academics and administrators at lower levels to display the desired behaviour. Time after time players at the decentralised level are able to frustrate central initiatives. Compatibility with base level values, beliefs and interests seems to be a precondition for the success of central initiatives.

One could presume the power of decentralised levels being substantial only at large universities such as Leuven or Gent, because implementation of central regulation is easier in smaller organisations. However, this hypothesis does not hold for Flemish universities, as is demonstrated by the following example. A vice-chancellor of a small university, which shall remain nameless, reached a compromise with the Minister of Education and his fellow vice-chancellors, but after a short while he was forced to retrace his footsteps by the decentralised powers at home.

It is questionable whether some of the goals of the pursued policies can be attained at all. The Flemish government for example is not willing to supply universities with permanent funds for lifelong learning. After the initial subsidies are spent, universities have to defray the costs themselves. The first option they have is a redistribution of the available financial resources or they can pass the costs on to the customers. The trouble with this is that academics do not have an interest in additional tasks, even if they get a reward for extra effort. The culturally determined main interest of academics is to obtain academic prestige by writing articles and books.

The governmental policies concerning the transparency and rationality of course supply run up against the hard core of university culture. Expressing wishes, for example, in a number of policy statements (by the former Minister of Education, Van Den Bossche, 1995, 1998), to diminish or integrate courses is easy; implementation within universities is not. Diminishing courses or integration of courses would imply that some academics and even departments would 'win' and others 'lose', which is unthinkable in an egalitarian culture where power is dispersed amongst many persons. Only collective strategies aimed at equal sharing of losses and gains are discussible. An intended rearrangement of programmes, which would imply a redistribution of financial resources, is still taboo. Furthermore, the ruling principle of non-intervention between academics makes it difficult to take collective decisions about abolishing, integrating or changing courses and programmes.

5.3   Reflection

The above discussion essentially amounts to the following. Instrumental analysis shows that there is a necessary condition for governing to be successful: that is, adapting to and making use of the possibilities provided by the context (see also Ten Heuvelhof & De Bruijn 1995). Instruments and tactics used by governments have to be related to available resources and motivation of the target group of a policy. On the one hand, the Flemish government embarked on a new course concerning transparency and rationalisation of programmes, lifelong learning and internationalisation. On the other hand, the Flemish government loosened the reins by introducing a state-supervising model. Expressing very specific policies, for example with regard to course supply and lifelong learning (Van Den Bossche 1998), does not fit in a steering model which allows institutions to shape their own future within a general system of quality control. From this point of view it is easy to comprehend that such a governmental policy will not be implemented without major transformations. A more rigid implementation without major changes is only possible after adaptation of the present steering model. But such one-sided control would ruin the much-improved relation between government and universities in Flanders.

To a large extent instrumental analysis considers implementation as a black box. Only the level of motivation of the target group in question is part of the analysis. The relationship between motivation and characteristics of the structure and culture of the target group, here the universities of Gent and Leuven, is left out of consideration. In contrast, cultural analysis points out which institutional mechanisms block implementation or transform governmental policies and therefore create new openings for more sophisticated interventions. In the case of transparency and rationality of course supply, instrumental analysis reached the conclusion that attaching conditions to funding or an intervention aimed at restructuring the institutional decision-making, are adequate tactics. These tactics are however not consistent with the new steering model of the Flemish government. Cultural analysis made clear that two factors hamper implementation of governmental policies, namely collective strategies aimed at equal sharing of losses and gains and non-intervention principles between academics, departments and faculties.

Finally it should be noted that instrumental and cultural analysis are not so much a matter of mutually exclusive perspectives, but of distinct perspectives that offer different explanations. Essentially instrumental analysis is about the characteristics of policy instruments, and cultural analysis is about the way of life in a certain social setting. Both perspectives deliver insights that are indispensable for scientific research and administrative performance.

References

Van Den Bossche, L., *Optimalisatie universitair aanbod in Vlaanderen, Besluitvorming n.a.v. de besprekingen met de rectoren en minister L. Van Den Bossche van het eerste voortgangsrapport van ere-rector Dillemans*, Brussel, 1998.

CHEPS (1998), *Scientific progress report, TSER-HEINE project*, Enschede: CHEPS, University of Twente.

Coens, D. (1985), *Werk maken van onderwijs*, Brussel: Ministerie van Onderwijs.

Clark, B.R. (1983), *The Higher Education System: academic organization in cross-national perspective*, Berkeley: University of California Press.

Coyle, D.J. and R.J. Ellis (eds) (1994), *Politics, Policy and Culture*, Boulder: Westview Press.

Douglas, M. (1970), *Natural Symbols: explorations in cosmology*, London: Barrie and Rockliff.

Douglas, M. (1978), *Cultural bias*, occasional paper no. 35, London: Royal Anthropological Institute.

Douglas, M. (1982), Introduction to grid/group theory, in: M. Douglas (ed.), *Essays in the Sociology of Perception*, London: Routledge & Kegan Paul.

Emerson, R.M. (1962), Power-dependence relations, *American Sociological Review*, vol. 27 pp. 31–41.

French, J.R.P. and B. Raven (1959), The bases of social power, in: D. Cartwright (ed.), *Studies in Social Power*, Ann Arbor: University of Michigan, pp. 150–67.

Gross, E. and A. Etzioni (1985), *Organizations in Society*, Englewood Cliffs NJ: Prentice Hall.

Grendstad, G. and P. Selle (1995), Cultural theory and the new institutionalism, *Journal of Theoretical Politics*, vol. 7, no. 1, pp. 5–27.

Heffen, O. van and P-J. Klok (1997), Policy as a result of instrumental tactics: resources, dependencies and power strategies, paper presented at the IPSA World Congress, Seoul, 17–21 August.

Hendriks, F. (1996), *Beleid, Cultuur en Instituties, Het Verhaal van Twee Steden*, Leiden: DSWO Press.

Hill, M. (1997), *The Policy Process in the Modern State*, London: Prentice Hall.

Hoppe, R. and A. Peterse (1993), *Handling Frozen Fire: political culture and risk Management*, Boulder: Westview Press.

Korsten, A.F.A. (1998), Beleidsbeëindiging, in: A. Hoogerwerf and M. Herwijer (eds), *Overheidsbeleid, Een inleiding in de beleidswetenschap*, Alphen aan den Rijn: Samsom, pp. 163–82.

Lindblom, C.E. (1959), The science of muddling through, *Public Administration Review*, vol. 19, pp. 79–88.

Lindblom, C.E. (1979), Still muddling, not yet through, *Public Administration Review*, vol. 39, pp. 517–26.

Maassen, P.A.M. (1996), *Governmental Steering and the Academic Culture: the intangibility of the human factor in Dutch and German universities*, Utrecht: De Tijdstroom.

Mintzberg, H. (1983), *Structure in Fives: designing effective organizations*, Englewood Cliffs NJ: Prentice Hall.

Olsen, J.P. (1988), Administrative reform and theories of organization, in: C. Campbell and B.G. Peters (eds), *Organizing Governance, Governing Organizations*, Pittsburgh: University of Pittsburgh Press.

Schmitter, P. (1974), Still the century of corporatism?, *Review of Politics*, pp. 85–131.

Selle, P. (1991), Culture and the study of politics, *Scandinavian Political Studies*, vol. 14, no. 2, pp. 97–124.

Ten Heuvelhof, E.F. and J.A. de Bruijn (1995), Governing: structure and process-contingent interventions, in: W.J.M. Kickert and F.A. van Vught (eds), *Public Policy and Administration Sciences in the Netherlands,* London: Prentice Hall, pp. 163–76.

Thompson, M., R. Ellis and A. Wildavsky (1990), *Cultural Theory*, Boulder: Westview Press.

Van Den Bossche, L. (1995), *Beleidsbrief 1995: School maken in Vlaanderen*, Brussel: Ministerie van de Vlaamse Gemeenschap.

Van Den Bossche, L. (1998), Optimalisatie universitair aanbod in Vlaanderen, Besluitvorming n.a.v. de besprekingen met de rectoren en minister L. Van Den Bossche van het eerste voortgangsrapport van ere-rector Dillemans.

Van Vught, F.A. (1995), Governmental steering in higher education: an international comparative analysis, in: W.J.M. Kickert and F.A. van Vught (eds*), Public Policy and Administration Sciences in the Netherlands*, London: Prentice Hall pp. 247–70.

Verhoeven, J. (1982), Belgium: linguistic communalism, bureaucratisation and democratisation, in: H. Daalder and E. Shils (eds), *Universities, Politicians and Bureaucrats*, Cambridge: Cambridge University Press.

Vlaamse Raad (1988), Regeringsverklaring van de Vlaamse Executieve, *Stukken*, 1988–89, vol. 19, no. 1.

Wildavsky, A. (1984), *From political economy to political culture or rational people defend their way of life*, paper presented to APSA, August/September.

Chapter 13

Integrating two theoretical perspectives on organisational adaptation

PETER MAASSEN AND ÅSE GORNITZKA

Key words: organisational change, resource dependency, neo-institutional theory

1.   INTRODUCTION

The aim of this chapter is to outline the theoretical framework applied in an international comparative research project on the relationship between governmental policies and organisational adaptation in higher education (referred to as HEINE-project), and to position the overall research question of the project in a more general theoretical landscape.

The overall research question in theoretical terms can be stated as follows: How do organisations change? And in particular: How do organisations change in interaction with government policies and programmes, i.e. government policies and programmes as impetus for change of higher education organisations. This is mirrored by the overall research design of our project, i.e. we do not approach this issue as one would do in a classical implementation study, following a given policy around from formation and implementation to the effects of the policy in question, assuming a linear causal chain of events. Rather we focus on public policy initiatives as possible inputs into organisational change processes at an institutional level. Our project consists of three main steps: first national case studies focusing on policy contents at a governmental (and European) level, followed by institutional case studies in the respective countries, and finally the comparative analysis.

The project is examining organisational changes in three areas: first, the relationship between higher education institutions and the economy in the area of traditional internal teaching activities of universities and colleges focused on traditional students. Second, new relationships between traditional internal teaching activities and the external needs for training and education leading to new educational and training structures for "non-traditional/life-long learning students". Third, the deliberate attempts to link external stakeholders to internal structural change processes as part of the adaptation of institutional governance structures.

Two basic assumptions can be made when addressing the question of organisational change. We could assume perfect flexibility or perfect inertia. Neither are very useful assumptions in themselves, nor does either of them constitute the starting point of the main theoretical perspectives on organisational change to be applied in this project: resource dependence theory and neo-institutional perspectives. In the following we will briefly go through these perspectives and point to their basic concepts and assumptions, while we will also discuss the additional theoretical building blocks to be used in this study.

2.   MAIN THEORETICAL PERSPECTIVES EXPLAINING ORGANISATIONAL CHANGE

Two of the main approaches in the study of organisational change and stability - resource dependency and the neo-institutional perspectives - share two basic assumptions: organisational choice and action are limited by various external pressures and demands, and the organisations must be responsive in order to survive. However, these theoretical perspectives seemingly do not converge on two central issues: first, to what extent are organisations capable of reacting to changes in their environment, and second, how do they do it, i.e. the mechanisms that couple environments to organisational change.

2.1   Resource dependency

Resource dependency theory (Pfeffer and Salancik 1978; Pfeffer 1982) shares
with earlier open systems theory the assumption that organisations are flexible.
Contingency theorists, for example, used a simple model of exchange where
organisational action is taken in response to the environment, but the
environment is not affected by organisational action (e.g., Lawrence and
Lorsch 1967). Organisations principally were perceived as reactive: if a
change in the environment threatens critical resource relationships, an
organisation will adapt its prevailing 'repertoire' of exchange relationships in
order to arrive at an equilibrium that guarantees a continuous flow of the
critical resources. Changing the resource flows and how they are structured
will then bring about organisational change; i.e. environmental transformation
induces organisational change.

A resource dependence perspective starts from a similar view, that is to
understand organisations one must understand how organisations relate to
other social actors in their environment. It denies the validity of viewing
organisations as essentially self-directed and autonomously pursuing their own
ends undisturbed by their social context. This perspective argues that
organisations are other-directed, constantly struggling for autonomy and
discretion faced with constraints and external control (Pfeffer and Salancik
1978, p. 257). However, it introduces concepts and arguments that set it apart
from a simple view of environmental determinism. It relies heavily on a
political view of inter and intra-organisational interaction, and the theory
departs from earlier open systems theory in its emphasis on how organisations
act strategically and make active choices to manage their dependency on those
parts of their task environment that control vital resources. Organisations thus
have a major capacity for change, but their response to demands from the
environment is not automatic and passive, but active and volitional. In HEINE
(1998) the core ideas from this perspective are presented in more detail.

The resource dependence approach implies that an organisation's responses to
external demands can to some extent be predicted from the situation of
resource dependencies confronting it. However, this perspective introduces
several factors that sever a deterministic and "automatic" link between an
organisation's resource dependencies and its actions.

First, organisations are usually in a position of interdependencies; the focal
organisation also controls resources that other organisations need. "The
potential for one organization influencing another, derives from its

discretionary control over resources needed by the other and the other's dependence on the resources and lack of countervailing resources and access to alternative sources" (Pfeffer and Salancik 1978, p. 53). Organisations then are not necessarily powerless entities totally malleable according to external demands. Instead, the underlying model is one of influence and countervailing power: the greater the power of external stakeholders the greater the environmental determinism, whereas greater organisational power suggests greater capacity for organisational choice (Hrebiniak and Joyce 1985).

Second, organisations have other options apart from complying with external demands. They can manage and manipulate their dependencies in several ways.

Third, environments are not treated as "objective realities". They become known through the process of enactment, i.e. how the context of an organisation is defined depends on how it is perceived, how aspects are given attention, and how the context is interpreted. How organisations learn about their environment and attend to it, and how they select and process information to give meaning to their environments are all important aspects of how the context of an organisation affects its actions. Furthermore, most organisations will find themselves in complex environments faced with competing demands, thus there are different criteria for assessing organisational performance, and the demands made will not always be consistent.

An important aspect of a resource dependence perspective is its emphasis on intra-organisational factors to understand how organisations react and interact with their environments: "the contest of control within the organization intervenes to affect the enactment of organizational environments. Since coping with critical contingencies is an important determinant of influence, sub-units will seek to enact environments to favor their position" (Pfeffer and Salancik 1978, p. 261). The combination of a focus on external control and dependencies and internal power and control relations is proposed to be the key to understanding and specifying the process of environmental effects.

This implies that for understanding organisational change it is not enough to investigate the "objective" resource dependencies and interdependencies. In addition it is necessary to examine the way organisations perceive their environments, how they act to control and avoid dependencies, the role of organisational leadership in these processes, as well as the way internal power distributions affect and are affected by external dependencies.

2.2   Neo-institutional theory

From an institutional perspective organisations operate in an environment dominated by rules, requirements, understandings, and taken-for-granted assumptions about what constitutes appropriate or acceptable organisational forms and behaviour (Scott 1987; Oliver 1997). Many of the studies and seminal theoretical contributions within neo-institutionalism emphasise the survival value of organisational conformity to institutional environments. It is argued that adoption of policies or programmes is importantly determined by the extent to which the measure is institutionalised - whether by law or by gradual legitimisation (Tolbert and Zucker 1983). In many respects this resembles the notion of organisational adaptability as found in resource dependency, only the focus is on how organisations adapt to norms and beliefs in their environments, not to resource dependencies. When organisations change according to institutionalised expectations, they do so in a context of taken for granted norms and beliefs, thereby showing little of the active choice behaviour that a resource dependence perspective would predict (Oliver 1991). As indicated by Oliver (1997, p. 700) "According to institutional theory, firms make normatively rational choices that are shaped by the social context of the firm, whereas the resource-based view suggests that firms make economically rational choices that are shaped by the economic context of the firm".

Furthermore, conformity is often of a ritualistic nature where organisations construct symbols of compliance to environmental change (DiMaggio and Powell 1983; Edelman 1992; Meyer and Rowan 1977). Organisations thus are seen to combine conformity to environmental expectations with organisational stability. In this respect a neo-institutional perspective will emphasise the stability of organisations and the barriers to change that exist within organisations. Neo-institutionalists, such as March and Olsen (1989), have given special attention to the latter and have demonstrated how deliberate attempts at organisational change are frustrated by organisational resistance, whereas most changes in organisations are the result of relatively stable routine responses that relate organisations to their environments (March 1988). However, there is a need for differentiating between the kind of organisational responses one can expect according to type of environmental change (Brunsson and Olsen 1990). This version of the neo-institutional perspective would particularly question the extent to which organisational change is the outcome of *reform*. Well-developed institutions with stable values, interests, perceptions and resources exhibit inertia or friction when faced with efforts at reform (Brunsson and Olsen 1990; March and Olsen 1984). Changes that are compatible with an organisation's institutional identity or culture can be responded to in a routine and non-upsetting manner. Organisational adaptation to environmental change is in these cases part of standard organisational procedures, which is not the case for major reform attempts that run athwart institutional (sub)cultures. For organisations to change as a result of government initiatives a normative match is necessary, i.e. congruence between the values and beliefs underlying a proposed programme or policy and the identity and traditions of the organisation.

3.   COMBINING THE TWO THEORIES

A central aspect of a resource dependency perspective is the attention it gives to the role of active agents and strategic choice in organisational responses to environmental change, an attention until recently lacking in the sociological institutional perspective. However, in an overview of empirical research on institutional effects on organisational structure and performance Scott (1995, p. 114-132) discerns a trend from the earlier institutional emphasis on organisational conformity towards more attention to variation in organisational response depending on their individual characteristics or connections. Combining the insights from both research and theoretical traditions a set of organisational responses to environmental changes can be identified. First, one can talk of collective responses to environmental pressures, often to redefine or reshape institutional demands. An example of the latter is associations of organisations that act to negotiate the content of legal requirements made by the state (Dobbin et al. 1993). In our case a comparable collective response would be if associations of universities or colleges actively got involved in negotiating the interpretation of higher education legislation. Second, organisations might respond individually in a number of ways to environmental demands and expectations ranging from passive acquiescing to active manipulation of external demands (cf. Oliver 1991, and HEINE 1998, where these strategies and responses are presented).

We would, according to Oliver (1991), expect organisational response to environmental pressures to depend on the following "external" conditions: 1) why pressure is being exerted ("cause"), 2) who is exerting pressure ("constituent"), 3) what the pressures consist of ("content"), 4) how and by what means they are exerted ("control"), and 5) where they occur ("context"). In the HEINE project, these conditions are studied as part of the analysis of national policies.

In addition we need to incorporate an understanding of the "micro-foundations" of institutional response. This constitutes a major focus of the institutional level case studies in our project. Although the perspectives outlined above have their specific analytical focus at an organisation level, the approaches facilitate the understanding of intra-organisation interaction and do not treat organisations as one unified entity. This is of particular importance when we take into consideration how a higher education organisation (i.e. a university or college) is structured and what the nature is of such organisations (c.f. section 4). Understanding the internal processes can be of vital importance for understanding why and how universities and colleges change, and how and why policies fail or are implemented successfully. In the following section some of the essential characteristics of higher education organisations, as identified by higher education research, and some of the organisational variables that we assume affect how organisations change and relate to their environments will be discussed. This discussion will make clear why we centralise the two theoretical perspectives introduced above, the resource dependence perspective and neo-institutionalism, in the framework of the HEINE project.

4.   THE NATURE AND STRUCTURE OF HIGHER EDUCATION ORGANISATIONS AS FACTORS IN ORGANISATIONAL CHANGE

There are some fundamental characteristics of higher education organisations that affect their ability and capacity for change. Some might see such organisations as being in a pathological predicament suffering from "institutional sclerosis". Whereas the same features of such organisations may be thought of as signs of strong, healthy organisations with the institutional confidence that enables them to resist shifting whims of outside constituents. The main point with respect to the theoretical framework used in the TSER project is not to determine the "diagnosis" of colleges and universities. Instead it aims at pointing to the characteristics of these organisations in such a way that can help us interpret and understand change processes within them. First, there are certain structural features that affect the capacity for collective action within universities and colleges, especially faced with competing interests, and makes them "hard to move". Second, the cultural identities and features of organisations in higher education should be seen as important factors in the context of this project. In the following we briefly go through this characteristics. (For a more thorough analysis, c.f. Clark 1983).

A first distinctive characteristic concerns *the governance structure* and *the distribution of authority* in higher education organisations. The primary source of authority is the professional expertise. These are organisations marked by professional autonomy (Minzberg 1983), both individually and collectively placed in the scholarly community. In higher education many decisions can only be made by the professional expert. In addition, there is the (Humboldtian) tradition that the function and objectives of universities and colleges are best served in an environment of academic freedom. This implies that such organisations are "bottom-heavy". Consequently the potency of collective action at an institutional level is low and there is generally a strong diffusion of power in decision-making processes in higher education organisations. This leaves a weak role for institutional leadership (Cohen and March 1974). A related characteristic usually attributed to higher education organisations is a high degree of structural differentiation, where "each department is a world in itself" which in turn can be understood as a consequence of the low degree of functional dependence that exists between different organisational sub-units. In general, the distribution of decision-making responsibilities and the degree of institutional fragmentation are important factors conditioning the extent to which co-ordinated change in as well as of higher education organisations is possible or likely. However, it has to be realised that the extent to which these characteristics are dominant will vary according to national differences and according to differences between types of organisations in higher education. Clearly we would expect such differences to be reflected in change processes concerning the development, for example, of new teaching programmes or changes in traditional degree programmes.

Furthermore factors such as *size* and the degree of *multiplicity of purpose* of (higher education) organisations influence the degree of decentralisation and fragmentation. Increasing size and heterogeneity affect institutional level collective action (c.f. Minzberg 1983). In general additional scrutiny and constraints on utilisation of power are associated with large size (Greening and Gray 1994, p. 490). Also, the size of an organisation can directly influence the way it responds to external demands - large organisations have sufficient resources and a scale enabling them to alter their context in a significant fashion (Pfeffer and Salancik 1978, p. 267).

Following the (re)discovery of the concept of culture in the social sciences, over the last ten to fifteen years also in the field of higher education research a growing interest in cultural aspects of university and college life can be observed (Maassen 1996, p. 38). Culture has been applied in a large number of studies focusing on the symbolic side of higher education. As is reasoned by Clark (1983, p. 72) "All major social entities have a symbolic side, a culture as well as a social structure, some shared accounts and common beliefs that define for the participants who they are, what they are doing, why they are doing it, and whether they have been blessed or cursed." In the light of the research question we are focusing on it is of importance to indicate how we interpret the cultural dimension of organisational change processes. This is also of relevance regarding the various applications and interpretations of culture in higher education studies. Following Scott (1995) we want to regard organisational change through a cultural lens as a form of organisational reproduction. This reproduction can be caused by individual as well as collective actions. The basis for these actions can be found in the cognitive frames the individuals or collectives use for their organisational operations. For our study it is of relevance to realise that the individual versus collective cognitive frame provides a basis for comparing the way cultural aspects play a role in organisational change processes in the eight countries involved.

The majority of the studies on culture in higher education focus on one specific source of cultural variation, for example, the discipline or the university. In these studies 'culture' is interpreted as the 'belief system' (Clark 1983) consisting of the specific values and norms that characterise the (members of the) academic profession. While, as indicated, this belief system is assumed to be affected by one dominating source, Clark (1983, p. 74-75) argues that there are four main variables affecting the academic belief system, i.e. the discipline, the higher education institution, the national context, and the academic profession at large. In his interpretation the academic belief system, or the academic culture (Maassen, 1996), is reproduced by the interaction of these four variables.

In our study we will examine the relation between individual and collective bases for change processes in higher education institutions as well as the effects of the four variables on the individual as well as the collective academic belief systems or cultures. We assume that there can be important differences in academic belief systems between disciplines, between higher education institutions, between countries, and between members of the academic profession and non-members, e.g. administrators, civil servants, and politicians. The intensity and nature of the differences will have an effect on the relationship between governmental policies and organisational change processes in higher education institutions.

5.   CHARACTERISTICS OF POLICY PROCESS AND CONTENT

While the central theme of this research project is about organisational change in higher education institutions, the concept of organisational change is examined in the context of government policies and programmes. Such a focus implies that we need to delineate the background and nature of each of the identified policy issues and describe programmes and policies with respect to more general characteristics. Hence, there is an additional need to shed light on characteristics of policy making complementary to the theories outlined above, and in this respect the body of social science literature on implementation and innovation can contribute to our understanding of change processes.

Whenever implementation studies and policy analyses are on the agenda, two basic conceptual problems are raised. Before moving on with the presentation of our framework we will touch upon them. First, *what is a policy*, i.e. by what criteria can one say that something among the many issues debated, texts written and decisions made, constitutes a government policy? In many instances it is assumed to be a fairly straightforward issue, where policy formation can be divided into many stages of policy-making culminating in a parliamentary decision to pursue a certain objective, such as a policy of merging higher education institutions, creating a unitary system or establishing a new university. In other cases it might be less obvious whether government talk or action represents a policy, for example, when there is no crucial decision or legally sanctioned text that can be pinned down as representing a policy. Some students of public policy have indicated that one criteria for action or activity to be called a policy is that there is a stated objective attached to it (Ranney 1968), or both intentions and actions/means are stated (Kjellberg 1977), whereas others would also give the label policy to 'non-policy'.   This project will rely on the following definition:

> *A policy is a public statement of an objective and the kind of instruments that will be used to achieve it.*

The latter part of this definition is probably the most problematic, given that one rules out government objectives that do not have a delineation of how goals are intended to be reached. Second, the definition begs the question of what constitutes a public statement. In most cases we could say that policies are the objects of political choice, in most systems an object of legislative choice, i.e. government policies are linked to a decision in an elected assembly at the national level and have a parliamentary stamp of approval. In these cases it is relatively tractable task to identify a specific policy.

The second issue is related to how one deals with the first one: *when does the process cease being policy formation and becomes policy implementation*? In their definition Pressman and Wildavsky (1971) interpret policy as a hypothesis, whereas programme signifies the conversion of a hypothesis into government action. The degree to which the predicted consequences (the 'then' stage) take place is called implementation, i.e. the forging of subsequent links in a causal chain so as to obtain the desired results. Thus, a programme becomes the intermediary stage between policy and implementation. In other parts of the implementation literature the conceptual distinction between formation and implementation has been challenged, especially by those who take an "adaptive" or "interactive" approach (cf. Mazmanian and Sabatier 1983; Barrett and Fudge 1981). If we assume that adjustments of policies take place continuously, it is difficult to distinguish empirically between formulating policies and carrying them out. We believe it could be useful to separate the two processes for analytical purposes, yet that does not imply that we take on a view of policy and implementation processes that fit the image of the perfect 'parliamentary chain of command', where an elected legislature makes a policy decision, whereupon an administrative agency executes them, and that policies travel untouched by the process of being carried out. Given the studies of policy processes and implementation of the last 20 to 30 years, the 'radical' position would be to assume that policies are not affected be the process of being carried out. Surely it would be sensational if implementation did **not** display evolutionary aspects. Post-policy formation negotiations or leeway for adjustment can be expected as part of the implementation process, but that does not necessarily imply that implementation stops being 'carrying out of policies' and becomes inseparable from policy formation. However, given the research design of our project, our study distinguishes processes by level of analysis more than by what stage a policy process is in. The national level analyses focus, for example, on governmental policy processes. Hence, there is little need to make a priori a sharp distinction between policy formation and implementation at this level, and to signal this we will for the national level case studies talk about policy processes and not of implementation versus formation processes. Furthermore the focus is on the institutional change processes in interaction with and response to government initiatives as opposed to a single focus of the fate of given governmental policies as they are implemented.

6.   POLICY PROCESSES

In our view higher education institutions have to be regarded as organisations that attempt to "manage" their environment for their interests of survival, growth and certainty. This implies that it does not suffice to take a policy as given. Attention should also be focused on the way in which the process of policy-design and policy-formation has taken place.

Policy making and policy change can be studied from similar perspectives as found in the outline above of a theoretical framework for the study of organisational change. We can take on an exchange view of policy making and see policy change as the result of changes in the political coalition and as the result of new bargains struck between policy making actors when resources are redistributed. Such a perspective sees policy formation as strategic goal directed behaviour and problem solving under conditions of conflicting interests. On the other hand, an institutional perspective would see policy change as driven by rules as well as taken-for-granted assumptions about appropriate behaviour. It would focus on how policy processes attempt to affect the values and beliefs about the nature of higher education and knowledge production and its role in society (Bleiklie *et al* 1995). Such a perspective then is more engaged in the study of how changes in and diffusion of values and ideas affect policy rather than changes in the resources and political clout of policy making actors. Furthermore, an emphasis is put on policy making as symbolic-expressive behaviour, i.e. policies are not simply guidelines for action but also expressions of faith, values and beliefs and instruments of (civic) education: 'Individuals and groups support the adoption of policies that symbolize important affirmations even where they are relatively unconcerned with the ultimate implementation of the policies" (Baier *et al.* 1988, p. 152). Proclamation of policies then can be more important to policy makers than their enactment[1].

---

[1]   In parts of the study of policy making (distributive theories of legislative organisations) the "neglect" of policy outcomes and primacy of policy decisions is built into the analytical model where the assumption is that policy makers utility function is defined over policy and not their outcomes (cf. Krehbiel 1992). In plain English: what politicians care about is

An institutional perspective would not see this as some anomaly but rather emphasise the way processes themselves are significant as a reaffirmation of the value of making policy decisions according to correct procedure and as a way of influencing society by affecting norms and beliefs (Olsen 1983; March and Olsen 1995).

It is beyond the scope of our project to do an in-depth analysis of policy processes. Yet a special focus will be placed on the role of higher education institutions in the policy process, given that being involved in policy formation is one way in which universities and colleges can 'negotiate' and 'create' environments (cf. e.g. chapters seven and eight in Pfeffer and Salancik 1978). In order to investigate this topic, we will give an overview of which participants are involved in the selected policy processes and what type of policy *arenas* within which policy is made (e.g. is policy formation the work of government commissions, inside parliament, bureaucracy at different levels). Second, the analysis will provide an overview of the *actors* that are involved and the main ideas, interests and resources they carry as well as the consequent degree and style of policy making *conflict*. The latter then would point to the degree of (political) conflict, and whether specific policies and programmes are considered controversial or unproblematic. The *sequence* of policy formation is important to reconstruct. Especially from a neo-institutional perspective it has bearing on the issue of diffusion of policy trends across sectors and national borders, i.e. a calendar of major policy events will be presented for each of the policy issues.

Central in this will be the emphasis on the extent to which national modes of policy-making as part of the national "state model" influence the policy formation process, especially the degree to which it accommodates the articulation of interests from the 'targets' of these policies, i.e. the higher education institutions and their representative groupings (see above).

7.   CHARACTERISTICS OF POLICY CONTENT

The analysis of the policy *content* will encompass an investigation of the policy theory underlying a specific policy. A policy theory has been identified as 'the total of causal and other assumptions underlying a policy' (Hoogerwerf 1990, p. 286), including its normative framework, i.e. policy

---

having their preferred piece of legislation passed and not whether a policy will produce some societal change (see also Olsen 1989).

ideology. A reconstruction of the total policy theories within our policy field is far beyond the scope of this study. Our analysis of each of the specific policies will be characterised according to a limited set of attributes and dimensions.

Why is such an analysis of interest in this connection? First, it will occasion a systematic presentation of the perception of means and goals of each of the policies in different countries and enable us to conduct a comparative analysis that can stand on its own merits. Second, policy content characteristics are selected in light of the focus of our theoretical framework. Following this framework, some form of identifying the 'policy theory' is essential for the investigation into different types of institutional response/action to government initiatives. However, some of the issues raised in section 2, such as the question of 'normative match' and resource dependencies, we would suggest are primarily to be treated as part of the institutional analysis, i.e. how institutions perceive policies and programmes, and not as an intrinsic property of a given policy. Nonetheless, conceptions of 'compatibility' and 'profitablity' of policies we assume are not totally unrelated to the character of a policy theory and ideology, as it can be reconstructed on the basis of policy documents and interviews of policy makers. The analysis of government policies will enable us to compare the policy theory of government programmes and policies, and the mental/cognitive maps/ means-ends thinking and normative foundation of the selected institutions within each of the policy areas. As such the analysis of national policies will constitute a valuable input to the institutional analysis.

Policy problems
What constitutes the societal problem that a policy is designed to redress? What conditions have been identified by people in and around government as the main policy issues and problems? From a comparative point of view, this is an interesting issue by which one can characterise different policies. In many instances one can see that policies are solutions that are more or less stable, but that the problems they are attached to vary both across time and different national systems. For example, life-long learning policies can be set out to address the issue of empowering underprivileged groups in society in some contexts, whereas in another context it is used to establish manpower more attuned to the needs of the labour market. From studies of decision-making this phenomenon is often documented, i.e. some policies are 'solution driven', rather than 'problem driven'.

Policy objectives

According to our definition of 'policy', a policy contains a statement of desired outcome. Policies can vary according to whether policies and programmes are directed *at changing, adjusting or maintaining behaviour* of target organisations or groups. This dimension pertains to the question of whether a policy can be considered an innovation or maintenance policy, the latter having standard operating procedures whereas the former takes on the shape of social experiment (Lane 1993, p. 104). Second, policies can be characterised according to the *level of change in the higher education system* it is aimed at: is a policy aimed at a system of higher education as a whole or at separate institutions, sub-institutions or individuals? Finally, the *functional breadth of change* is important to investigate, i.e. does a policy consist of one or several programmes ('functional complexity')? (Cerych and Sabatier 1986).[2] How many different aspects of higher education activities are intended to be affected by a policy?

These policy characteristics are related to the type of change a policy is aiming at. The overall proposition we could make is that the more a policy departs from the existing behaviour and procedures, the more resistance it will encounter when implemented and the more it will be affected by the tendency to transform a reform back towards the established order. The Cerych and Sabatier (1986, p. 12) study of implementation of higher education reforms in Europe in the 1970s, concludes that the degree of success of implementations is highest in cases of policies aiming at mid-level change both in terms of breadth and depth. They conclude that there is a curve-linear relationship between scope of change and implementation success. Their conclusion is derived from the empirical results without providing a theoretical explanation as to the underlying mechanisms that produces the curve-linear pattern. It is so far unclear whether either the neo-institutional perspective or resource dependence theory could explain such a pattern. Yet it is rather evident that when we use theories that assume that organisations seek stability, the type of change that government attempts aim at will affect institutional response. Elaboration of predictions according to the theoretical framework could be spelled out, at least we are able to hypothesise, as stated in 2.2, that adjustment policies and 'familiar' policy measures can be handled by organisations' standard operating procedures for change, and in that sense they are much more likely to be successfully implemented.

---

[2]   However, a policy's value on this variable is dependent upon how one defines 'one policy'. In cases where boundaries of a policy are difficult to identify, it is also not altogether straightforward to characterise the functional breadth of change that a policy is aimed at.

Policy objectives vary in the degree to which they are explicit/clear versus 'implicit'/ambiguous. Outcomes of policies depend on their intentions, they are more likely to succeed if their intentions are focused and well defined rather than ambiguous (Olsen 1989, p. 12). Nonetheless, as noted by several studies, policies tend to have multiple, conflicting and vague intentions because the policy formulation process is marked by contending parties with different interests and values. The price one pays for accommodating them are policies with inherent tensions and contradictions (Majone and Wildavsky 1978, p. 182; Cerych and Sabatier 1986; Olsen 1989). There is very little point in lamenting the fact that policy objectives are often unclear. In pluralistic political systems it is 'in their nature' to be so. Furthermore, one could argue that having unclear and ambiguous intentions with policies creates a leeway for institutional transformation of policies (Edelman 1992). As such ambiguity will be a precondition for getting things done in cases where clarity would bring contending parties involved in both policy making and implementation to a stalemate and consequent non-action. On the other hand, ambiguity of policy goals makes it difficult for policy makers to gather information about and pass judgement on goal attainment, i.e. it is hard to tell whether implementing institutions are complying or not. Following Meyer and Rowan (1977), the latter phenomenon is a prerequisite for ritualistic compliance to external institutional requirements.

What is the normative basis of a policy?
What values and beliefs are policies and programmes based on? This aspect of policies can be read out of both the types of objectives attached to a policy and the problems it is designed to solve. According to institutional theory the normative foundations of a policy are of importance to unravel, since they relate to the issue of whether there is a normative match between a specific government initiative and the values and identities of institutions a policy is targeted at (cf. section 2 and below). Doctrinal assumptions and ideological preferences underlie and direct policies within a subsystem (Mathisen 1997; Elzinga and Jamison 1994). In many policy areas these are hard to identify because they are integral parts of policy subsystems and policy networks to the extent that they are taken for granted. Analysis of policy discourses and the language of policy are one way of disclosing such normative frameworks, especially when policy languages and discourses are changing. Dickson's (1984) study of changes in science policy has demonstrated how the concept of the role of science policy making has changed: science gone from being conceived and talked about as an undirected activity to an economic commodity. An even more apparent change of policy ideology is found in economic policy when a Keynesian framework was replaced by monetarist mode of policy making (Hall 1993).

Policy instruments

How and by what means are government pressures to conform to policy and programmes being exerted? Hood's (1983) 'NATO-scheme' categorises instruments in the following manner: Nodality (information); Treasure (money); Authority (legal official power); Organisation. These, Hood argues, are government capabilities, i.e. the fundamental mechanisms by which government influence society. Nodality refers to the central position of governments in societal communications and its ability to 'send out' information which it judges to be necessary or relevant. Authority refers to the ability of governments to issue binding laws, i.e. to formally restrict the behaviour of the targeted subjects. Treasure refers to government control of money and other resources. Organisation refers to the public bureaucracy and its ability to implement programmes, and to monitor environments.

Few real life policy instruments are pure examples of government tools as discussed by Hood. A given policy instrument can draw on two or more of these capabilities simultaneously. It is, for instance, hard to think of how the tool of organisation can be an instrument without some kind of money or funding attached to it. Often organisation is a prerequisite for governments to employ information or funding as a policy instrument (Linder and Peters 1990, p. 307). Nevertheless, this categorisation can be used to identify the dominant policy instrument(s) attached to a given policy and to identify the blend of different policy instruments within each policy/programme. Furthermore, we can use it to describe how restrictive each policy instrument is, given that the four types of government tools display varying levels of constraint with respect to the aimed at behaviour of societal actors (Maassen 1996, p. 68).

A neo-insitutional perspective would typically focus on the presence of legal coercion and legal sanctioning of state initiatives, or on the other hand on voluntary diffusion of 'institutionalised' norms. From a resource dependence perspective, organisational adaptation to external demand can be seen as a clever strategic response to external constraint that is dependent upon the sanctioning capacity of environmental actors. This theory would then lead us to highlight the 'structure' of sanctions and rewards, and in particular the extent to which rewards and sanctions are 'issued' by an environmental actor who controls scare resources. Successful implementation then can also be seen as being positively related to the extent to which new policies are considered profitable by the implementing organisation (Levine 1980; Van Vught 1989). If we assume organisations to be driven by their self interests, a simple, natural proposition to make is that the more profitable, the more likely institutions will be to adopt a new policy. Any other hypothesis would break the self-interest assumption. The effect of types of policy instrument must then be considered together with the implementing organisation's dependence upon the pressuring constituency, either for legitimacy or economic viability (Oliver 1991:166). Furthermore, absolute measures of the degree of profitability are confused by policy-makers' tendency to oversell the merits of a programme: 'reforms cannot be successfully marketed unless they promise more than they can deliver' (Olsen 1989, p. 14). This aspect is not first and foremost to be considered as an inherent quality of policies, but what is profitable is relative to the interests and resources of the implementing institution. Thus we would assume that the role government initiatives play in organisational change processes in higher education is significantly influenced by the overall dependencies within which organisations in higher education find themselves. It might be the case that institutions choose to adapt to some minor government initiative, which in itself might not seem very 'profitable', in order to appear legitimate and responsive in the long run in the eyes of a government agency who controls vital resources.

Nonetheless, the analysis of government policy means and ends, and instruments, will give us the basis for studying in a later stage of our project the 'input' upon which institutional decision makers pass judgements on the profitability of a policy.

The attention to policy instruments will include a special focus on the instruments that are directed especially at the *process* of implementation, in other words, whether special arrangements surround the implementation process: are existing institutions used as framework for implementation or are there separate implementation organisations/task forces? One finding that is fairly consistent in the study of implementation is the importance of making sure that there are some kind of organisational arrangements buffering policy implementation against short term fluctuations in attention. This can be hypothesised to be especially important in case of comprehensive policies (March and Olsen 1983). In studies of single agency reform a prerequisite for the success of organisational reform has been political or organisational leadership giving top priority to the implementation phase and bypassing ordinary routines (Egeberg 1984, 1987; Christensen 1987). Cerych and Sabatier (1986) point to the importance of having "fixers", i.e. key persons who are able to hold an implementation process together and exercise governance. A fixer is an actor from outside the implementing organisation who is committed to policy objectives, who has the capacity to monitor implementation and the political resources to intervene.

Policy linkage

The degree of *coherence/consistency* of policies and policy *linkage* over time and over policy fields, is different from the first characteristic because it measures the extent to which the content of policy is breaking with or continuing the content of other government policies, and not the behaviour of policy 'targets'. As Foss Hansen's (1990) study of implementation of the Danish Modernisation programme in the field of higher education suggests: former policies are the biggest barriers to implementation, not institutional characteristics *per se*. This aspect is relevant from a resource dependence perspective on organisational change because linkage between policy fields pertains to issues of how different types of policy agencies and other environmental actors are connected. In most higher education systems universities and colleges face many constituents, including different government actors, whose expectations are usually not unitary and coherent. Instead universities and colleges may find themselves in a jungle of conflicting requirements from different types of government policies and programmes. The overall characterisation of an organisation's environmental multiplicity and dependence primarily belongs to the institutional case studies. Yet the overview of the overall degree of "policy-coherence", makes up an important intake into the way that environments of higher education institutions are being linked in our area of study. This aspect of policies is also relevant as far as the neo-institutional perspective is concerned, because it relates to the issue of whether policies are connected to broader trends in society and public policy. From this perspective it is argued that reforms can only succeed if they try to change institutions in ways consistent with long term trends in society, i.e. success of comprehensive policies is dependent upon policy not going against the "tide" (Olsen 1989, p. 11). An example of specific higher education policies that are part of a broad tide are, e.g., budgetary/organisational reforms in the Nordic countries that had their particular expression in the higher education sector, but were explicitly linked to broader policy trends in the 1980s in the shape of large public sector 'modernisation programmes' (cf. Foss Hansen 1990; Larsen and Gornitzka 1995).

8. SUMMARY

In this article a conceptual framework has been presented for studying the following question: *How do organisations in higher education change in response to or in interaction with government policies and programmes?*

Two main perspectives on organisational change have been outlined. First, a resource dependence perspective that emphasises how organisations are externally controlled and how organisational action is to a large extent determined by the dependence on external resources and the exchange relationships an organisation is involved in. Organisational change must be understood by looking at how organisations perceive their environments and how they act to control and avoid dependencies in order to maintain organisational discretion and autonomy of action. From this perspective the role of leadership and the internal power distribution are major factors that determine how organisations change in the context of external demands and expectations.

On the other hand applying a neo-institutional perspective for the study of change in higher education organisations will lead us to focus on the cognitive and normative elements in the environment that shape organisational action. When organisations change according to institutionalised expectations, they do so in a context of taken for granted values, norms and beliefs. We have argued that both perspectives represent valuable perspectives for study and that these can be combined fruitfully assuming the following. First, organisational response to environmental expectations is shaped by intra-organisational factors such as power distributions and institutional values, identities and traditions. Second, organisational actors seek actively to interact with environmental constituents in order to shape and control dependency relations. They exercise strategic choice within the constraints imposed by their environment, but also the opportunities the organisational environments provide. On the basis of an integration of the two theoretical perspectives and underlying approaches to the study of organisational change, we can discern a set of strategies that organisations can use when faced with environmental demands. These range from relatively passive responses such as organisational conformity to active defiance and manipulation of external relations. We see these strategies as conditioned both by what characterises the overall exchange and dependence relationships that organisations in higher education find themselves in, and the internal characteristics that influence the "micro-foundations" of institutional response.

References

Baier, V.E., March J.G. and Sætren H. (1988). 'Implementation and ambiguity', in March, J.G. (ed.), *Decisions and Organization*. Oxford: Basil Blackwell, pp. 101-166.
Barrett, S. and Fudge, C. (eds.), (1981). *Policy and Action*. London: Methuen.
Bleiklie, I., Marton, S. and Hanney, S. (1995). *Policy Arenas, Network and Higher Education Reforms. The Cases of England, Sweden and Norway*. Bergen: LOS-Senter, Notat 95/40.

Brunsson, N. and Olsen, J.P. (1990). *Kan organisasjonsformer velges?* Bergen: LOS-Senter, Notat 90/6.

Cerych, L. and Sabatier, P. (eds.) (1986). *Great Expectations and Mixed Performance.* Stoke: Trentham Books.

Christensen, T. (1987). 'How to Succeed in Reorganizing: The Case of the Norwegian Health Administration', *Scandinavian Political Studies* 10(1), 61-77.

Clark, B.R. (1983). *The Higher Education System.* Berkeley: University of California Press.

Cohen, M.D. and March, J.G. (1974). *Leadership and Ambiguity,* 2nd Ed. Boston, Massachusetts: Harvard Business School Press.

Dickson, D. (1984). *The New Politics of Science.* New York: Pantheon Books.

DiMaggio, P.J. and Powell, W.W. (1983). 'The Iron Cage Revisited: Institutional Isomorphism and Collective Rationality in Organizational Fields', *American Sociological Review* 48, 147-160.

Dobbin, F.R., Sutton, J.R., Meyer, J.W. and Scott, R.W. (1993). 'Equal Opportunity Law and the Construction of Internal Labour Markets', *American Journal of Sociology* 99, 396-427.

Edelman, L.B. (1992). 'Legal Ambiguity and Symbolic Structure: Organizational Mediation of Civil Rights Law', *American Journal of Sociology* 97, 1531-76.

Egeberg, M. (1984). *Organisasjonsutforming.* Oslo: Tano.

Egeberg, M. (1987). 'Designing Public Organizations', in Kooiman, J. and Eliassen, K.A. (eds.), *Managing Public Organizations. Lessons from Contemporary European Experience.* London: Sage, pp. 142-157

Elzinga, A. and Jamison, A. (1994). 'Changing Policy Agendas in Science and Technology', in Jasanoff, S. (ed.), *Handbook of Science and Technology.* Thousand Oaks: Sage.

Greening, D.W. and Gray, B. (1994). 'Testing a Model of Organizational Response to Social and Political Issues', *Academy of Management Journal,* 37(3), 467-498.

Hall, P. (1993). 'Policy Paradigms, Social Learning and the State: The Case of Economic Policy Making in Britain', *Comparative Politics* 25, 275-96

Hansen, H. Foss (1990). 'Implementation of Modernization: Paradoxes in the Public Control of Higher Educational Institutions-The Case of Denmark', *Scandinavian Political Studies,* 13(1), 37-56.

HEINE (1998). 'Theoretical framework', Gornitzka, Å. and Maassen, P.A.M., *Interim report to the European Commission DG XII,* Enschede: Center for Higher Education Policy Studies (CHEPS).

Hoogerwerf, A. (1990). 'Reconstructing Policy Theory', *Evaluation and Program Planning* 13, 285-292.

Hood, C.C. (1983). *The Tools of Government.* London: MacMillan.

Kjellberg, F. (1977). 'Politics of redistribution and equalization', *Politico* 28, 77.

Krehbiel, K. (1992). *Information and Legislative Organization.* Ann Arbor: The University of Michigan Press.

Lane, J.E. (1993). *The Public Sector.* London: SAGE Publications.

Larsen, I.M. and Gornitzka, Å. (1995). 'New Management Systems in Norwegian Universities: the interface between reform and institutional understanding', *European Journal of Education* 30(3), 347-361.

Lawrence, P.R. and Lorsch, J.W. (1967). *Organization and Environment: Managing Differentiation and Integration.* Cambridge, Mass.: Harvard Business School.

Levine, A. (1980). *Why Innovation Fails.* Albany: State University of New York Press.

Linder, S.H. and Peters, B.G. (1990) 'Policy Formulation and the Challenge of Conscious Design', *Evaluation and Program Planning* 13, 303-311.

Maassen, P.A.M. (1996). *Governmental Steering and the Academic Culture.* Utrecht: De Tijdstroom.

Majone, G. and Wildavsky, A. (1978). 'Implementation as Evolution', in Freeman, H. (ed.), *Policy Studies Review Annual.* Beverly Hills: Sage.

March, J.G. (1988). 'Footnotes to Organizational Change', in March, J.G. (ed.), *Decisions and Organizations.* Oxford: Basil Blackwell.

March, J.G. and Olsen, J.P. (1995). *Democratic Governance.* New York: The Free Press.

March, J.G. and Olsen, J.P. (1989). *Rediscovering Institutions.* New York: The Free Press.

March, J.G. and Olsen, J.P. (1984). 'The New Institutionalism: Organizational Factors in Political Life', *American Political Science Review* 78, 734-749.

March, J.G. and Olsen, J.P. (1983). 'Organizing Political Life. What Reorganization Tells Us About Government', *American Political Science Review* 77, 281-296.

Mathisen, W.C. (1997). *Diskursanalyse for statsvitere: Hva, hvorfor og hvordan.* Oslo: Department of Political Science, University of Oslo, Working Paper 01/97.

Mazmanian, D.A. and Sabatier, P.A. (1983). *Implementation and Public Policy.* Glenview, IL.: Scott, Foresman & Co.

Meyer, J.W. and Rowan, B. (1977). 'Institutionalized Organizations: Formal Structure as Myth and Ceremony', *American Journal of Sociology* 83, 340-363.

Oliver, C. (1991). 'Strategic Responses to Institutional Processes', *Academy of Management Review* 16(1), 145-179.

Oliver, C. (1997). 'Sustainable competitive advantage: combining institutional and resource-based views', *Strategic Management Journal* 18(9), 697-713.

Olsen, J.P. (1989). *Modernization Programs in Perspective - Institutional Analysis of Organizational Change.* Bergen: LOS-Senter, Notat 89/46.

Olsen, J.P. (1983). *Organized Democracy.* Stavanger: Norwegian University Press.

Pfeffer, J. (1982). *Organizations and Organization Theory.* Boston: Pitman.

Pfeffer, J. and Salancik, G. (1978). *The External Control of Organizations; A Resource Dependence Perspective.* New York: Harper and Row Publishers.

Pressman, J.L. and Wildavsky, A.B. (1971). *Implementation.* Berkeley: University of California Press.

Ranney, A. (1968). *Political Science and Public Policy.* Markham Publishing.

Scott, W.R. (1995). *Institutions and Organizations.* Thousand Oaks: Sage.

Scott, W.R. (1987). 'The Adolescence of Institutional Theory', *Administrative Science Quarterly* 32, 493-511.

Tolbert, P.S. and Zucker, L. (1983). 'Institutional Sources of Change in the Formal Structure of Organizations: The Diffusion of Civil Service Reform, 1880-1935', *Administrative Science Quarterly* 30, 22-39.

Vught, F.A. van (ed.) (1989). *Governmental Strategies and Innovation in Higher Education.* London: Jessica Kingsley Publishers.